Philosophy
in the Classroom

Philosophy
in the Classroom
Second Edition

Matthew Lipman

Ann Margaret Sharp

Frederick S. Oscanyan

Temple University Press

Philadelphia

Temple University Press, Philadelphia 19122
© 1980 by Temple University. All rights reserved
Published 1980
Printed in the United States of America

Library of Congress Cataloging in Publication Data

Lipman, Matthew.
  Philosophy in the classroom.

  Bibliography: p.
  1. Curriculum planning.   2. Education—Philosophy.
I. Sharp, Ann Margaret, 1942–   joint author.
II. Oscanyan, Frederick S., joint author.   III. Title.
LB1570.L57   1980   370′.1   80-12157
ISBN 0-87722-177-4
ISBN 0-87722-183-9 (pbk.)

Photographs: Joseph B. Isaacson

Portions of Chapter 1 first appeared in *The Social Studies*, published by Heldref Publications, Washington, D.C., and are reprinted by permission. Chapter 4 is reprinted by the permission of the publisher from *The Oxford Review of Education* 4, no. 1 (1980).

Contents

Preface

Philosophy has become a respectable feature of elementary school education. This has been a fairly sudden development, since there was no such thing as philosophy in the schools prior to the 1970's. And since philosophy has for many centuries been taught exclusively on the college or graduate school level, what now induces elementary school administrators to add philosophy to the already crowded school day?

It is well to remember that when philosophy emerged in Greece in the sixth century B.C., it did not burst suddenly out of the Mediterranean blue. The development of societies of reasoning creatures—what we call civilization—had been a process to be measured not in thousands but in millions of years. Human beings became civilized as they became reasonable, and for an animal to begin to reason and to learn how to improve its reasoning is a long, slow process. So thinking had been going on for ages before Greece—slowly improving itself, uncovering the pitfalls to be avoided by forethought, endeavoring to weigh alternative sets of consequences intellectually. What happened in the sixth century B.C. is that thinking turned round on itself; people began to think about thinking, and that momentous event, the culmination of the long process to that point, was in fact the birth of philosophy.

But what the early Greeks recognized is much the same as what many teachers and administrators are beginning to realize today: just as the perfection of the thinking process culminates in philosophy, so too is philosophy, *par excellence*, the finest instrument yet devised for the perfection of the thinking process. Perhaps, then, a brief consideration of the dawn of philosophy in Greece 2,500 years ago can throw some light on the dawning in the 1970's of the important role that philosophy can play in the future of elementary education.

For the greater part of their history in Western civilization, literature and philosophy have been estranged from one another. But this was hardly the case during those early centuries in Greece that saw the emergence of philosophical thinking. Prior to Aristotle, in fact, philosophy was virtually always

xi

embodied in some literary vehicle. There were the aphorisms of Heraclitus and the poetry of Parmenides, just as there were later to be the dramatic dialogues of Plato.

Moreover, there were literary events taking place in Greece that, while not themselves philosophical, had much to do with the philosophical consciousness and reflection that characterized Greek culture. One thinks here of the work of Homer, or of the dramatists of the fifth century, for these most certainly laid the groundwork for the systematic philosophical thought that followed.

But Homer was no philosopher. How can he be credited with a major contribution to philosophical consciousness?

Let us recall that the *Iliad* recounts the end of a war that presumably had occurred some three centuries before Homer's day. We think of it as a war between the Greeks and the Trojans, but that is not quite correct. Before the war, there were only individual city-states on the peninsula that was to be called Greece. It was the war that made the inhabitants of those city-states think of themselves as Greeks, just as it was the American Revolution that caused the colonists of the thirteen states to think of themselves as Americans.

Our own American Revolution is only two hundred years behind us, but we still have strong feelings about it. We shake our heads incredulously upon learning that what we think of as a "war for independence," the British refer to as the "rebellion of the Colonies." In other words, we are still passionately partisan about that war, and so, evidently, are the British. Yet we consider ourselves sophisticated and civilized—especially when we contrast ourselves with the Greeks of the twelfth century B.C., still a tribal people, hardly out of barbarism. The Greeks of Homer's day, a few centuries later, were presumably not much more civilized. They too must have looked back upon the war with Troy as the major unifying experience in their national history. So crude and fierce a people, we are inclined to think, would be no less hostile to a disparaging depiction of their ancestors than we are today.

So we are surprised, when we read the *Iliad* for the first time, to discover Homer's even-handed treatment of Greeks and Trojans alike. Here are heroic Trojans and cowardly Greeks; here too, brave Greeks and treacherous Trojans. Each side loses at least as much as it wins. Amidst all the petulance, stupidity, cunning, and ferocity, only one individual stands out as noble—but he is not Greek, and his end is anything but a happy one. One would think that the Greek people of Homer's day would have persecuted him for such an unflattering portrait of their patriotic heroes, but apparently the Greek populace embraced the *Iliad* joyously. What manner of people could these have been?

Homer was no philosopher—but he treated the war impartially and objectively and detachedly. He admired what he thought admirable, whether it was

Greek or Trojan. He depicted people as he saw them, regardless of nationality. It was a depiction that could have appealed only to a people that wanted to be told the truth about itself, regardless of how much it hurt, just as the chief protagonist of *Oedipus* was later to demand to know the truth at all costs.

The impartial, objective pursuit of truth that the Greeks apparently recognized in Homer must have molded their own consciousness and must have whetted their appetite for a still greater independence of thought, so that the beginnings of philosophy in the sixth century were not, usually, greeted with persecution. The pre-Socratic "nature philosophers" of the sixth century may be scientific in their inspiration, but they are aphoristic and at times poetic in their manner of expression. Thus, when philosophy does finally make its appearance, it is at once philosophic in its originality and autonomy, scientific in its concern to propose statements as to the nature of things, and artistic in its mode of presentation.

Moreover, it is simple and popularly accessible, rather than technical or esoteric. Early philosophy was not for specialists, nor for a technical elite or a monastic minority. The aphorisms of the sixth century were rich and multileveled—yet at some level anyone could understand them.

It was only in the fifth century that philosophy came to be identified specifically with dialogical inquiry. Clearly, a major responsibility for this development lay with Socrates. It is not only that Socrates set an example to his fellow Athenians of what it would be like for a person to pursue the thoroughly examined life through public discussion; without Socrates, the great dialogical dramas of Plato would probably have been unthinkable. What was so different and so important about the life of Socrates?

In the first place, whatever Socrates urges us to do, he shows us how to do. Thinking is work, and it is a kind of work no one can do for anyone else. Socrates models intellectual inquiry for us, yet refrains from imposing upon us the products of his own intellectual inquiry. Recognizing the partnership of theory and practice, he recommends nothing to us as desirable without indicating the steps by which it may be attached. Socrates does not *say*, "Make all necessary connections and draw all necessary distinctions!" for he knows the worthlessness of such a command. Instead, he operationalizes whatever he recommends: if there is a concept to be discovered—of friendship, of courage, of love, of beauty—then there are specific and sequential steps that can be taken to flush that concept out of its concealment. Nothing about Socrates is so contagious as the calm confidence he exudes, that those to whom he talks are as capable of thinking—and of thinking excellently—as he is.

Moreover, we should know ourselves, we should know our lives, Socrates tells us. That is, we should know what matters in life, for it is evident that our chances of obtaining whatever of excellence life has to offer are greater if we know what these things are than if we do not. So intellectual inquiry begins with matters of the most intense interest to each of us: what is worthwhile in life, and what good reasons are there to support the claim that these things matter most? The interest of the individual in the improved management of his own life must be acknowledged to have first priority, for we can have no better incentive than to see our lives improve upon our thinking them through.

Third, Socrates engages people in conversation: it is a fact that, on the surface, at least, appears to be quite unremarkable. But in the context of his lifelong insistence that we live reflectively, the urgency of conversation becomes more understandable and significant. When we engage in dialogue, we must be intellectually on our toes—no place here for slovenly reasoning or unwitting remarks or mindless banter. We must listen carefully to others (for listening is thinking), we must weigh our words (for speaking is thinking). And then we must rehearse in our minds what we and others have said, and reconsider what we might have said, or what others might have said. Thus, to engage in dialogue is to explore possibilities, to discover alternatives, to recognize other perspectives, and to establish a community of inquiry. As the members of that community reflect upon the procession of ideas and the logic of their emergence, they each replicate the original conversation, but with new emphases, because the angle of vision of each individual is different. Some think that Socratic dialogue is only casually or accidentally related to his pursuit of intellectual understanding, but this is certainly a misapprehension. If individuals are to be encouraged to think for themselves, he seems to be saying, then there is no better way for them to begin than by conversing with one another in a spirit of reasonableness.

Finally, thinking must be rigorous. Socrates demonstrates that each belief must be subjected to the tests of logic and experience. It does not matter whose opinions they are, or whose ideas they are—they must submit to the requirement that they be internally consistent, and their proponents must divulge the evidence that supports them. Intellectual inquiry is thus a discipline that has its own integrity, and is not to be dissolved into scientific inquiry, nor permitted to masquerade as a political or religious ideology. Socrates does not deceive himself into thinking that, because he converses with a general, he is discussing strategy, or that, because he converses with a statesman, he is discussing statecraft. He knows he is dealing with the *assumptions* of these disciplines, and these assumptions must be treated philosophically. Thinking must be rigorous, and philosophical thinking is a unique discipline that must be carried on independently of other intellectual pursuits, however much such pursuits may ultimately benefit from reflection and dialogue that are distinctively philosophical.

Insofar as we know Socrates from the writings of Plato, these characteristics appear to describe him. They are features of his life to which he characteristically returns; they are not, however, features from which he never deviates. Those who wish to emulate Socrates should take most seriously his depiction of himself as a "midwife," for we shall resemble him most not by imitating him (just as it is unlikely that he imitated anyone), but in thinking for ourselves. In summary, those educators who wish to learn from Socrates should take the following lessons to heart:

1. All major concepts should be operationalized, and these operations should be properly sequential.
2. Intellectual inquiry should begin with the interests of the student.
3. One of the best ways of stimulating people to think is to engage them in dialogue.
4. Excellent thinking is logical and founded upon experience. (It is also, as we know from Plato, imaginative.) Thinking skills programs should, therefore, stress both formal and creative reasoning.

In the sixth century, prior to Socrates, each philosopher had issued his own pronouncements as though he alone existed; philosophy needed a more dialectical tension. It was literature and drama that first provided what was needed. Thanks to Aeschylus, Sophocles, and Euripides, philosophers were able to learn how to organize ideas dramatically; how to put them into sparkling interaction. And no one learned this lesson better than Plato.

But Plato also learns from Socrates, and learns, among many other things, that if the life of philosophy is dialogue, then the life of the philosopher is that of a teacher-learner, that philosophy is teaching as much as it is learning.

Ever since Plato, efforts to present philosophy in a manner that is popularly accessible and yet that has authenticity and integrity have been few and far between. Nevertheless, we must take the Greek experience seriously and apply its lesson to the problem of our own age. For we too are in a society that is philosophically deprived—long on knowledge but short on wisdom. Philosophy comes to too few people, and, even to those, it often comes too late.

But philosophy cannot be force-fed to people; they must want it. And they must somehow be motivated to want it—perhaps by the sorts of literary devices the Greeks employed. For the secret of the Greeks was not some special genius that was bestowed by nature on Athenian infants of the fifth century; it was more likely the happy legacy of Homer, whose fairness gave the Greeks a glimpse of justice, whose even-handedness gave them a glimpse of objectivity, and whose honesty gave them a glimpse of truth. A people that wants its posterity to be wise can do no better than create a vast repertory of artistic activities embodying those values whose pursuit it wishes to inculcate, much as the *Iliad* embodied the values prized by later generations of Greeks. Of foremost importance in that repertory will necessarily be a variety of new curricula that will help children think for themselves, curricula that will provoke children to make and say and do more imaginatively and more thoughtfully than any of our curricula have done in the past.

I

Encouraging Children to be Thoughtful

1   The Need for Educational Redesign

A visitor from a planet whose inhabitants were all incorrigibly rational would no doubt find in our educational system much cause for wonder. It is not that we are unaware of the inefficiency of that system. Rather, the cause for wonder would be the method with which we seek to come to grips with that inefficiency. Over and over again, we have recourse to remediation rather than to redesign. And when the remediation turns out to be inefficient, compensatory approaches proliferate in an effort to remedy the ineffectual remediation. The fundamental source of the system's failure to distribute education effectively —the faultiness of its basic design—remains unexamined, and increasingly vast sums are poured into efforts to compensate for the inefficiency of the system, into attempts to compensate for the inefficiency of the compensatory efforts, and so on and on in the direction of futility.

If the educational process were to be redesigned, what criteria could be used to determine that the new design would be of optimum serviceability? We would say that the overall objective of such redesign would be an educational system of maximum intrinsic value (as contrasted with a system whose values are purely instrumental and extrinsic), maximum meaningfulness and rationality, and maximum methodological unity and consistency. In the remainder of this chapter, we will endeavor to spell out the reasons for suggesting such criteria, and some of the ways in which they can be met.

Educational Dysfunction

Whatever the deficiencies of an educational system may be, it is apparent that they most cruelly and harshly affect precisely those portions of the population that are already educationally disadvantaged. The system thus affects the student population differentially, so that there is significant student vulnerability to systematic dysfunction. It would seem that students vary greatly in their susceptibility to the harmfulness of ineffectual educational processes, just as the population at large is differentially susceptible to outbreaks of influenza, and just as tendencies toward suicide are differentially distributed through-

3

out the society. Some cultural groups are not much harmed by inadequate public education, and many of their members may succeed in spite of it; the system can thus not take credit for their success. Other cultural groups may succumb to miseducation very readily, and the system bears some responsibility for their failure. In any event, consideration of the factors to be taken into account in redesigning education must involve the dysfunctions of the educational process that make compensatory education seem necessary. An analysis of those dysfunctions and their consequences that makes use of the epidemeological metaphor holds more promise than taking as a starting point allegations of differences in cognitive capacities based upon ethnic or socio-cultural differences.

The theory implicit in current practice with respect to compensatory education is that the most extreme and obnoxious symptoms of an inadequate educational system may be remedied or redressed by means of a countervailing educational thrust that would make up for ground lost, and would bring the lagging population up to a par with the remainder of those undergoing educational processing. Unfortunately, the methods employed in compensatory education generally turn out to be much the same as those in the existing system itself. With no clear understanding of the causes of the miseducation now prevalent, compensatory education as currently practiced tends to be preoccupied with little more than the alleviation of symptoms.

It would hardly be correct to imply that the system is without its critics. But although they are numerous, they are generally unconstructive. They are content to carp, but see no way to correct. Apologists for the system, on the other hand, point an accusing finger at cultural or at socio-economic conditions as the true causes of miseducation. Since there are few signs that our society is planning any major improvement in such socio-economic conditions, such apologists imply that no major amelioration can be expected with respect to the education of those in the society who are economically disadvantaged.

Failure of Remedial Approaches

So from both sides come counsels of despair. Hence, too, the desperateness of the remedial approaches. Each is touted too much, oversold, and overly relied upon: classroom walls are put in and taken out; technological innovations are introduced or discontinued; parents are involved or not involved; teachers are paid more or exhorted more; teacher aides are brought into the classroom; the list stretches on and on. One cannot help feeling that, even if all these remedial approaches were to work, they are like so many Band-Aids: fine for superficial abrasions, but risky if the real problem is an underlying internal injury.

We begin, therefore, with a different premise from the prevalent one. We begin by assuming that the only way to make compensatory education work is not to approach it as a merely compensatory device at all, but to design it so as to promise educational excellence for all young people. Just as there is no field called "compensatory medicine," there should be no such field as compensatory education. Just as the intensive care facilities available in hospitals to those who are seriously ill are the model of lesser facilities elsewhere for those whose medical needs are less severe, so the care and attention we give to the educational development of the disadvantaged or highly vulnerable members of our society should be a model of excellence, representing the best in services available to all. There is no effective strategy for compensatory education that is not at the same time an effective strategy for all education.

What is clear is that education must reconstruct itself so that the socio-economic conditions can never be the excuse for purely educational deficiencies. It must reconstruct itself so that diversity of cultural conditions will be regarded as an opportunity for the system to give proof of its excellence, rather than as an excuse for its collapse. It must reconstruct itself so that no significant fraction of those affected by it should ever be able to say, "It failed to help me discover the full range of options that were open to me." Or, "I grew. But I would have grown anyway. It failed to increase my capacity for growth by synchronizing my abilities so that they would reinforce each other rather than cancel each other out." Or, "When I entered the educational system, I brought curiosity and imagination and creativity with me. Thanks to the system, I have left all these behind."

One should expect neither too much nor too little of educational redesign. One should not expect it to be followed by drastic social changes, but one should at least be able to expect it to work, in the sense of producing measurable educational improvement. It would be inconsistent to deplore the measurable deficiencies of the existing system, while not requiring alternative approaches to justify themselves in ways that are publicly verifiable.

Meeting Expectations

But what expectations can be attributed to the children who attend the schools and to the parents of those children? Children frequently complain that their courses lack relevance, interest, and meaning; it is to this interpretation, at any rate, that their remarks most readily lend themselves. Parents can be equally succinct: schools exist to "make kids learn." Of course, what the parents and the children are saying amounts, in practice, to the same thing, since, if the educational process had relevance, interest, and meaning for the children, there would be no need to *make* them learn.

Learn what? We are often told that what is to be learned consists in the essentials of the heritage of Western civilization. That education should, in fact, be limited to an initiation of children into the cultural traditions of their society is hardly self-evident, although it would be difficult to show that it should be any less than such an introduction. Children are in no position to gauge the importance of cultural transmission to their society; they can only assess its meaningfulness to them. They are capable of being quite unenthusiastic about those aspects of Western or any other civilization for which many people now dead and some now living have felt great respect. Seldom are they interested enough or critical enough to ask why we revere a great many of the deeds of people of the past, whereas the same deeds performed today would be considered the height of barbarism. Children take our word for it that we revere what we say we revere, and have too little self-assurance to wonder if we might be incorrect. When they do protest (more often by what they fail to do rather than by what they do or say) that they fail to see what all this means, we soothe them with the remark that "it will all make sense eventually," and for yet a little while longer they may go along, their hands in ours, hoping it might be so.

Would children be wrong to expect that the entire educational process—as a whole at every stage, and in its development from stage to stage—be meaningful? If the school cannot help children to discover the significance of their experiences, if that is not its function at all, then there may be no alternative but to turn the educational system over to those who can most craftily engineer the children's consent to being manipulated into a state of mindless beatitude.

If, on the other hand, it is meaning for which children thirst and have a right to expect from the educational process, then this enlightens us about the legitimate incentives that might be employed in motivating them. Their self-interest demands profits in the form of meanings; no person in business expects to persist in a chronically unprofitable enterprise. But now we are compelled to acknowledge that the school must be defined by the nature of education, and not education by the nature of the school. Instead of insisting that education is a special form of experience that only the schools can provide, we should say that anything that helps us to discover meaning in life is educational, and the schools are educational only insofar as they do facilitate such discovery.

Discovery

Emphasis upon the term *discovery* is hardly coincidental. Information may be transmitted, doctrines may be indoctrinated, feelings may be shared—but meanings must be *discovered*. One cannot "give" another person meanings. One can write a book that other people may read, but the meanings the readers come up with eventually are those which they take from the book, not necessarily those put into it by the author. (The writers of textbooks often assume that the meaningfulness for them of the subjects with which they deal is automatically conveyed to their readers, when in fact the text as a delivery system transmits little that is retained.)

You attend a discussion, are provoked and excited by it, participate by making several comments, then later, when asked about the event, proceed to sum it up by recounting your own comments. As a comprehensive and objective account of the discussion in its entirety, your report must be considered one-sided. But what you may be trying to suggest is that you did take the entire discussion into account; your own remarks represent, to you, your appraisal of the gist of the event, and your pronouncement upon it. It is, after all, a very human experience that all of us have had—after a general discussion, reflecting particularly upon our own remarks. But those remarks embody the meanings of the event that we made ours, meanings that we do not consider merely "subjective," for they did not merely issue from us (or from our "minds"), but were, from the entire dialogue.

So it is with children. The meanings they hunger for cannot be dispensed to them the way wafers are dealt out to communicants at a mass; they must seek them out for themselves, by their own involvement in dialogue and inquiry. Nor is that the end of the matter, for meanings, once found, must be cared for and nurtured, as one might care for one's house plants, pets, or other living and precious treasures. But the children who cannot make sense of their own experience, who find the world alien, fragmentary, and baffling, are likely to cast about for shortcuts to total experiences, and eventually may experiment with drugs or succumb to psychoses. Possibly we could teach children before they reach out for such desperate remedies by helping them find the meanings so lacking in their lives.

Frustration

If those researchers who conduct experiments aimed at producing frustration in animals were asked to organize an educational process along the same lines, it is likely that they would insist that all subjects be taught as discrete entities, not even remotely connected with one another, so that children, with their needs for wholeness and completeness, would have to perform the heroic feat of synthesis all by themselves; their frustration would be guaranteed. But then, what difference is there between such a hypothetical system and the one that presently exists? Is there any persuasive reason why education cannot be a process that moves from whole to part, from general to specialized, from the comprehensive to the specific, rather than the other way around?

Like everyone else children crave a life of rich and significant experiences. They want not merely to have and to share, but to have and share meaningfully; not merely to like and love, but to like and love meaningfully; children want to learn, but to learn meaningfully. We see them glued to the television set, and we ascribe this behavior to a love of thrill and excitement, preferring not to note that, whatever else popular entertainment may be, it is at least presented in the form of dramatic wholes, not in the form of inscrutably estranged fragments. These meanings may often be superficial, but they are better than no meanings at all. But this is simply another instance of adult imperception of or misinterpretation of childhood experience, like seeing children as whimsical and capricious rather than experimental, as rash rather than adventurous, as irresolute and indecisive rather than tentative, as illogical rather than as sensitive to conflicts and ambiguities, as irrational rather than as resolute in protecting their own integrity.

Meaningful Experiences

Once it is acknowledged that, as far as children themselves are concerned, no educational plan will be worthy of the name unless it results in meaningful school and after-school experiences, we can feel some confidence in having arrived at one of the significant criteria for the evaluation of an educational design. It has already been indicated that meanings emerge from the perception of part-whole relationships as well as of means-end relationships. To present something part by part while merely promising eventually to provide the whole that would give each part its meaning is to build an educational system upon the model of a jigsaw puzzle—which is to say that it is great, but just for those few people who happen to like jigsaw puzzles. To specify the ends of an educational design without specifying the means by which they are to be attained is to have concocted something that is quite pointless. Yet again, to specify both ends and means, but to be unaware of the unintended consequences likely to emerge from the use of such means must be considered irresponsible, for the implementation of such a plan may generate meanings, as perceived by those affected by it, quite incompatible with the intended meanings.

Part-whole relationships—such as the meaning of a particular play in a game to the game as a whole, or the meaning of a word in a sentence, or the meaning of an episode in a movie, are meaning-laden relationships. Since the meaning is acquired concomitantly with the perception of the relationship, such meaning is generally spoken of as "intrinsic." (In this sense, what has no context has no meaning.) "Extrinsic" meaningfulness occurs when means are related to ends in an external or instrumental fashion. This is the sense in which a gasoline can found at the scene of a fire is meaningful, or the sense in which labor and wages are related to one another (where one is done for the sake of the other, but the one is not a meaningful part of the other).

Now a purely didactic textbook would have to be considered as being only extrinsically meaningful. We must ask, regarding its use: (1) does it actually achieve the goals that it is intended to achieve, and (2) does it produce unintended, counter-productive consequences as well? And we must specify the context. For in the case of a highly motivated student, a didactic textbook approach may be serviceable, and may involve relatively minor inconveniences in consequence. But in the case of students of less intense motivation, the use of such instruments may be viewed with apathy, or with downright revulsion. Mere utility has a low degree of intrinsic meaningfulness: the patients in the dental chair are aware of the instrumental value of the drill, but can be excused if they fail to be enchanted by it. It is inexcusable to expect a child who is only modestly motivated to "love knowledge for its own sake" when such knowledge is presented like bad-tasting medicine—as something that may be useful some day. That this dreary book will enlighten them eventually is something children cannot deny, just as they cannot deny that the nauseating substance in that spoon will eventually produce a cure. But we are not born with an awareness of the future: such an awareness is what adults construct out of past experiences and verifications. Children have little future to count on; they only know that the present makes sense or does not make sense, on its own terms. This is why they would appreciate having educational means that are meaning-laden: stories, games, discussions, trustful personal relationships, and so on. If the didactic textbook for children should eventually die out, it will be a death most richly deserved, the only regret being that it did not happen sooner—provided that its replacement is a textbook that children will find enjoyable for its own sake.

Need for Adventure

The textbook should be an adventure filled with discoveries; indeed, it should be a paradigm of discovery in practice. But why cannot the child's entire school experience be an adventure? It should be chockful of opportunities for surprise, with the tension of exciting possibilities, with tantalizing mysteries to be wondered at as well as with fascinating clarifications and illuminations. Must the school day necessarily be comprised of lockstep routines in which children are benevolently imprisoned? Routine and adventure are, of course, polar opposites. Routine is interminable, whereas adventure has a beginning, middle, and end. Routine is inherently meaningless, although we engage in it for the sake of values extrinsically related to it. Adventure is satisfying in and of itself; indeed, one dwells so often in memory on one's past adventures that it is as though they somehow contained, like dreams, the secret meaning of one's entire life. Routine is a matter of rote; adventure, never free of risk and delightful uncertainty, is what the child's reveries suggest life ought to be. It seems obvious that if the image children had of education were more consonant with adventure than with routine, the problems of truancy, delinquency, and in-school restlessness could be significantly alleviated.

It is a touching thing, of course—children's expectations of life experiences meaningfully organized, as it is likewise touching for them to expect that people intend no harm and will do them no harm. In time children will discover the ambiguities of experience, as they may discover ample grounds for interpersonal mistrust. But there is no reason why we cannot prepare them to cope with ambiguities and complexities: to teach them that everything is simple is only to give them still stronger grounds for mistrust later on.

As for the parents' reaction to all this, it would be difficult to assert that parents are intensely concerned that children have a meaningful school experience. Our culture encourages parents to acquire augmented self-esteem from the "successes" of their children, but threatens the parents with diminished self-esteem as a result of their children's "failures." When the parents grumble, as they often do, "Don't they teach you *anything* in that school?" their question may simply be symptomatic of their anxiety that the child may grow up to be irresponsible, and therefore a discredit to the family.

But what does the parent perceive to be the guarantor of responsibility in the existing educational set-up? Certainly not the manner in which the child's affective life is developed—that hardly appears relevant. No, what is more likely is that the parent clings to the hope that the schools will develop the child's *cognitive* processes. Parents will sometimes acknowledge as much when they admit that what they want the schools to do is not so much educate their children as "knock some sense into their heads." Granted, then, parents assume that the long years spent in school will convert their willful offspring into responsible adults. It is a bit disconcerting to find parents seldom demanding that the school train the child in Reasoning, much as parents do everywhere demand the other three R's for the children. Why the lack of attention to the drawing of inference, the citation of reasons for beliefs, the quest for evidence, the formation of concepts? Perhaps the answer lies in the prevalent notion that reasoning (in the form of logic) either cannot be taught *per se* to children, or should not be. Alternatively, the answer might lie in the assumption that the child's rationality is already sufficiently cultivated by such disciplines as mathematics (the assumption of transfer from mathematical to logical or linguistic reasoning being a good deal easier to make than to prove).

Meaning versus Rationality

We have tried to show that education, both from the child's point of view and from the parents', should be imbued with thoughtfulness and reasonableness. The child's claim can be seen as a demand for meaning, the parents' as a demand for rationality. The existing educational process can only be a disappointment to both, for children are not disciplined in such a way as to enable them to engage in effective reasonings, nor are their school experiences contextually structured so as to make available to them a rich and tempting array of meaning.

An education that has been structured for thoughtfulness promises to be an academically superior education, in behaviorally measurable terms, and even more valuable as an instrument for beyond-school experience. There are benefits in addition to the intrinsic delights to be found in such a process. It should not be overlooked that the development of the child's resources can enormously strengthen this self-concept, which in turn intensifies the child's sense of purpose and sense of direction. It is rather pointless to exhort children to be proud of themselves (to have a "positive self-image") without helping them to develop those competencies and powers of which they would like to be proud. It is similarly pointless to assure them that they have the dignity and worth of human beings, when what children more immediately and precisely need is to be helped to express the individuality of their experience and the uniqueness of their personal point of view. This applies with all the more forcefulness to economically disadvantaged children, for they have few other resources to call upon in life than their wits, and when these are disparaged, what else are they to fall back upon?

2 Thinking and the School Curriculum

The Child's Hunger for Meaning

All of us—not just children—have known what it is for things to lack meaning. It is a deeply disturbing experience, much more so than simply being puzzled.

When we are puzzled, we suspect there is an answer somewhere that will yield understanding. But meaninglessness can be terrifying. Children who sit at their desks and are inundated with factual information that seems jumbled, pointless, and unconnected to their lives have a direct sense of the meaninglessness of their experience. Meaninglessness is a much more fundamental problem than simply not knowing what to believe. Children who are experiencing it desperately search for clues that would give them guidance of some kind. Adults in this condition will often turn in their desperation to astrology and other quick and easy nostrums. But children don't know where to turn. And since school is compulsory, many children find themselves imprisoned in a nightmare.

People often think that the problem lies not in the educational process but in the fact that so many children today are bored and apathetic, and that this is a direct result of their home environment. But if the home environment were not at least initially stimulating, children would come to kindergarten bored and apathetic. They don't. Whatever their environment, they come to kindergarten bright-eyed, curious, and ready to learn. By third grade, however, many children's inquisitiveness is beginning to dissipate, and by the middle school years, they are beginning to suspect that they are being compelled to remain in school—not because it does them any good, but simply as a baby-sitting operation, and to keep them out of the labor market. Not that schools are totally joyless; it is in school that one meets one's friends and enjoys a social life with people of one's own age with whom one can communicate. But if school experience were as rich and meaningful as it is capable of being, we would not see children detesting their lives in school, as so many in fact do.

The relationship between education and meaning should be considered in-

12

violable. Wherever meaning accrues, there is education. This may happen in school, at home, in church, on the playground, or in any dimension of a child's life. On the other hand, the relationship between school and education is a highly contingent one. Schools may or may not provide education. But those schools that consider education their mission and purpose are schools that dedicate themselves to helping children find meanings relevant to their lives.

Meanings cannot be dispensed. They cannot be given or handed out to children. Meanings must be acquired; they are *capta*, not data. We have to learn how to establish the conditions and opportunities that will enable children, with their natural curiosity and appetite for meaning, to seize upon the appropriate clues and make sense of things for themselves. Many teachers will say that they are already doing this, and no doubt they are. But the educational process, from schools of education where teachers themselves are trained on through to the actual school classroom, does not operate in this fashion. Something must be done to enable children to acquire meaning for themselves. They will not acquire such meaning merely by learning the contents of adult knowledge. They must be taught to think and, in particular, to think for themselves. Thinking is the skill *par excellence* that enables us to acquire meanings.

Thinking Skillfully

When we are comfortably relaxed, a sequence of thoughts, often accompanied by images, will be the immediate object of our attention, and we may wave off the child who tugs at our sleeve by saying, "Don't interrupt me, I'm thinking"—as if when we later get up to drive the car, do some shopping, write a letter, read the newspaper, or prepare a meal, we are *not* thinking. The truth is, of course, that in the process of making things or doing things we are always thinking: there is no way a living, active human being can obliterate the thinking process. Why then is there the illusion that it is only during moments of relaxation, when we attend to the leisurely movements of a train of thoughts, that we engage in that peculiar activity people call thinking?

Consider an analogy. You are watching a film. The movements of the actors are completely lifelike. But something is wrong with the projector; it begins to slow down. Now the film is moving so slowly that the illusion of movement is gone, and you observe only individual frames, each completely static, slowly drifting in front of your eyes.

So it is with thinking. When we are physically active, or involved in an animated discussion, our thought processes are moving so rapidly that they can no longer be identified as a series of discrete individual thoughts, different from our bodily activities. The thinking that goes into waving goodbye to a friend or turning on the shower is so meshed with the action, and so swift, that we cannot isolate it, except perhaps as a blur.

Thus the thinking that goes on when we are relaxed and physically inactive is not at all typical of thinking; instead, it is highly atypical. It represents thinking moving at a heavy, lumbering pace, so slow that we can actually visualize the individual thoughts. But these slow-moving entities are not at all characteristic of thinking as it usually occurs.

You can prove this for yourself by paying attention to the way you engage in a lively conversation. Notice the sequences of flurries of mental acts that are required to listen to a comment, extricate implicit assumptions, draw inferences of what the speaker sought (or did not seek) to imply, speculate about the various possible intentions the speaker may have had, develop your own intention in response to the comment, rehearse various possible ways of responding so as to fulfill your intention, decide on the kind of remark to make (exclamation? question? ironical suggestion? tactful changing of subject?), choose the first word of your sentence, then the second to go with the first, and so on. The sheer density of mental activity in even the simplest of question-answer interchanges is enormous, because of the volume of thoughts involved in such an interchange and the rate of flow of the individual thought processes. But we are so alert, so attentive to what is being said, that we are unaware of the thinking, or aware of it only as a blurry periphery to our field of consciousness.

If the thinking that goes on in a conversation is densely structured and textured, that which goes on in the act of writing can be even more so. In writing we have in mind not just one audience but many possible audiences, each of whose possible responses to what we write must be anticipated. And we are concerned with a parameter of literary style that hardly comes into play in the course of spoken conversation, but that introduces a vast number of considerations that must be taken into account with the choice of every word.

Like breathing and digesting, thinking is a natural process—something everyone does. From this we are unfortunately prone to conclude that nothing much can be done to improve thinking. We infer that we already do it about the best we can, just as we feel we cannot improve on the way we breathe or digest.

But this is simply not the case. Thinking is natural, but it can also be recognized as a skill capable of being perfected. There are more efficient and less efficient ways of thinking. We are able to say this with confidence, because we possess criteria that enable us to distinguish between skillful and clumsy thinking. These criteria are the principles of logic. By means of such rules, we can tell the difference between valid and invalid inferences.

It may be thought at this point we are suggesting children learn logic so as to be able to think more efficiently. But this is not so. Children learn logic along with their learning of language. The rules of logic, like the rules of grammar, are acquired when children learn to speak. If a very young child is told, "if you do that, you will get punished," it is assumed that the child understands, "if I don't want to get punished, I shouldn't do it." That assumption is usually correct. Very small children, in other words, recognize that the denial of the consequent requires the denial of the antecedent. Although this is a very sophisticated piece of reasoning, children are capable of it in very early stages of their lives.

To draw invalid inferences may not qualify as thinking well, but nevertheless it is thinking. To fail to draw appropriate conclusions, to define and classify badly, to assess facts uncritically, all of these are instances of thinking— but of poor thinking. The pedagogical problem is, at least in its first stage, to transform the child who is already a thinking child into a child who thinks well. A reliable thinking skills program would do more than enable children to deal effectively with immediate cognitive tasks, such as problems to be solved, or decisions to be made. It would seek to consolidate children's cognitive potentials so as to prepare them for more effective thinking in the future. The aim of a thinking skills program is not to turn children into philosophers or decision-makers, but to help them become more thoughtful, more reflective, more considerate, and more reasonable individuals. Children who have been helped to become more judicious not only have a better sense of when to act but also of when not to act. Not only are they more discreet and considerate in dealing with the problems they face, they are also capable of deciding when it would be appropriate to postpone dealing with problems or to circumvent such problems rather than confront them head on. Thus one of the aims of a thinking skills program should be the improvement of judgment. For judgment is the link between thinking and action. Reflective children are apt to display good judgment, and children with good judgment are unlikely to perform inappropriate or inconsiderate actions.

The integration of thinking skills into every aspect of the curriculum would sharpen children's capacity to make connections and draw distinctions, to define and to classify, to assess factual information objectively and critically, to deal reflectively with the relationship between facts and values, and to differentiate their beliefs and what is true from their understanding of what is logically possible. These specific skills help children listen better, study better, learn better, and express themselves better. They, therefore, carry over into all academic areas.

A thinking skills program must help children think both more logically and more meaningfully. These two requirements are closely connected with one another. Since to a great extent what a statement means consists in the inferences that can logically be drawn from it, the capacity to draw inferences correctly is of the highest importance in establishing the meaningfulness of those activities that children engage in both in and outside of school. The richer the array of inferences that can be logically or linguistically inferred by children from what they read, perceive, or otherwise experience, the more satisfying and more wholesome will those experiences seem to them.

Thinking Skills and Basic Skills

The thinking process is a vast and intricate family of activities: there is mathematical thinking and historical thinking; practical and poetical thinking; thinking as one reads, as one writes, as one dances, as one plays, as one speaks. Reading and mathematics are sometimes called the "basic skills" because they are said to be able to unlock and to reinforce other cognitive skills. But reading and mathematics are simply two expressions of cognitive processing; performance in these areas can be no better than the thinking skills that underlie them. From an educational point of view, the improvement of thinking skills is of crucial and foundational importance. The child who has gained proficiency in thinking skills is not merely a child who has grown, but a child whose very capacity for growth has increased.

Reading to Find Meanings

There is rather general agreement that children with reading problems are also likely to be hampered in their thinking. Improving the way such children read, it is believed, will likely improve the way they think. But it is our contention that reading and thinking are interdependent. Each ministers to the other. Consequently, helping children think can very well result in helping them to read.

The concern about children's reading should not be shrugged off as an anxiety about something superficial or unimportant. If reading and thinking are interdependent, there is reason to be concerned if children are far less proficient in reading than they could be, or if even competent readers seem to care little about reading.

Now, what motivates children to read? What is the incentive? What do they get out of it? No answer to these questions is more plausible than that one reads to get meanings. If we try to read a book and become more and more convinced that it is meaningless, we throw it aside. The child does the same thing. Children who cannot find meaning in what they read simply stop reading.

But what kind of meanings do children look for? The meanings they are hungry for are those that might be relevant to—and might illuminate—their lives. Some of these problems are unique to the stage of growth through which they happen to be passing. Others are problems common to all human beings. Children wonder about both sorts of problems. They wonder about their own identities. They wonder why they are expected to go to school every day; they wonder how the world began and how it might end. Sometimes they may wonder what to do about their own appetites and emotions.

Children are often reluctant to talk about their problems—they often have a sense of discretion and privacy that we must respect. But many such children would still like to engage in discussions where problems like their own might come up. For example, take what the jargon of psychology identifies as "sibling rivalry." Many times, children in the same family who are not getting along with one another will be unable to discuss these conflicts with each other. But they'll love to read fairy tales about sister princesses who don't get along, or about princes in the same royal family who are rivals for parental affection. Somehow, it takes the sting out of the problem when it can be understood as part of a story that begins with "once upon a time. . . ." In the make-believe setting of the fairy tale, the problem of sibling rivalry can be considered more detachedly, just as Homer helped the Greeks see themselves more objectively in his great account of their war with Troy.

So, if children are to develop a sustained interest in reading, it must be meaningfully relevant to their major concerns—to the things that matter most to them in their lives. What counts is not just learning to see words and say them, but learning to grasp the meanings of words, phrases, sentences, in the contexts in which they appear.

Beginning readers have to learn to find connections—connections that are often extremely difficult to pinpoint. It is not just what a sentence *says* that is important. What does it suggest? What does it imply? For example, suppose a mother says to you about one of your students: "Oh, I'll admit he's not very good in *spelling*!" What is she suggesting? Isn't she hinting that spelling's not all that important anyway, but that her son's quite good in certain other subjects? Or take a statement like, "*Everyone's* going to the party!" Taken literally, it could mean merely that "everyone's going, so I'm going too." But it may also be taken as suggesting that everyone "who counts," everyone "who's anyone," is going. Or, accompanied by tears, it may mean, "everyone else is going, so why can't I?"

To discover meanings in written passages, a child has to be sensitive to meaning, and has to know how to *infer* it or draw it out. Inference is reasoning from what is given literally to what is suggested or implied. If someone says, "Oh, you're Norwegian, so you must like snow!" you should be able to infer that he is assuming that all Norwegians like snow. If you read that "only women are excluded from the club," you can legitimately infer that all men are admitted. Or, if you know that today is Tuesday the 14th, you shouldn't have much trouble inferring that tomorrow will the Wednesday the 15th.

At every moment of our lives, we draw inferences. If you are crossing the street and hear a horn, you infer a car is coming. If you see an empty glass coated with milk on the inside, you infer that someone has had a glass of milk. Thanks to inference, we can draw a myriad of meanings from what we see, hear, taste, touch, and smell, as well as from what we think.

Naturally, the more readily children can draw inferences, the more meanings they will be able to extract from what they read. This in turn should make their reading more satisfying. And the more satisfied they are by what they read, the more often they are likely to read—whether for entertainment, for comfort, or for understanding.

Reasoning as a Foundational Skill

No one knows for sure how it happens, but thinking is so intimately connected with language that it is widely suspected that learning to speak, learning to think, and learning to reason are all tied in with one another. It could well be that part of the explanation of how children learn to reason is to be found in observing how they learn to talk.

Certainly the child's achievement in learning to organize words into grammatical sentences is utterly magnificent. That this feat is performed every day by children all over the world, in every imaginable language, is one of the most extraordinary facts we know. It is not only learning words that is so remarkable, but organizing them as they are spoken into grammatically correct structures—and this by virtual infants. The relating of thoughts to one another logically, as well as grammatically, is yet another striking achievement.

Evidently children bring with them these dispositions to organize their thinking and speaking grammatically and logically. But just as children must be taught the difference between using language well and using it badly (for example, ungrammatically), so they must be taught the difference between reasoning soundly and reasoning sloppily.

We spend a great deal of time helping children see the difference between well-constructed and badly constructed prose, or between properly executed and improperly executed exercises in arithmetic, but we hardly devote any time at all to teaching children to tell better reasoning from worse. This is not because children do not need to know how to reason, or lack the ability to learn it. It is because we ourselves are generally unacquainted with logic, and are embarrassed to admit we have so much difficulty in understanding it.

We have been saying that one reason children cannot read better than they do is that we do not teach them reasoning. And without reasoning, they cannot figure out what they're reading.

Reading, of course, is the focus of much attention at present. Critics accuse the schools of not teaching reading well, and many schools respond by paying greater and greater attention to reading, but often at the expense of other educational objectives.

It is odd how reading has become an end in itself. There was a time when it was considered simply a means. Parents wanted their children to grow up to be intelligent adults; to develop the child's intelligence, what better means could there be than reading? But increasingly the stress is on reading, while the thinking processes it was supposed to build are neglected. We "redouble our efforts, having forgotten our aims."

It may seem strange that we urge the teaching of reasoning to improve children's reading, and that we urge that reading be seen in turn as a means to helping children think, rather than as an end in itself. We reply that reasoning and reading are skills that can be taught, and that reinforce each other. Whether thinking can be taught is debatable, but it certainly can be encouraged. And instruction in the procedures of reasoning can be helpful in developing the art of thinking.

But how is reasoning taught? Schools often maintain that they are already doing it, and doing it well. To justify their claims, they cite mathematics and language arts programs. Arithmetic and reading can contribute usefully to good thinking. But, by themselves, they are insufficient. The fact that Johnny adds, subtracts, multiplies, divides, and can race through comic books—or even *Stuart Little*—does not mean he can reason clearly. It does not mean he is developing habits of efficient thinking, or of arriving at independent judgments. Something more is needed.

In our own program, we try to sensitize children to sloppy thinking at the same time that we try to help them think well. We give them examples like these:

> My father's been reading in the papers that smoking causes cancer, so he says he's going to give up reading.
> Whenever I see Elinor, I ask her what she thinks of Joe, and she gets real embarrassed. Boy, does she have a crush on me!
> I've been told that one child out of every five that's born in the world is Chinese; I have three brothers, so I figure the next baby in our family will probably look pretty Oriental.

Or we ask them absurd questions such as these:

When is a straight line crooked?
Why are dolphins such stupid fish?
Is it warmer in the summer or in the city?

Children can easily learn to spot the flaws in examples like these. But they need to discuss what is wrong under the supervision of someone trained to distinguish between thinking effectively and thinking confusedly.

Obviously, we need to develop attractive ways of presenting matters of intellectual quality without compromising the integrity of the subject. Our objective should not be to confront children with two isolated entities—the structure of logical thought on the one hand and the urgent and bewildering problems of life on the other. What we must do is allow children to discover how delightfully and how fruitfully thought can play on its subject matter. We must help them see how reasoning about matters of importance to them can be a richly rewarding experience. At times such reasoning can be inspiring, even if it does no more than reformulate the basic issues more insightfully.

Thinking Skills and Other Academic Disciplines

Experimental research has shown that introducing philosophy to children in a sustained and rigorous way by trained teachers can make a significant impact on basic skills. (See the summary of experimental research in Appendix B.) But can it make a substantial or significant difference when integrated into other academic disciplines?

Two areas that are of major importance in the junior high school curriculum are language arts and social studies. In both cases, philosophy for children can be useful, not only in order to raise preliminary questions about the underlying assumptions of the discipline, but in order to develop critical habits and methods of inquiry essential to student proficiency in these areas.

Consider the case with language arts. We have already noted the problems apparent in the teaching of reading; there is similar widespread dissatisfaction with the effectiveness of existing approaches to writing. A further problem is the declining sense of relevance among school children of the literary tradition to their performance of the basic reading and writing skills. Teachers complain that students are inadequately motivated to learn and students complain, on the other hand, that teachers insist too much upon mechanics of reading and writing but fail to make such skills relevant to their lives.

One way of overcoming the teacher's objection that students are inadequately motivated would be to use a novel instead of the traditional didactic text, a novel whose plot would be one the students could readily identify with. Let the plot be one in which a student experiences a complete block when it comes to writing poetry or literary prose, and let the novel demonstrate how classroom discussions and well-chosen exercises provided by the teacher can be helpful in dissolving such a block.

In general, children resist doing what they do not understand. To be told they have to write a poem or a composition is for some children horrible. They don't see why they should do it; nor do they see the fundamental issues involved or the relevance to their lives. A philosophy course prior to or concurrent with the regular language arts program could explore just these considerations. Children could be given an opportunity to discuss criteria of good writing, the difference between poetry and prose, the relationship between experience and meaning, the relationship between feeling and expression, and the distinctions between fact and fiction and between explanation and description. Further, children could explore such notions as adventure, imagination, attention, perception, definition, communication, possibility, meaning, liberation, surprise, and perfection.

What would discussion of these notions do for the child? By themselves, they do nothing. Such discussions are helpful only when they emerge in a course that is seriously concerned with helping children come to grips with their own life situations and with helping them to see the connection between those situations and the literary skills that they are being asked to acquire. If literature and writing are presented to children as things only adults or highly motivated bright children do, then they will tend to strike most of the members of the class as alien and alienating. The student has got to want to appropriate the work of literature and to identify with the motives of the writer.

The student must also see that there is no conflict between literature and thinking. All too often, children view poetry as an inventory of someone else's feelings and perceptions. That thinking went into the poem and can be shared with the reader—something the reader can re-enact and even do for himself—is something of which many children are not aware. A review of the writing that children do engage in will quickly show their readiness to express their thoughts and to formulate their convictions about life in the world in literary form. Philosophy for children would support this native inclination on the part of children by providing the conditions for such expression.

In the case of social studies, much the same would be true regarding the need to encourage children to reflect upon their own life situation as the primary matrix out of which the study of social studies should develop. But a course in social studies would concern itself with sociological and political aspects of these student life situations. The classroom discussions would involve concepts such as democracy, society, justice, anarchy, education, property, law, crime, social ideals, division of labor, institutions, tradition, responsibility, authority, and freedom. Social studies to a child often appears as a course in data, an endless inventory of facts whose relationships to one another are vague and confusing. What philosophy can do is give the child an intellectual sense of direction so that the materials of the course can be approached with a greater confidence. When children can be helped to understand the ideals and values and criteria that are taken for granted in a society, they are equipped to judge how well the institutions and practices in that society are operating. This is not the case when they are encouraged to study those institutions and practices without the critical apparatus that would enable them to judge and would give them a sense of perspective and proportion in dealing with the vast amount of material of this kind.

This approach, moreover, would help to bridge the gap between the institutions in the society at large and the situations of the student in the classroom. All too often, students see no connection between what they are studying, what they do in their lives, and what society at large does. These factors must be brought together in a meaningful way in order for children to begin to have a conception of themselves as social and political beings.

The Relationship between Dialogue and Thinking

Since we often assume that thinking is private and internal, we also come to view it as something mysterious and baffling. Under these circumstances, people are unable to apply criteria that would enable them to distinguish better thinking from worse thinking because the reality itself is not apparent to them.

Moreover, when thinking is construed as something wholly "mental" and "private," there is apt to be considerable misunderstanding as to how it may be improved. For example, consider the relationship between thinking and dialogue. The common assumption is that reflection generates dialogue, when, in fact, it is dialogue that generates reflection. Very often, when people engage in dialogue with one another, they are compelled to reflect, to concentrate, to consider alternatives, to listen closely, to give careful attention to definitions and meanings, to recognize previously unthought of options, and in general to perform a vast number of mental activities that they might not have engaged in had the conversation never occurred.

Ask yourself if this is not true. What are the most memorable and intellectually stimulating events of the school day? Study hall? Lectures? Presentations? Paper and pencil tests? Or classroom discussions where everyone is involved and talking about what matters to them as human beings? Following such a discussion, the participants reflect on what they themselves have said and what they might have said; they recall what other people have said, and try to figure out why they might have said it. Moreover, the participants reproduce in their own thought processes the structure and progress of the class conversation. This is what is meant when it is said that thinking is the internalization of dialogue.

When we internalize dialogue, we reproduce not only the thoughts that we have just heard the other participants express, but we also respond in our own minds to those expressions. Further, we pick up from the audible dialogue the ways in which people draw inferences, identify assumptions, challenge one another for reasons, and engage in critical intellectual interactions with one another. In a dialogue, slovenly reasoning is attacked and criticized; it is not allowed to pass unchallenged. Criticial attitudes towards what other people say are developed in the participants of the discussion. But these critical attitudes are then turned upon one's own reflections. One considers carefully what others might say about one's contribution, once one has learned the techniques of critical examination of other people's thinking processes and modes of expression.

Insistence that the formation of a classroom community is of crucial importance to the encouragement of thinking is not without a basis in cognitive or in social psychology. If one turns, for example, to the work of George Herbert Mead (see *Mind, Self and Society*) or to the work of Lev Vygotsky (see *Mind in Society*), one will find both philosophical and psychological support for the thesis that thinking is the internalization of dialogue. Vygotsky, for example, clearly recognizes that there is a difference between children's ability to solve problems as individuals and their ability to solve such problems in collaboration with their teacher and their classmates. Like Mead, Vygotsky sees the formation of a classroom community as indispensable for stimulating students to think and do at higher levels of performance than they would display if acting individually.

This does not mean that all instances of dialogue are instances of communities of inquiry. Children are perfectly capable of giggling, chattering, not paying attention, or starting to talk all at once. Even when they all talk in sequence, they may not listen to what each participant has to say and try to build on one another's contributions. To the extent that certain children are concerned only with what they have to say regardless of how the dialogue unfolds, they are not full participants in the community of inquiry. Further, to the extent that they fail to put forth an effort to follow the dialogue and make a contribution that seems relevant and meaningful, they are not participants. Mead points out that there is a difference between merely imitative behavior and internalizing the processes of the group. When you enroll children in a nursery school where the other children are playing a game, the new children may imitate what the others are doing without really understanding the process. They understand the process only when they understand and internalize the rules of the game, the roles of each participant, and the meaning that the game has for the group as a whole.

Now it may be asked why a child would want to participate in a community where there are such rules and regulations. Mead would argue that children come to school already equipped with social impulses awaiting the opportunity for expression. The child does not have to be converted from a barbarian into a social being. The child is already social, but requires a milieu in which these social tendencies can be expressed in a constructive manner. Thus, children who often are mute in class are not children who have no desire to talk; instead they are usually children who fear that what they have to say will be dismissed by others as unimportant. Should a genuine community of mutual respect emerge in the classroom, where students such as these will find the opportunities to speak and be listened to with respect, they will likely come out of their shells and engage voluntarily in the community dialogue. Very often the non-verbal child is simply one who is daydreaming about how wonderful it could be if he were at the front of the room addressing the class about some matter of importance.

The role of classroom discussion in motivating children to engage in academic activities has often been underestimated. For example, a teacher may assign a topic to the class and require a paper and pencil essay the next day. But children very often have to go through a transitional process of verbalizing various ways of approaching a particular topic in order to prime their intellectual pumps. They have to try out their ideas on one another, listen to the feedback, overcome the feeling that what they have to say is absurd or irrelevant by testing it on the group so as to learn from one another's experiences and begin to feel a sense of excitement as the implications of the topic begin to seep in. It is only then that the assignment begins to seem enticing to them. We should never assume that because we, as adults, can write something without discussing it with anyone else, or read something and comprehend it without discussing it with someone else, that such refined end-products of the educational process are proper models for the process itself. Dialogue is one stage of that awkward and gross processing of experience that must take place if raw experience is to be converted into refined expression. For children, at any rate, dialogue is an indispensable phase of the process.

Teachers would do well to keep in mind the powerful connections that exist between reading and speaking on the one hand and between writing and speaking on the other. In addition, there is an intimate relationship between speaking and listening, that if one does not listen attentively to the meanings that are being expressed, but rather attends to less essential components of the conversation, one will probably misunderstand the speaker. Those who learn to listen to the points other people are making and to discern the meanings that are to be found in the conversation are likely to be those who grasp what they read as meaningful rather than meaningless.

Thinking Well about Things That Matter

Philosophy is a discipline that contains logic and therefore is concerned to introduce criteria of excellence into the thinking process, so that students can move from merely thinking to thinking well. At the same time, the philosophical tradition that stretches back to the sixth century B.C. has always dealt with a specific body of concepts that have been thought important to human life or relevant to human knowledge. Examples of such concepts would be justice, truth, goodness, beauty, world, personal identity, personhood, time, friendship, freedom, and community. Some of these concepts are still ill-defined, and many of them are highly controversial. But they represent the combined efforts of a great many philosophers over many generations to bring order and clarity into our understanding. Without concepts such as these to function as regulative ideas, we would have considerably more difficulty in making sense of our experience. What especially distinguishes civilization from barbarism is that civilized peoples are *concerned* about differences between beautiful and ugly, good and bad, truth and falsity, justice and injustice. If human beings did not think the concept of beauty meant anything, it is hard to see why they would have persisted, as they have, in struggling to build beautiful cities and beautiful works of art. If they did not believe in justice, they would not have struggled to create more acceptable forms of social organization. Philosophy deals with the ways in which these concepts regulate our understanding of the things we do in our lives. The acquisition by children of such concepts is indispensable if they are to make sense of the social, aesthetic, and ethical aspects of their lives.

There is a mistaken notion that children are not interested in philosophical notions, but wish only to prattle about trivialities or to master facts. Adults too often assume that children are curious merely in order to acquire specific information rather than to understand the reasons that things are the way they are.

Unfortunately, philosophy has traditionally been reserved for adults on the apparent assumption that children would not be interested in a subject matter so abstract, and would not in any case be capable of dealing with it since it is so technical. But the fact is that philosophical issues are not restricted in their interest to adults, and need not be formulated in such a technical fashion that they cannot be dealt with by children. Indeed, one of the things that is so wonderful about philosophy is that people of any age can reflect upon and discuss philosophical issues profitably. Children are as fascinated by such notions as friendship or fairness as adults are, and both children and adults can recognize that no one as yet has said the last word on these topics. The possibility that adults and children can together explore philosophical possibilities is one of the most refreshing and encouraging consequences of elementary school philosophy.

A philosophical thinking skills program, in addition to encouraging children to be rigorously critical, will encourage them to speculate imaginatively. When children discuss the way things are, there should always be a concomitant effort to explore with them how things might be. We should avoid giving children the impression that things could not be other than they are. Even in the case of facts, not to encourage children to think about what kind of a world it would be if such facts did not exist is to lose an opportunity to strengthen their capacity for independent and creative speculation.

One of the major problems in the practice of education today is the lack of unification of the child's educational experience. What the child encounters is a series of disconnected, specialized presentations. When language arts follows mathematics in the morning program, the child can see no connection between them, nor can he or she see a connection between language arts and the social studies that follows, or a connection between social studies and physical sciences.

This splintering of the school day reflects the general fragmentation of experience, whether in school or out, that characterizes modern life. It is also due, however, to the enormous increase in the factual dimension of human knowledge, for insofar as education involves a transmission of information to the child, it must be simplified and schematized by specialists. The result is that each discipline tends to become self-contained, and loses track of its connections with the totality of human knowledge, in an effort simply to present a bare outline of that particular field.

Since such specialization is likely to prevail for the foreseeable future, there needs to be some way of establishing continuity among the different disciplines that make up the school curriculum. Normally, the burden of establishing continuity is laid upon the teacher, who unfortunately is seldom trained to see continuities among different subject areas. Thus to expect the teacher to be able to establish such continuities for the child is unreasonable. The teacher may not have been trained to be aware of the formal resemblances between grammar, mathematics, and logic; or to be aware of the methodological continuities that connect the physical and social sciences; or to see the connections between the literary description of social life and the sociological descriptions of social life. Furthermore, it is unrealistic to ask the teacher to create the continuities between the different subject areas for children when specialists have for so long been unable to organize and express such continuities.

Ultimately each discipline will have to recognize its connections with the other areas of human knowledge. There is no good reason why every specialized curriculum should not contain bridges to the other disciplines that will enable the child to confront the interconnections of human knowledge as a fact rather than as a piously hoped-for ideal.

But the immediate step to be taken is to lift the burden of establishing continuity from the teacher and transfer it, at least in part, to the child. This can be done by building upon children's natural curiosity, their natural desire for wholeness, their natural inclination to continue questioning until they are satisfied, whether such inquiry on their part stays within the bounds of prescribed disciplines or not. Children have the motivation and the interest to insist that their understanding be unified and complete. What both children and teacher therefore need is guidance from the curriculum that would indicate to them how to make the connections that they are looking for.

The question arises, How can philosophy satisfy this need for continuity for both teacher and children? The answer seems clear: If children's chief contribution to the educational process is their inquisitiveness, and if philosophy is characteristically a question-raising discipline, then philosophy and children would seem to be natural allies. What could better connect children with the formal structure of human knowledge than a discipline that has traditionally concerned itself with the interrelationship among the different intellectual disciplines, and with the raising of ever more penetrating questions about how human experience is to be understood and interpreted?

In other words, philosophy encourages the intellectual resourcefulness and flexibility that can enable children and teachers alike to cope with the disconnectedness and fragmentization of existing curricula. Its traditional concerns with ethics, with the nature of knowledge, and with the nature of reality are concerns that transcend existing disciplines and at the same time are basically related to the subject matters with which existing disciplines deal.

The peculiarity of philosophy is that the questions it raises deal with the nature of human knowledge in a way that is, so to speak, directly at right-angles with the distribution of non-philosophical subject matters. That is, following the accepted division of knowledge into such academic subject matters as physical science, life science, mathematics, history, and the like, children may be encouraged to ask such questions (if they are encouraged to ask questions at all) as, What is colonialism? What is gravitation? What is long division?

A philosopher, on the other hand, raises questions that are metaphysical, epistemological, aesthetic, or ethical, and what is unique about these questions is that they cut directly across the diverse subject matter areas. To ask what is ethical is to ask a question that applies equally to the sciences, the arts, the professions, and every other aspect of human activity. Likewise, every subject matter area has an aesthetic dimension, an epistemological dimension, a metaphysical dimension. The mathematician may insist that children begin by learning simple arithmetical operations, but the children may stagger the teacher by asking, "What is number?"—an immensely profound metaphysical question. The teacher of history may wish to concentrate on the history of the Roman Empire, but the children, with seeming innocence, may first want to know "what is history?" and are duly suspicious of proceeding without an explanation. Similarly with such questions as "What is an explanation?" "What is obedience?" "What is goodness?" The teacher who insists that students "get the facts" should be willing to engage in discussion with the child who asks, "But, what is a fact?" In other words, every time children call into question the fundamental assumptions of the subject matter they are studying, they raise metaphysical questions. Every time they want to know how they can be sure of anything, they are raising epistemological questions. Every time they want to know why, on what grounds, their parents or teachers recommend, say, Tom Sawyer over James Bond, they are raising aesthetic questions.

Now, of course, there is a good deal of controversy as to what answers you give to the question, "What is number?" or "What is a fact?" Nor are we altogether clear what history is, or what an explanation is, or what the mind is, or what human individuality is. In fact, philosophy involves precisely this perpetual effort to come to grips with questions that permit no simple solution and that require continual rephrasing and reformulation. But the fact that there are no ready answers to these philosophical questions that children continually raise is no justification for dismissing such questions when the child asks them. Such questioning represents children's search for wholeness and completeness, their healthy disregard of artificial categories and barriers to understanding. Not to encourage and nurture children's search for comprehension by systematically introducing them to philosophical dialogue through which their curiosity can be nourished and their insights clarified is to compel them to accept the aridity of the overspecialized view of knowledge as presently found in the schools, rather than the rich, synoptic, comprehensive philosophical view that their questions suggest they prefer.

The "philosophy for children" approach thus involves the view that children's questions tend to be extraordinarily sweeping in scope and grandeur. To ask a question, "How did the world begin?" or "What is everything made of?" or "What happens to people when they die?" is to raise issues of enormous metaphysical import. The fact that children can raise such questions indicates that they begin with a thirst for holistic explanations, and it is patronizing, to say the least, not to try to help them develop concepts equal in generality to the questions they ask. Philosophy is therefore of enormous benefit to persons seeking to form concepts that can effectively represent aspects of their life experience. The teacher who recognizes and respects the sense of totality that children demand will endeavor to help them develop the greatest possible intellectual flexibility and resourcefulness. Children will respect the teacher who takes their questions seriously, even if this means no more than answering a question with another question. Thus, if the child asks, "Is the world made of matter?" the teacher may ask the child, "What do you think matter is?" Or if the child asks, "How did the world begin?" the teacher may ask, "How can you tell that it had a beginning?" This forces the teacher into a role of questioner or searcher like that of the child.

To be asked by a child, "What is death?" is to be compelled to ask oneself what is life. To be asked by a child, "What is mind?" is to be compelled to ask oneself what matter is. In other words, every question that implies a one-sided, partial view of things requires an answer that is more exhaustive, and compels us to look at the matter through a richer and more varied set of perspectives.

In summary, it is commonplace to deplore the fragmentation and over-specialization that seems to be endemic in education. It is now becoming clear that the solution to this problem will not come from those who are themselves practitioners of these very specializations, because they are themselves already too overspecialized to devise a solution. On the other hand, it is impractical to thrust the burden of generalization and continuity upon teachers who have not themselves been trained to raise the more general questions or to see continuities among the various subject matters. Philosophy in the classroom must be seen as a countervailing force to the overspecialization rampant in the educational system, and the burden of introducing philosophy into the classroom will be borne more than willingly by the children themselves, since the meanings philosophy represents are among those the children cherish most. Obviously, the future of philosophy in the classroom is dependent upon the training of teachers not only to understand the philosophical dimensions of educational subject areas that the teacher presently teaches during the school day but also to learn how systematically to nurture and sharpen (and not merely to tolerate) this philosophical quest on the part of students.

Children need comprehensiveness and a sense of perspective. But they can develop these only if the educational process itself challenges their imaginations and gives scope to their intellectual processes while at the same time providing the pathways by which the various subject matters of the curriculum can be integrated with one another. These are two essential requirements for a general education program, and philosophy for children can satisfy both. It provides children with the intellectual and imaginative tools they need, and it provides the mode of transition from subject matter to subject matter that bridges and connects the various disciplines to which the child is exposed during the course of the school day.

3

Philosophy:
The Lost Dimension
in Education

Philosophy Begins in Wonder

As adults, we have learned to accept the perplexities that emerge from our daily experience, and to take them pretty much for granted. Many of us no longer wonder why things are the way they are. We have come to accept parts of life as puzzling and enigmatic because that is the way they have always been.

Many adults have ceased to wonder because they feel that there is no time for wondering, or because they have come to the conclusion that it is simply unprofitable and unproductive to engage in reflection about things that cannot be changed anyhow. Many adults have never had the experience of engaging in wondering and reflecting that somehow made a difference in their lives. The result is that such adults, having ceased to question and to reach for the meanings of their experience, eventually become examples of passive acceptance that children take to be models for their own conduct.

Thus the prohibition against wonder is transmitted from generation to generation. Before long, children now in school will themselves be parents. If we can somehow preserve their natural sense of wonder, their readiness to look for meaning and their hunger to understand why things are the way they are, there might be some hope that at least this upcoming generation will not serve as models of unquestioning acceptance to their own children.

At every moment of a child's life, events impinge upon that child that are perplexing or enigmatic. Consider a small girl from the very moment she wakes up. Perhaps she discovers her mother is angry with her and she is not aware of having done anything to deserve this anger. She is bewildered. On her way to school, she may observe many more things whose meanings are obscure to her: the firehouse flag is at half-mast, garbage cans are rolling around the street, some children she knows are walking away from school rather than towards it, one of the street corners is flooded with water, a merchant is opening a series of locks to his store, and so on. Perhaps if she had an adult companion who would be willing to take the time to answer the ques-

31

tions that each of these incidents might provoke, the child would gradually begin to piece together some larger understanding of how the world works. Insofar as an education aims at providing young people with such an understanding, its greatest resource is the child's perpetual curiosity.

Things are wonderful when we can think of no way of explaining them. It may be a magician's card trick, or a caterpillar turning into a butterfly, or a Schubert trio. It may be a quasar in outer space, or it may be the activities of a virus under a microscope. But whatever it is, if we find it inexplicable, we are inclined to call it marvelous, and wonder at it.

When we find the world wonderful, it is because we seem to be confronted not by soluble problems, but by utter mysteries. You may know ever so much about heredity, but it matters little when you step before the mirror and confront your face. Ah, now there's a mystery! Where did it come from? How did it get to be the way it is? To what extent are you responsible for it? Surely questions like these have occurred to you from time to time.

They occur to children constantly. Because children wonder not only about themselves, but about the world. Where did it come from? How did it get to be the way it is? To what extent are we responsible for it? And if not we, then who?

Children look at their fingernails, and wonder where they came from. How does something like a fingernail grow out from one's body? But then, everything about their body seems fascinating to them.

Likewise, a snail is fascinating to them—or a mud puddle—or the dark spots on the face of the moon. It is only gradually that a crust or scale will grow over their minds, and they will take these things more and more for granted, until from marvelling at everything, they marvel at nothing.

Wonder and Meaning

To explain something, and thus dispel our puzzlement, we must somehow find the surrounding circumstances that might explain it, the conditions accountable for it. Or we must find a context or frame of reference to which the puzzling thing belongs, for we can understand it if it is a meaningful part of a larger whole.

For example, suppose you had planned to go to a movie with some friends, but you got there late—just in time for the last scene, by which you were completely bewildered. So you turn to your friends, as the lights come up, and you say, "What did it mean? What did it mean?" They tell you all that had happened before your arrival—and suddenly the last scene snaps into place. Its meaning becomes clear to you as you see it as a part in a larger whole.

But suppose you had not been late at all. Suppose you had been on time, and had seen the whole film with your friends. But you found the film an enigma from beginning to end, so you turn to your friends and ask, "What did it mean?" Unfortunately, there is not much they can tell you. You saw the whole film, and there is no larger framework to put it in. In this sense, all you can do is try to understand it on its own terms, lacking as it does the larger context that would give it meaning.

Since children do not have a fully formed frame of reference into which to place each experience as it happens, each such experience takes on for them an enigmatic, puzzling quality. No wonder, then, the children wonder at the world.

Now, there are three ways that children try to cope with the mysteries or marvels they find around them. The first is through a scientific explanation. The second is through a fairy tale or story that offers a helpful interpretation on a symbolic level. The third is by formulating the matter philosophically—in the form of a question.

Scientific Explanation

The scientific approach usually appeases the child, but if the explanation offered is only partial, the child's appetite for understanding will hardly be satisfied. "Why's there that rainbow on the surface of the puddle?" you are asked. "Because there's a film of oil on the water," you reply. The child may say no more. But the puzzlement can remain. What has oil got to do with rainbows? Why should one cause the other? You have not really dealt with the problem for him; you have merely postponed it.

Nor is there really anything wrong with what you have done. You can destroy a child's curiosity by overkill. You want to help children find out as much as they need to know about the problem they are presently dealing with, without damaging their curiosity itself by telling them more than they want to know.

There are those who say that small children are not interested in getting scientific explanations—that is, explanations in terms of causes. Children, it is claimed, want to know the *purpose* behind everything, not just the cause. And surely this is often the case. You may observe to a two-year-old how pretty the sky is, and she may reply, "Yes—who painted it?" She sees things made to be pretty, and concludes—by analogy—that the sky must have been made for the same purpose. Pretty things are made by people who paint. The sky is pretty. It must have been painted by someone. So she reasons.

But it would be a mistake to assume that children who ask for explanations necessarily want them in terms of purposes rather than causes. Suppose, for example, the same little girl were to ask you why a cantaloupe has those lines on it. And suppose you decide to tease, so you say, "That's to show us where to cut the slices." But she may not take it as a joke at all. She may take it quite seriously. Small children can *reason*, as Shulamith Firestone has argued, but they are painfully short on *information* and experience. The fact that the child believes you does not mean she wanted an answer in terms of the *purpose* of the lines on the cantaloupe; it may simply mean that she is not yet able to distinguish between explaining by causes and explaining by purposes. But she may still be looking for a causal or scientific answer to her question.

Put yourself in the child's place. Suppose something perplexes you. There was a fire in your building. You want an explanation. You may think in terms of holding some human being accountable—an arsonist, for example, or someone in the building who fell asleep while smoking. Or you may just be looking for a physical cause—such as a short circuit in the wiring. But whether you discover that the fire was intentionally set, or began unintentionally, is of less concern to you than that you want your mind to be put at rest as to how it happened.

So with children. They want to know how things happen. So they ask why. Do not assume that they are looking either for scientific—or for non-scientific—explanations; they may have no idea of the difference. They are simply looking for explanations to put their mind at ease.

What they can do without is teasing—unless you can somehow convey to them that you are joking. If a child asks why you have a nose, and you answer, "To hold my glasses up," the child may squeal with laughter. But the question is still unanswered.

Or, when the child asks, "Why does the moon follow us as we drive along the road?" you may think it appropriate to answer, "Because it likes us," or some such effort at humor. But you have merely avoided having to deal with a question you cannot answer; you have not satisfied the child's curiosity at all.

Symbolic Interpretation

Children, then, are often curious about the world, and their curiosity is partially satisfied by factual information and by explanations that provide them with causes or purposes of things. But children sometimes want more. They want symbolic interpretations as well as literal ones. For these they turn to fantasy and play, to fairy tales and folklore—to the countless levels of artistic invention.

Children's folklore is a subculture all its own. Generation after generation of children pass through that culture, acquire a taste of its saucy doggerel, then pass on, forgetting it almost completely as they enter adolescence or maturity.

Have you forgotten the limericks you knew as a child, the gaily naughty jokes and riddles, the mad nonsense verse? Perhaps you have forgotten:

> Ladies and gentlemen,
> Take my advice,
> Pull down your pants,
> And slide on the ice

but your students will acknowledge knowing it, if you ask them, although they will be surprised you should want to know about such a trifle.

Children's folklore is sometimes ribald, and often zany, but one thing it is not: it is not children's literature written for children by adults. It comes from children themselves. It is an indigenous comic vision—although the sheer wackiness of much of it is laced with a grim echo of black or gallows humor. The Opies have shown in detail the richness of children's folklore, and Erikson has amply shown how children's play and children's games can be understood as their efforts to come to terms with their experience.

On the other hand, children's literature is generally written *for* children rather than *by* children. And the chef d'oeuvre of the world of children's literature is the fairy tale.

The themes of fairy tales are so basic to human fantasy (whether children's or adults') that their origins are lost in the origins of civilization itself. The love of the beautiful girl turns the beast back into a handsome prince, as the kiss of the handsome prince turns the sleeping beauty into a wide-awake one. Either we are beautiful but convinced at heart we are toads, or we are toads but at heart convinced we are beautiful. The themes are countless, and each is infinitely rich in the possibilities it spreads out for interpretation.

The point to note, however, is that the authors of fairy tales are grownups, and every grownup is a potential spinner of such tales. "Tell me a story," children beg, and who can resist obliging when confronted with such pleading?

In doing so, however, one should know what one is doing. The fairy tale is captivating and beguiling. It fascinates its listeners, and casts a spell over them, from those very first words, "Once upon a time. . . ." The parent who invents stories for children nevertheless runs the risk of so indulging his own imagination as to pre-empt the child's imagination. We find delight in the creativity with which we express ourselves in such stories (and in the illustrations that go with them). But to what extent do we rob children of *their* creativity by doing their imagining for them?

If adults *must* write for children, then they should do so only to the extent necessary to liberate the literary and illustrative powers of those children. For example, we have resisted putting illustrations in the children's books we publish because we feel that to do so is to do for children what they should do for themselves: provide the imagery that accompanies reading and interpretation.

It remains a fact, of course, that our children's books are also adult-authored. Our excuse is, first, that there is nothing wrong with adult stimulation of the powers of children—but such stimulation should be encouraging rather than overwhelming. We feel that our children's books encourage children's imaginations rather than pre-empt them.

Second, our purpose is not to establish an immortal children's literature, but to get children thinking. If this purpose is attained, the instrument can self-destruct, as a match burns up once it has lit the fire. If our approach is correct, the fairy tale written by professional authors and the textbook written by professional scholars may eventually give way to children's books written by teachers and children themselves, yet incorporating the imagination and insight and understanding that such children acquire at each stage of their development.

What is important is that the imagination be de-professionalized: that children be encouraged to think and create for themselves, rather than that the adult world continue always to think and create for children. There is something unwholesome, even parasitical, in the thought of adults seeking to hold on to their own creativity by pre-empting the creativity of their own children.

But until we can devise effective ways of getting children to think for themselves, the least we can do is write books for them that will promote their creativity rather than diminish it.

Philosophical Investigation

Finally, children look for meanings that are neither literal (like scientific explanations) nor symbolic (like fairy tales), but which can only be called philosophical.

There are a great many types of questions that your children can ask you that can be called philosophical questions demanding philosophical answers. Obviously it is not going to be easy for you to answer such questions, just as it would not be easy for you to answer their arithmetical questions if you had no arithmetic.

Those philosophical questions that children most often raise are likely to be either metaphysical, logical, or ethical. Let's look at some briefly.

Metaphysical Questions

Metaphysical questions are very large questions, and most difficult to come to grips with. Metaphysics is philosophy at its most comprehensive. It involves issues of maximum generality.

You may wonder that your small children can raise such big issues. Yes, it is wonderful that they do. But equally remarkable is the fact that you probably used to do so yourself at one time, and have virtually forgotten how.

For example, suppose you ask your child what time it is. It is a simple question, and you hope you will get a simple answer. Instead you find yourself under interrogation. "What's time?" the child asks. It is really quite stunning, when you come to think of it. "What's time?" How does one answer? Refer the child to St. Augustine or Einstein? Read St. Augustine or Einstein oneself? The options look quite unpromising. So you say, "I didn't ask you what time was, I asked you what *the* time was." There, now—that should hold the little creature! For the moment, you have escaped. But you are beginning to recognize how formidable a child can be.

Or suppose you ask your children what the distance is between your home and the grocery store at which you shop. Since you have asked a very specific question, you expect a very specific answer—such as "a quarter-mile," or "six blocks." But to your surprise, they ask you "What's distance?" Not a particular distance, mind you, but distance in general. Now there you have a philosophical question—to be exact, a metaphysical question.

This manner of upstaging the normal level of dialogue by leaping to a more general level is typical of metaphysics. Instances of other metaphysical questions your children may already have posed you (or are quietly preparing for you) are these:

What's space?
What's number?
What's matter?
What's mind?
What are possibilities?
What's reality?
What are things?
What's my identity?
What are relationships?
Did everything have a beginning?
What's death?
What's life?
What's meaning?
What's value?

What makes questions like these particularly difficult to answer is that they involve concepts so broad that we cannot find classifications to put them in—we just cannot get a handle on them.

Normally, when we define terms, we do so by finding some broader context to which the given term belongs. For example, suppose you're asked by your children to define "man." Well, you might say that man is an *animal*. But if they keep after you, and insist on knowing what *kind* of animal man is, you might answer by saying that man is the animal that thinks. (Or you might answer by saying that man is the animal that laughs and cries, or any of a number of possible answers.)

But obviously, when your students ask you, "What's space?" you're going to have a pretty hard time trying to figure out a larger context in which space can be put. The same with words like "time" and "number." So questions like these are apt to be quite perplexing.

You may say, "Well, now, just because my students ask questions I don't know how to answer, that doesn't make them philosophers, does it? Surely they don't know they're asking metaphysical questions!"

They may not know it, but that is not the point. What is to the point is that children, with their need for wholeness and comprehensiveness, together with their naïveté and lack of information, have a way of reaching out for total answers. It is all or nothing with them; not just how did this or that begin, but how did everything begin? Not just what is warm or cold, but what is temperature? Not just what is better or worse, but what is it for something to be perfect?

For example, this conversation about *perfection* was recently reported from a sixth-grade classroom:

Teacher:	How would it be if, as Tony says here, everything were as clear and simple as it is in arithmetic?
1st student:	It'd be perfect!
2nd student:	But if it were perfect, nothing would need to be done!
3rd student:	It'd be dull if there weren't anything to do!
4th student:	Yes, and besides, if everything were perfect, you'd have perfect fools, and perfect messes. . . .

How quickly they got to the point of asking just what *perfection* might actually be like!

Logical Questions

Logical questions generally have to do with reasoning. In *Harry Stottlemeier's Discovery*, the grade 5 novel in the philosophy for children program, the children usually raise logical questions whenever they ask, "So what?" or "So what follows from that?" or "What can we figure out based on what we already know?"

For example, you are using logic when, having read a sign that says, "Closed Sundays," you figure that the place is open Mondays through Saturdays.

You are using logic when you see that "spaniels bark" follows from the sentences "dogs bark" and "spaniels are dogs."

The relationship of logic to thinking is somewhat like the relationship of grammar to language. Grammar sets out the rules to conform to if we want to speak well. Logic sets up the standards that apply if we want to reason well.

One of the standards logic is concerned about is *consistency*. If your students mention to you that they did their homework, and then say a little later they have not yet done it, surely they would seem to be speaking inconsistently. What logic can do is emphasize the importance of consistency in our thinking, speaking, and acting.

Ethical Questions

"What's good?" children want to know. "What's right?" "What's fair?"

Maybe they do not ask you. Maybe they do not even ask these questions ordinarily of one another. But they ask such questions of themselves. And if you get into a philosophical discussion with your students, you will find out soon enough that they are concerned about morality, just as most people are. They want to know what matters and what does not matter. They want to know what things are of importance—and therefore worth pursuing—and what things are not.

Generally, when they want to know what is right to do, they do not bother to ask you: they just observe what you do, and do likewise. For example, suppose you frequently stress to them the importance of honesty, and they also observe that you respect other people's property. What will they learn from you?

Not just two things, but three. They will learn to advocate honesty, just like you. They will learn to respect others' property—just like you. And they will learn how to keep their actions consistent with their pronouncements—just like you.

But now suppose that you take them on a class trip and upon packing to leave the hotel, they notice you stuffing hotel towels and ash trays into your luggage. What will they now learn from you? Well, once again, three things. They will continue to advocate honesty—just like you. Also, they will fail to practice it—just like you. And they will come to believe that there should be inconsistency between what one preaches and what one practices.

So an understanding of consistency is important if children are to learn moral integrity. But the consistency has to be *practiced* by those whom the children take as their models of correct conduct—it will not be effective if it is merely *advocated* to them, or taught to them.

Nevertheless, it is logic that can best explain to us the nature of consistency: what it is for thoughts to be consistent with other thoughts; what it is for thoughts to be consistent with actions; and what it is for actions to be consistent with other actions. Training in logic can develop in children an *appreciation* for the consistency that is a basic condition of moral integrity. And training in logic can also develop in children an awareness of sound reasoning such that, should departures from consistency be called for, children will recognize that they should have good reasons for making such departures.

4   Some Educational Presuppositions of Philosophy for Children

Concern for the educational possibilities of philosophy as an elementary school subject suggests that attention should be given to what this curious innovation must presuppose. Exploring such presuppositions might in turn throw new light on the always murky connections between education and philosophy.

In the past, discussions about philosophy for young people have assumed that the students would be no younger than of secondary school age. The prospect of encouraging philosophical reflection among elementary school children was literally unthinkable. Such discussions have further tended to assume that the difficulties hitherto experienced in presenting philosophy to young people lay in the inherent complexity of the subject, to say nothing of an abstractness that made it much too dreary and forbidding for children. Consequently, efforts to introduce philosophy to young people were limited to seeking ways of making the subject simpler and more palatable. But of course one can go only so far in *that* direction, and so it was assumed that one should concentrate upon providing philosophical enrichment to the concluding secondary school years of some of the brighter students.

These presuppositions were of course part and parcel of an older theory of education, for which the learning process consisted in nothing more than the transmission of the contents of human knowledge from the old to the young, much as a parent bird might drop bits of food into the yawning mouths of its offspring. The alternative theory of education—that more or less taken for granted by proponents of philosophy for children—has it that the educational process must generate thinking activities among those so taught. Accordingly, it is presumed that as the proper teaching of history generates historical thinking and the proper teaching of mathematics generates mathematical thinking, so the proper teaching of philosophy must generate philosophical thinking, regardless of the age of the students. It is characteristic of this approach to assume that philosophical thinking involves, on the one hand, an appreciation of ideas, logical arguments, and conceptual systems and, on the other, a manifest facility in manipulating philosophical concepts so as to be able to take them apart and put them together in new ways.

41

Those who contend that philosophy for children is capable of encouraging philosophical thinking generally express assurance that virtually all children have both the interest and the ability to engage in such activity. Our traditional reluctance to discuss matters philosophical with children is the product of our reliance upon an archaic theory of education. Having observed few children eager to browse through Kant or even to peruse the livelier passages of Aristotle, having met with little success in our efforts to convey directly the impact and urgency of the greatest happiness principle, we have been led to draw the irresistible inference that there is an unbridgeable chasm between the disciplined reflection that is philosophy and the unbridled wondering characteristic of childhood. It is clear that the plausibility of this inference is now under attack.

Underlying the newer approach is the notion that there are ways of engaging children in philosophical repertoire. The paradoxes of appearance and reality, permanence and change, unity and diversity are enchanting to them from early childhood, perhaps a decade or two before they are prepared to tackle Heraclitus or Parmenides. Like the pre-Socratics, children tend to be terse. But in the animated classroom dialogues in which children love to participate, such economies of phrasing add a welcome sparkle to the discussion. Children for whom the formal presentations of philosophy are anathema may find hints of the same ideas entrancing when embedded in the vehicle of a children's story. Young people who find the writing of a philosophical essay unthinkable can be induced to express philosophical notions in verse form with little apparent reluctance.

If one educational premise that philosophy for children takes for granted is that there is a clear distinction between thinking *about* a subject and thinking *in* a subject, another such premise is that there is a distinction, although one that is not so easily demarcated, between thinking and thinking for oneself. Since the latter is an instance of the former, it is subject no less than the former to appraisal in terms of logical criteria. But if one of the things thinking in its broader sense entails is figuring out what follows from premises, then thinking for oneself involves inferring what follows from one's own premises. Thinking for oneself implies the intensified focus upon the child's own interests and point of view that is a prerequisite for presenting philosophy to children in an appealing fashion. It enables one to work out one's own beliefs and discover good reasons for their justification; to figure out what follows from one's own assumptions; to hammer out in one's mind one's own perspective on the world; and to be clear about one's own values, one's own distinctive ways of interpreting one's experience. Philosophy for children does not assume that thinking for oneself, because it is thinking that is relevantly applied, needs any greater emphasis than one would give to encouraging children to acquire more general sorts of reasoning skills. But certainly, in the case of children, it does not require any lesser emphasis.

Philosophy for children can be expected to flourish in a heterogeneous classroom where students speak out of a variety of life styles and experiences, where different beliefs as to what is important are explicit, and where a plurality of thinking styles, rather than being deprecated, is considered inherently worthwhile. The slow thinker with the sound argument is accorded no less respect in the philosophy classroom than children who present their views quickly and articulately. The child who arrives at beliefs analytically is respected neither more nor less than the child who arrives at beliefs intuitively and speculatively, although for certain purposes—such as the justification of beliefs—one intellectual style may be preferable to another. Thus the variety of thinking styles in the classroom, coupled with a variety of backgrounds, values, and life experiences, can contribute significantly to the creation of a community of inquiry. Furthermore, shared inquiry comes to be seen as the positive counterpart to thinking for oneself. When widely different approaches to problems are openly accepted, then invidious competition diminishes and the inputs from the different participants are welcomed.

One of the greatest obstacles to the practice of philosophy by children is the formidable terminology of the tradition. To engage in philosophical activity as a college undergraduate or graduate student is to learn to operate with a technical vocabulary sanctioned by 2,500 years of usage. The prestige and power of that vocabulary are quite overwhelming. They certainly suffice to intimidate any child happening to venture between the covers of a philosophy book. For this very reason, philosophy for children requires the bypassing of that vocabulary. As nearly as possible, philosophical thinking among children should be encouraged to take place in the terms and concepts of the ordinary language with which children are comfortable.

Preserving the Integrity of Philosophy as a Discipline

It is not uncommon for proponents of a new approach to find themselves in a quandary as to the identification of the tasks to be done and the priorities to be assigned to each task. In the case of the educational innovation known as philosophy for children, perplexities of this kind are fairly prevalent. An example is the tension between those who are concerned to preserve the integrity of philosophy as a discipline, regardless of the ages of the students, and those for whom the value of philosophy is to be found in its intensifying the reflective dimension of the existing curriculum. The latter proponents contend that children need to be encouraged to be more thoughtful and more critical in their approach to history, political science, mathematics, language arts, and the like. They therefore prize philosophy for its instrumental merits, while others perceive its value to be intrinsic, insisting that it be introduced and retained as a separate subject within the revised curriculum.

There is really no need to choose between these two meritorious approaches, since they are not incompatible with one another. Those who have taught philosophy as a separate and distinct discipline to children have noted that it almost inevitably spills over into other disciplines. Children who have been taught to be systematically inquisitive and reflective naturally tend to import such behavior into the remainder of their learning activities. Any inquiry into the presuppositions of philosophy for children would do well to consider the justification of both these approaches. But the approach that is the more seriously threatened, and hence in greater need of defending arguments, is the one that seeks to retain philosophy, even in the elementary school, as an integral discipline.

Every discipline possesses a consummatory aspect—an aspect in which its materials are apprehended and enjoyed for their own sake. Thus if the intrinsic values of architecture—the delights to be found in the various possible arrangements of volumes in space—were not taught in a discipline having its own integrity, the instrumental and utilitarian values of architecture would be jeopardized, and would have far less impact upon our lives. So it is with the teaching of philosophy. Children's philosophical practice may take many forms: there is the play of ideas that is sometimes casual and spontaneous, at other times studied and architectonic. But whatever the specific form their philosophical activity may take, not to encourage them to work with ideas and to cherish them for their own sake is to be educationally irresponsible.

Among those who emphasize the instrumental function of philosophy, there are some who contend that philosophy for children can result in enhanced academic achievement in a wide range of disciplines. Whether or not this contention is correct depends upon suitable educational experimentation and measurement. Such research in the humanities has seemed inappropriate to many people. Thus it has been argued, in some instances very properly, that humanistic studies should not be compelled to justify themselves by virtue of empirical evidence that they promote academic improvement. Literature, for example, should not have to justify itself by showing that its study results in better grades in social science or in mathematics. One might well make the same case for philosophy: it is a humanistic subject whose acquisition represents an enrichment that needs no other justification.

But this argument is not likely to be persuasive to the vast majority of school administrators who must make the actual decisions as to which new courses to introduce and which to cut back. If philosophy is to be admitted into the curriculum under present-day conditions, it will succeed in doing so only if it can demonstrate to those who run the schools that it can make a significant difference in the child's overall performance. What effect does the study of philosophy have upon reading proficiency, upon reasoning, upon creativity? What changes, if any, does it produce in attitudes towards oneself, towards one's going to school, and towards one's classmates? Unless some such results are available, and unless they are of substantial importance, one should not have any illusions about the readiness of educational administrators to bring philosophy into the classroom.

Converting the Classroom into a Community of Inquiry

When children are encouraged to think philosophically, the classroom is converted into a community of inquiry. Such a community is committed to the procedures of inquiry, to responsible search techniques that presuppose an openness to evidence and to reason. It is assumed that these procedures of the community, when internalized, become the reflective habits of the individual.

The construction of a community of inquiry is a more substantial achievement than the mere contrivance of an open environment. Certain conditions are prerequisites: the readiness to reason, mutual respect (of children towards one another, and of children and teachers towards one another), and an absence of indoctrination. Since these conditions are intrinsic to philosophy itself, part of its very nature, as it were, it is not surprising that the classroom should become a community of inquiry whenever it serves as an arena for the effective encouragement of children's philosophical reflection.

This is not to say that philosophy for children entails an equalizing of the status of teacher and students. In the normal course of philosophical inquiry, such as in a classroom dialogue, the teacher may be presumed to possess authority with regard to the techniques and procedures by which such inquiry is to be prosecuted. It is the teacher's responsibility to assure that proper procedures are being followed. But with respect to the give-and-take of philosophical discussion, the teacher must be open to the variety of views implicit among the students. The students must be urged by the teacher to make such views explicit, and to seek out their foundations and implications. What the teacher must certainly abstain from is any effort to abort the children's thinking before they have had a chance to see where their own ideas might lead. Manipulation of the discussion so as to bring the children to adopt the teacher's personal convictions is likewise reprehensible.

That children should be encouraged to think for themselves and that teachers should be open to a variety of viewpoints may strike some educators as mischievously abetting a reflective relativism even more deleterious and subversive than a mindless relativism. Under the banner of "pluralism," it may be contended, the convergence of views is precluded, agreement and assent are ruled out, and intellectual diversity becomes the order of the day. But this ignores the presupposition of the practice of philosophy that dissent is a right, not an obligation. Certainly the right to disagree is no greater than the right to agree, and the right to pursue unanimity is to be respected no less than the right to pursue intellectual diversity. Moreover, the teacher's readiness to encourage intellectual variety is balanced by a consistent emphasis upon the common practice of the procedures on inquiry.

Teachers have a responsibility to see to it that their pupils have the means, in the course of a philosophical discussion, to defend themselves. Thus one justification for teaching logic, other than to compel children to think rigorously themselves, is that it enables them to compel their opponents to think rigorously as well. The same may be said for making available to children an armory of philosophical concepts: one ensures thereby that they do not become helpless pawns when in discussion with other children possessing superior rhetorical or logical ability. For example, suppose a teacher in the classroom is confronted with a suggestion that none of the students opposes—that the metaphysical issue under discussion be "decided" by a vote. There would seem to be good reason in such a case for the teacher to question the appropriateness of such a procedure when applied to philosophical matters in contrast to political issues. In short, where student dialogue fails to materialize, the teacher may be compelled to intervene, by introducing philosophically relevant considerations, so as to safeguard the integrity of inquiry.

Preparing the Teacher and the Curriculum

Such an instructional performance obviously demands considerable skill and astuteness, and it is a reasonable question whether existing elementary school teachers can be entrusted with such responsibility. The answer is that with rare exceptions they cannot. Without appropriate training, most teachers cannot be entrusted to deal with the rigors of logic, or the sensitive issues of ethics, or the complexities of metaphysics. This is not to say, however, that teachers cannot be educated to handle such issues appropriately at the level at which they teach. The problem is not that teachers-in-training lack the intellectual potential that would convert them into effective teachers of philosophy in the elementary school classroom. It is rather that existing teacher-training programs completely fail to prepare the teacher for this responsibility. For example, teachers are sometimes provided with courses in philosophy of education. On rare occasions they may even take a course in logic or philosophy. But such courses by themselves are worthless when it becomes a matter of preparing the teacher to encourage children to think philosophically. A college-level course in philosophy does not equip the teacher to translate the concepts and terminology of philosophy into a presentation that children will understand. Unless teachers are trained by means of the identical instructional approaches as those that they will be expected to utilize in their own classrooms, their preparation will be a failure. If teachers are expected to conduct dialogues, then they must be provided with opportunities to engage in philosophical dialogues themselves and exposed to models who know how to facilitate discussions in a philosophical manner. If teachers are expected to elicit questioning behavior on the part of their students, then they must be taught by educators who themselves model such behavior in the teacher-training sessions. If teachers are expected to teach children how to reason, then they must be given practice in reasoning such as they will expect of their students. And needless to say, teachers in training must be encouraged to respect the procedures of inquiry if they are to induce their students to care about such procedures.

It is likewise evident that for effective classroom treaching, the basic curriculum in which the teachers themselves are trained should not be substantially different from the curriculum material they will employ in the elementary school. This is not to say that the teachers are not to be trained in greater depth than the children. Nuances and complexities of logic and philosophy can be explored more fully with the teacher, although in most situations these are not likely to come up explicitly in the classroom. But if the teacher is not familiarized in the training process with those materials, whatever they are, which will be used to encourage philosophical thinking among children, then again the problem of translation is placed wholly upon the shoulders of the teacher, and it is a burden no teacher should be asked to support.

It would be very difficult to construct a philosophy program for children without a moral education component, since questions of value are so frequently encountered in other aspects of philosophy and are of such importance to children. On the other hand, if it is to be included, it would be difficult to define it otherwise than as ethical inquiry. Students must not only be encouraged to express their beliefs as to what they consider important, but to discuss and analyze them, considering the reasons for and against holding them, until they can arrive at reflective value judgments that are more firmly founded and defensible than their original preferences may have been. Such inquiry necessarily will involve students in examining the criteria employed in favoring one value over another, and even can lead to children's investigating the criteria by which criteria themselves are selected. Giving children practice in determining the grounds on which some reasons are to be preferred over other reasons in justifying moral beliefs, training them to recognize inconsistencies in argument and getting them to see the relationship between theory and practice are likely to be of considerably more value than exposing children to the traditional schools of ethics that are taught in courses for adults.

We have said that philosophy without ethics cannot readily be taught. Conversely, the suppositions that moral education can be taught without exposing the child to other branches of philosophy is even more dubious. Ethical inquiry necessarily involves logical considerations such as consistency and identity, metaphysical considerations such as the concept of a person or a community, aesthetic considerations such as part-whole relationships, as well as a whole range of epistemological considerations. Children, to all of whom the playing of games comes very easily, can be helped in a philosophical classroom to see the similarities and differences between the ways rules function in a game and the ways they are supposed to apply to moral conduct. Children's moral imagination may be fired by tales of saints and heroes, but if we are going to expect them to engage in moral conduct in a reflective and responsible fashion, they are going to have to have some degree of philosophical understanding as to what sainthood and heroism are about. In short, the key concepts of ethics can no more be grasped by the child without the assistance of philosophical interpretation than they can be grasped at the adult level.

Our discussion concerning the presupposition of philosophy for children has made no mention of the types of social settings that would be a prerequisite to the success of the program in elementary schools, as contrasted with those types that might dispose it to failure. Those who are venturesome enough to initiate such a program would do well to acquaint themselves in advance with the values and expectations of the community in which the program is being introduced. Philosophy presupposes a commitment to open inquiry, and such inquiry might or might not be welcome in certain areas. It can be contended, of course, that this is a good reason to expect the spread of philosophy for children to be extremely limited. But this is largely a matter of timing in educational innovation. A district with strong conventional values might not be the best place to initiate a program whose supporters cannot show a solid record of improved academic performance. On the other hand, once one can demonstrate the academic benefits from the program and can allay parental fears that philosophy will aggravate parent-child tensions or undermine parental values, the problem of introducing such a program into elementary schools becomes much less formidable. Let the case of the hard-nosed administrator or parent be admitted: if philosophy for children is not good education, it has no place in the schools. The burden of proof is then shifted to the program itself to demonstrate the differences it can make in the students to whom it is taught.

II

Aims and Methods of Philosophy for Children

5   The Philosophy for Children Curriculum

Description of Curriculum

Let us assume that the discipline known as philosophy, until now a college-level subject, is to be constructed so that it can be integrated into the elementary and secondary levels of education. Obviously there would be needed, to bring this about, a concerted effort to prepare teachers to teach philosophy on these levels, and a new curriculum. The preparation of teachers will be discussed in a later chapter and in Appendix A. For the moment, let us consider what such a curriculum would look like.

Since as yet there is only one philosophy for children curriculum—that published by the Institute for the Advancement of Philosophy for Children—the remarks that follow will draw upon that program for illustrations and recommendations. The IAPC program originated in 1969 and has been expanding steadily since 1974. It is now being implemented in thousands of classrooms throughout the world. Examination of the IAPC program as it now exists can assist us in visualizing what such a program might be when fully developed.

Let us first consider how the introduction of philosophy can be "staged" throughout grades K–12.

K–2nd Grade.   Curriculum here consists of a story or stories together with a manual of activities and exercises for the teacher's use. The stress is on language acquisition with particular attention to the forms of reasoning implicit in children's everyday conversation. Also, there is an emphasis on intensification of perceptual awareness, sharing of perspectives through dialogue, classification and distinction, and reasoning about feelings.

Grades 3–4.   This curriculum, consisting of a philosophical novel with a manual containing activities and exercises for the teacher, continues the emphases of K–2, and aims to bring the children at this level up to a point at which they can be introduced to the formal reasoning of the next stage. Greater attention is paid to semantic and syntactical structures, such as ambiguity,

51

relational concepts, and abstract philosophical notions such as causality, time, space, number, person, class, and group.

Grades 5–6.   This curriculum consists of a novel, *Harry Stottlemeier's Discovery*, and a teacher's manual, *Philosophical Inquiry*. Here the stress is on the acquisition of formal and informal logic. The novel offers a model of dialogue—both of children with one another and of children with adults. The story is set among a classroom of children who begin to understand the basics of logical reasoning when Harry, who is not paying attention in class, says that a comet is a planet because he remembers hearing that comets revolve around the sun just as planets do. The events that follow in the classroom and outside of school are a recreation of the ways that children might find themselves thinking and acting. The story is a teaching model, non-authoritarian, and anti-indoctrinating. It respects the value of inquiry and reasoning, encourages the development of alternative modes of thought and imagination, and suggests how children are able to learn from one another. Further, it sketches what it might be like to live and participate in a small community where children have their own interests, yet respect each other as people and are capable at times of engaging in cooperative inquiry.

Philosophical Inquiry, the manual for *Harry Stottlemeier's Discovery*, identifies the leading philosophical ideas of each chapter of the novel and provides for their classroom implementation by offering a variety of exercises and activities for each idea. In this way, the philosophical content of the novel is put into practice through discussion plans and activities that promote the formation in the classroom of a community of inquiry such as is modelled already in the novel.

Grade 6.   This curriculum consists of a novel, *Tony*, which explores the underlying presuppositions of scientific inquiry. It is through discussion of these fundamental premises of the scientific enterprise that children can come to recognize the aims and benefits of which science is capable. Students who have had the opportunity to discuss such concepts as objectivity, prediction, verification, measurement, explanation, description, and causality will be better prepared to deal with the content of science courses and will be better motivated to engage in scientific inquiry. This curriculum will be accompanied by a teacher's manual, *Scientific Inquiry*.

Grades 7–9.   With this curriculum, the stress is on elementary philosophical specialization in the areas of ethical inquiry, language arts, and social studies. Each has a novel and manual.

The ethical inquiry curriculum for students in grades 7–9 consists of the novel, *Lisa*, and its teacher's manual, *Ethical Inquiry*. *Lisa* is a sequel to *Harry Stottlemeier's Discovery* and focuses upon ethical and social issues such as fairness, naturalness, lying and truth-telling, and the nature of rules and standards. Other issues explored include the rights of children, job and sex discrimination, and animal rights. *Lisa* is concerned with the interrelationship of logic and morality. The curriculum helps students establish good reasons in justifying their beliefs as well as in justifying certain departures from normal patterns of conduct.

Suki is a novel about the same group of children, who are now freshmen in high school. Faced with assignments in writing prose and poetry, Harry Stottlemeier protests that he cannot write at all. The novel explores the way in which this writer's bloc is dealt with and overcome. At the same time, it considers such underlying issues as experience and meaning, criteria for the assessment of writing, relationship between thinking and writing, the nature of definition, and the distinction between craft and art. The manual, *Writing: How and Why*, concentrates on the writing of poetry, with numerous exercises and activities.

Grades 8–10. The fictional characters in *Mark* are now high school sophomores. One of them, Mark, is accused of vandalism. In an effort to ascertain who is guilty, Mark's class find themselves impelled to inquire into a number of general social issues such as the function of law, the nature of bureaucracy, the role of crime in modern society, the freedom of the individual, and alternative conceptions of justice. Again the manual, *Social Inquiry*, puts these and many other concepts into practice through classroom activities and exercises.

Grades 11–12. This curriculum would consist of a number of approaches, each representing a more advanced area of philosophical specialization. Five separate novels, each with its own manual, would be constructed in the areas of ethics, epistemology, metaphysics, aesthetics, and logic. Each of these would carry on and re-enforce the thinking skills and the techniques of applying such skills that had been developed in previous exposure to philosophy for children.

Aims and Objectives of Philosophy for Children

The main purpose of a program in philosophy for children is to help children learn how to think for themselves. But how does one accomplish this? What specifically can be accomplished by offering children a course in philosophical thinking?

Figure 1.

K–2	3–4	5–6	6	7–10	11–12
General Philosophical Foundations			Elementary Philosophical Specialization		Advanced Philosophical Specialization
Language Acquisition	Language Acquisition	Acquisition of Formal and Informal Logic			

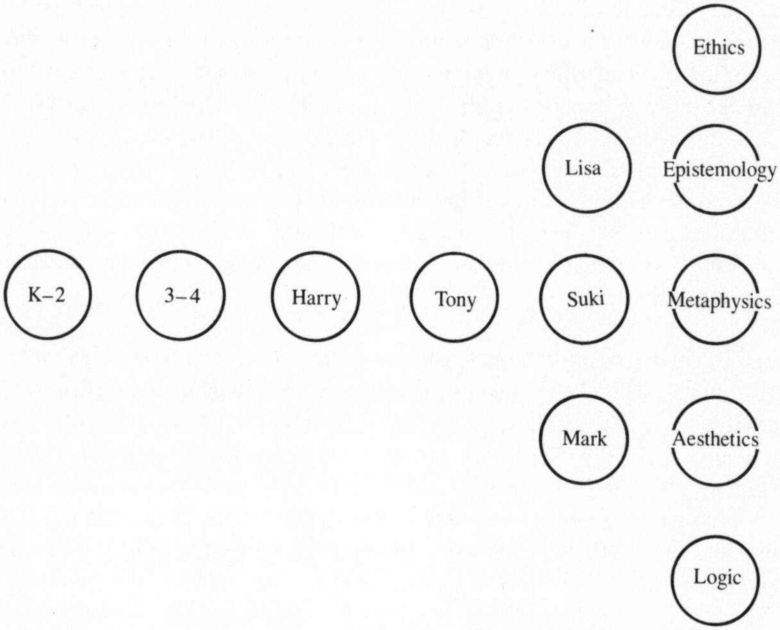

Improvement of Reasoning Ability

The Origins of Reasoning

Reasoning is too vast a topic to be discussed in a few paragraphs, and the cultivation of reasoning presents almost as many problems as reasoning itself. In a sense, reasoning tries to do for the mind what medicine does for the body; both are remedial arts, trying to heal the frailties or injuries that mind or body are subject to. Think of the thousands of years that are spanned by the history of medicine. How much of that time was spent—and is still spent—in searching for specific remedies to specific ills. Here a tribe (or a "medicine man") finds an antidote to a poisonous substance; somewhere else another tribe devises potions intended to ward off disease. The aggregation of these preventive and curative stratagems, as thousands and hundreds of thousands of years are piled one upon the other, is simply overwhelming. The desperate, on-the-spot ways of curing become tributaries to medical understanding, and eventually the broad mainstream of medicine as a systematic discipline emerges.

But the savage must have recognized that there were errors of reasoning just as surely as there were bodily ills. Had he not thought so, and had he not thought both were corrigible, how could we ever have moved beyond savagery? But the way is tricky. The savage may have reached a point where he recognized that the proper approach for solving a problem is to treat the cause rather than the effect. He may also have reached a point where he realized that dirt breeds infection and that cleanliness is necessary for healing. And now he has an opportunity to put these two great realizations together. Here is a wound, and here is the knife that caused it. So he industriously scrubs and cleans the knife rather than the wound.

The path to rationality is not an easy one. Errors such as the one just recited are made by supposedly civilized people every day, as well as by savages. What is important, however, is the effort to correct, the struggle to rectify, the impulse to improve. Primitive man must have slowly become aware of the difference between better and worse reasoning, as he became aware of, say, the difference between harmless and poisonous mushrooms. We are not speaking here of the invention of formal logic, which is only a few thousand years old. We are speaking of the slow, painful growth of awareness that there are certain pitfalls that one must beware of in listening to others, just as there are pitfalls dug by hunters that other hunters must beware of. Indeed, the stratagems of early man must not have been limited to trapping game, but must have been devised to outwit his fellow men as well, and such wily maneuvers must have invited counter-stratagems. We are referring then to that particular form of folklore known as non-formal logic, which may well have begun in early man's primitive efforts to weed out unproductive forms of thinking, and rid himself of the forms of thought he associated with unsuccess.

It is unlikely that reasoning is limited to humans. What seems more plausible is that humans discovered their own capacities to discover, explore, and infer. That they invented tools was perhaps less important than that they discovered that they had the *capacity* to invent tools and all sorts of other things. That they invented language was perhaps less significant than that they employed it to analyze, to discuss, to reflect, and to speculate—all of which then expanded and re-enforced the languages they had invented.

Thus part of what we call reasoning consists of homely warnings descended from ancient times concerning the danger of accepting advice from people who are not authorities on the subject, or concerning the gullibility of those who are easily flattered, or concerning the mistake of thinking that if one event precedes another, the first must inevitably be the cause of the second. What we today call civilization very likely could not have occurred had there not been primitive men who cared about the hygiene of dialogue, and who could assert, "Just because you're a good fisherman, it doesn't mean you know anything about hunting wild boar," or "Just because you say an incantation every evening, it doesn't mean you make the stars come out at night," or even, "Flattery won't help you persuade me."

The sum of this kind of lore is what we have been speaking of as non-formal logic. It embodies our suspicions of certain forms of reasoning as being unsound and to be avoided. It consists less of recommendations for correct reasonings than of prohibitions against incorrect reasonings. It identifies fallacies as the reefs and sandbars upon which the ship of reason can all too easily run aground—but it is as yet a ship with neither mast nor rudder. These appear only with the beginnings of philosophy.

We are naturally more struck by the lurid and colorful aspects of life than by the prosaic, and there is no doubt that the drama of good versus evil, the clash of moral values, strikes us much more forcefully than the dry bones of logic. We prick up our ears at "Thou shalt not lie," forgetting that the broad human context of such an injunction has to do with the need for consistency in human discourse. The rough lessons of experience must have provided evolving man with wisdom enough to see that inconsistencies are trouble-makers. One must get one's story straight—that is, consistent with the facts, and the parts of it consistent with one another. Moralists may denounce lying as immoral, but folklore sees it as inexpedient. From the point of view of practical sagacity, the counsel not to lie is like the counsel not to contradict oneself, except that the self-contradiction is more flagrantly disadvantageous. There is, of course, considerably more to morality than the logical aspect we have been pointing to. There are components of self-respect and respect for others that have not been alluded to at all. But the point is that these latter components, though valid enough, are not so easily demonstrated to children as the need to avoid self-contradiction and the need for consistency. Mutual respect can best be taught children by encouraging them to engage in activities in which they discover its merits, rather than by explaining it to them or by exhorting them to it. But consistency can be both practiced *and* explained. There is thus a distinct advantage to stressing in elementary education the logical underpinnings of morality.

Naturally there are objections that can be cited with regard to the above approach. It seems to appeal to expediency and to the child's selfish interests, rather than to character, conscience, and duty. But exhortations to duty and conscience appear to be increasingly less promising as sources of moral dispositions. If moral character is to be constructed, it will have to employ the child's interests as its means and materials.

Consistency is only one of the features stressed by a philosophically oriented education. It is of equal generality and importance to help the child see connections and make distinctions. We help children perceive connections when we give them practice in grouping and classifying, and show them how their everyday behavior presupposes the ability to make such classifications. We help them make distinctions when we encourage them to say both *what* does not belong to a given group or class, and *why* it does not.

Connections can also be thought of as relationships, and along with instance-kind class relations, there are two other major families of outstanding importance in education, requiring particular attention from the teacher. The first consists of cause-consequence connections; the second consists of part-whole connections. It is unfortunate that our emphasis upon science has led us largely to ignore the second of these types, while giving the bulk of our attention to the first. Our notion of intelligence is all too often addressed only to matters of practical control over practical affairs, and understanding of cause-consequence connections seems most appropriate to such control. But intelligence is no less a matter of perceiving what the parts of a situation are, how they relate to one another and to the whole to which they all belong; it is also a matter of understanding how to *construct* wholes out of materials that then come to serve as parts. Every art class in the school is a laboratory for such intelligence, and if education has as one of its goals the enlargement of intelligence, then the stress on the understanding of part-whole relationships should be emphasized no less than the understanding of the relationship of causes and consequences. It is because philosophy treats both forms of intelligence as valid and important (unlike science, which stresses only the one, or art, which stresses the other), that it is so eminently valuable as a methodology of educational practice.

Reasoning in Childhood

Wondering at what age an infant begins to reason is a bit like wondering at what age an embryo becomes a person. Both questions presuppose that a particular age can be specified at which these monumental changes occur, and we know so little about the pre-natal and the early post-natal life of the child that it is extremely difficult to specify the origins of infantile reasoning.

We can say that reasoning begins with inference, but it is no simple matter to distinguish the early stages of inferential behavior from instinctual behavior. There is the anecdote, no doubt apocryphal, attributed to the ancient Roman writer Sextus Empiricus, that a dog can be said to draw an inference if, when following a scent, he comes to a fork in the road, and after sniffing the first two paths with negative results, proceeds down the third path *without sniffing*. But what of the infant who reaches for the breast of someone who picks him up? We attribute it to instinct, but why can it not be the conclusion of a practical syllogism: In the past, breasts have nourished me; this is a breast; therefore it nourishes, where the action of reaching is tantamount to the conclusion? It is true that the child would not have had the facility with language to formulate the premises linguistically. But this is not necessary, so long as the child has acquired habits translatable into such premises. In other words, children can be said to think inductively and deductively long before they begin to use language. What language does is to symbolize such behavior and permit its formalization.

Likewise, a single counter-instance may be sufficient to alert an infant to the inapplicability of the habit that is the non-verbal counterpart of a generalization. Thus the infant may have developed a particular habitual response to a configuration of behavior that it identifies as its parent. This response is a trusting response, let us say. Now a traumatic event occurs. The parent carelessly puts the child in a bath that is too hot. Result: a substantial loss of trust by the infant in its parent. The generalization about the parent's trustworthiness no longer holds, so the infant infers that its own trusting response is no longer called for.

Obviously one could go on and on with examples of this kind, in which habitual rules are learned, then modified in the light of counter-instances. One could explore the rudiments of psychological associations, or the tendency of children to complete perceptual patterns, for all of these represent the manner in which the child moves from what is immediately given to what is not. Hence all of these represent the foundations of inference, which is to say they represent the foundations of reasoning.

But when, it may well be asked, does the child begin to reason *philosophically*? For although all philosophical activity involves reasoning, it does not follow that all who reason are engaged in philosophical activity. Children begin to think philosophically when they begin to ask why.

The word "why" is surely one of the small child's favorites. Yet its uses are anything but simple. There are two main functions that, it is generally agreed, are performed by the question "Why?" The first is to elicit a causal explanation, the second to determine a purpose.

To explain something causally is to allude to conditions that give rise to that thing or event. You explain the ice on the sidewalk by referring to the cold front that arrived during the rainstorm last night. You explain the burning of the factory by referring to the match that started it, or to the fact that the building had just been struck by lightning.

To ask to know the purpose is to ask what a thing is made for, or what an activity is done for. The purpose of the bridge is to convey traffic. The purpose of a pen is to serve as an instrument for writing. Weatherstripping is put around a door in order to conserve heating fuel.

Among questions to determine purposes, some ask for what purpose a person does something he chooses to do. Explanations that account for choices are called justifications, and are said to provide reasons rather than causes. If we ask why an arsonist set a fire, we are presumably asking for his reasons. The answer, however, could cite either a purpose or a cause. If the answer is that he is a pyromaniac and has an uncontrollable obsession, then we are being given a causal explanation of his behavior. But if the answer is that he set the fire on purpose, *in order to* collect the insurance, then the answer is in the form of a reason.

Children are interested in both purposes and causes, and they constantly blend these usages of the question "Why?" or seek to distinguish one from the other. Thus the child may ask why there was a hailstorm, and may appear to accept the meteorological explanation offered by a teacher about the causes of hailstorms. But the child may very well have been looking for a justification rather than an explanation. "For what behavior was the hailstorm sent as a punishment?" may have been the question he had in mind. On other occasions, of course, the reverse may happen. He wants a causal explanation for the disappearance of his drum, and instead we give him a justification.

We endeavor to help the child distinguish between justification and explanation when we try to teach him the difference between things done "on purpose" and things that are "just accidents." Children are taught that they are accountable for what was done deliberately, but not for what happens accidentally. Accidents can be explained, and one need not justify one's conduct if one has been involved in a genuine accident. On the other hand, children learn, one can be punished for deliberately doing what one had been warned not to do, for doing such things on purpose.

To the Stoic philosophers of ancient times, this distinction was of major importance—knowing the difference between what lies within one's power to do and what does not. For one can feel totally absolved of responsibility for what happens outside one's power. The child's "why?" can be seen as a similar effort to identify what should be accounted for by reasons, and to distinguish this from the realm of causal explanations.

The child asks "why?" very early in childhood, and so can very early be considered to be engaged in philosophical behavior. Indeed, the young child is so persistent at this that, in comparison with the lack of curiosity characteristic of adults, we are tempted to speak of the individual's philosophical behavior as declining with increase of age. This contrasts sharply with the child's increase of information and facility in the use of conceptual instruments.

No doubt the child's capacity to perform certain tasks set for him by experimenters increases with age, from relatively simple arithmetical tasks to more complex ones, and still more complicated ones. Since experimenters tend to assume that gradations of intelligence conform to gradations of ability to perform these tasks, they view growing up as a unilinear pilgrimage from incompetence to competence. Losses are nowhere taken into account. The decline of imagination, of one's sense of harmony with surroundings, of one's curiosity about the world, these are not considered losses at all, when maturity is equated with doing tasks considered to be the hallmarks of responsible adulthood.

Thus it is that normal children are said to mature through acquiring language, forgetting that the language would be useless did the infant not have dispositions to acquire and utilize it. Thus too children are said to acquire rationality, although the masses of information they acquire would be useless did they not have dispositions to process it so as to discover its relevance and meaning. Only in the area of children's art is it admitted that children possess abilities—a power of organization and a feeling for form—which gradually disintegrate until they are in danger of being altogether lost. But when art is not taken seriously as an index of rationality, the decline of artistic power in the middle years of childhood is deemed irrelevant to the growth of intelligence, and in any event no great loss.

Since our culture characteristically defines intelligence in terms of the ability to answer questions rather than the ability to ask them, and in terms of competence in solving problems rather than competence in recognizing and formulating them, it is little wonder that philosophy and childhood are generally thought to be mutually exclusive. Philosophy has been traditionally conceived to be the preserve of the elderly. By a curious perversion of logic, we ignore authentic manifestations of philosophical reasoning in childhood, we virtually ignore children's need to be challenged and assisted to develop their philosophical powers, and then we conclude that philosophy is inherently unsuitable for young people, that they have neither talent for it nor interest in it.

The intellectual progress typically credited to children occurs, not when they learn to think for themselves, but when we note with satisfaction that the content of their thought has begun to approximate the content of our own—when their conceptions of the world begin to resemble ours. Until children view reality as adults do the richness and preciousness of their views of the world are repeatedly disparaged and discouraged. This is particularly true of prevailing conceptions of "moral development," where certain notions such as universalizability are taken to represent the summit of moral thought. In other words, children whose moral views approximate those of the psychological researchers are assigned a higher level on the scale of moral development than those whose views differ from the moral outlook of the investigators.

The child who displays originality and independence of thought is likely to come to unpopular conclusions, and may very well arrive at some conclusions that are in fact quite wrong. It is easy enough to correct a wrong conclusion; it is quite something else to sustain originality, or to revive it in a child who has been led to suppress it.

Adults sensitive to philosophical implications and to philosophical originality are much more likely to nurture children's speculations and insights than adults lacking such experience and sensitivity. Not long ago, a Chicago mother, with some background in philosophy, reported that her four-year-old daughter, when told to turn off the water in the bathtub, had replied, "Don't worry, it won't run over, because from the water to the top of the tub, it just keeps getting less." No one familiar with the paradoxes of Zeno can fail to recognize here that offbeat way of looking at the world, such as is exemplified in the parable of Achilles and the Tortoise. (Trying to catch the tortoise, Achilles halves the distance between it and himself with every step, thus being assured of never overtaking it.) In this instance, the child's conclusion is *literally* wrong: the water *will* overflow the tub. But what thoughtful originality nonetheless. Such a remark as this little girl's, if listened to seriously, could be the point of departure for an exciting discussion of the ways and processes of nature (after turning off the water!).

Or take this comment reported by the father of a seven-year-old Parisian boy: "When we are dead, we dream that we are dead." Such a remark might well be dismissed by an adult with no interest in philosophy as being meaningless. Yet it would seem to represent an insight enormously rich in metaphysical implications, indicating that the child may have a powerful speculative imagination. Children generally do not develop their intuitions systematically. But the teacher can encourage children to explore the implications of their original insights, so that the treasure of their perceptions and intuitions may not be lost.

Not long ago, in reviewing a videotape of a classroom dialogue, we picked up an interchange between two boys ten years of age, regarding personal identity. One boy remarked that it is our thoughts that make us the persons we are. The other replied, "No, because last night I dreamt I was dead, and yet here I am." Obviously this latter child has intimated, with this remark, a much more systematic notion than he has expressed. His comment begs for elaboration and interpretation: if he *is* his thoughts and he has thought (dreamed) he is dead, then he really must be dead. But here he is, alive, though he has dreamed he is dead. So he cannot just be his thoughts. There is use of an important logical pattern here, of stating a hypothesis (as an "if . . . then . . ." statement), then denying the second part of it and thereby showing the first to be false.

As part of our own curriculum for grades 5 and 6, we present a discussion plan on children's rights that begins with the question "Did you ask to be born?" It is a question many children have themselves raised. In the context of classroom discussion, the question being thrown back at them, the children may at first treat it with ridicule. How indeed *could* someone not yet born ask to be born? Then other voices are heard, suggesting that perhaps the question is not quite as silly as it sounds and that perhaps the issue of the child's consent should not be dismissed without serious discussion.

Estimations of childhood intelligence have often been the work of investigators whose approach to the problem is wholly observational and detached. Very often, we measure children's abilities to do things *we* want them to do, rather than assess their capacities to do what they themselves choose to do. We set them tasks and then measure their responses; yet these tasks can seem to them like chores to be avoided. Merely regarding what children do in response to adult demands is a poor substitute for evaluating what they can do when their own interests and their own problems come to the fore. The merit of philosophy for children is that it allows the classroom to become a forum for an airing of issues relevant to children's own problems, diverse enough so that the appeal is not just to the manipulative aspect of a child's intelligence, but to the contemplative and creative aspects as well. Adult intervention need not be aimed at bringing the child strictly into line with the adult perspective of reality, but rather at facilitating children's explorations of their own thoughts and experiences through the use of philosophical techniques derived from the inexhaustibly rich philosophical tradition.

Reasoning and Inference

One of the most serious difficulties experienced by elementary school children is in the area of the drawing of inferences. The child may have a problem with perceptual inferences, logical inferences, or evidential inferences.

Inferences from Single Perceptions.   Children may have 20-20 vision and yet have difficulty drawing inferences from what they see. They come home to a house where the doors are normally kept locked and find the door open, yet it may still not occur to them that something is different. The child perceives adequately, but fails to draw the obvious perceptual inference. The child's hearing may be perfectly all right, he hears the car horn, yet he fails to infer that a car is coming at him. These difficulties are not limited to children: there are adults who likewise have trouble drawing basic inferences from what they see or hear or taste or smell.

Logical Inferences. Another type of difficulty a child may experience has to do with the drawing of an inference from one or more *statements*. For example, if someone tells him that winters at the equator are never cold, the child should be able to infer that the statement, "Last winter was cold at the equator," is false. And a child should know that given the statement, "Some people are tall," it does *not* follow that "All people are tall."

Inferences from Various Types of Data. Sometimes a person is confronted by groups of facts of various sorts. For example, a child visits a foreign country, observes parades, children with flags and banners, speeches and singing, and concludes that "it must be some sort of national holiday." This is an inference drawn from a variety of observations, and requires the ability to synthesize.

Children who experience difficulties with any or all of the above-mentioned types of inferences are likely to experience academic difficulties as well. The child may be able to read well, but does not interpret what has been read because of a difficulty with drawing inferences from the material. A child may do good work in a laboratory when given specific directions but then be at a loss when asked about the meaning of what was done: the child observes effects but has trouble inferring causes. Or the child may observe countless instances of the same kind but not infer that there may be a rule or a law involved.

Such children may be experiencing an "inference block," and this kind of block very likely *cannot* be resolved by repetitious exercises or memorization of rules of thinking. In fact, there is no easy solution to an "inference block." This course in philosophical thinking can perhaps contribute to an alleviation of the problem, by helping children to engage in processes of inferring by creating a milieu that encourages them to do so. Philosophy for children should encourage them to draw better inferences, help them to identify evidence, and assist them in recognizing inferences that are faulty. Much can be accomplished if children can be brought via their own experience to understand the feasibility of going beyond what they see and read by developing the capability for drawing inferences. As long as they are stuck with the concrete perceptions and verbal expressions that surround them, they may feel so overwhelmed by it all that they cannot bring themselves to get up and over the content and facts and begin the process of thinking. It is for this reason that teaching which emphasizes content to the exclusion of the *process* of inquiry is so damaging to children in the long run.

Development of Creativity

It is an unfortunate part of traditional education that training in logical rigor is often assumed to take place only at the expense of imagination and creativity —as if, for the child's logical proficiency to be developed, spontaneity and imaginativeness would need to be suppressed. The approach taken in this program supposes on the contrary that logical thinking can be encouraged by means of creative activity and, conversely, that creativity can be fostered with the development of logical ability. The two go hand in hand.

In this program, we have endeavored to suggest various kinds of creative play activities: games, dramatizations, puppetry, and other art forms, all of which directly or indirectly contribute to children's ability to express their experience and to explore the consequences and meanings of such expressions.

Adults are too frequently prone to underestimate the heavy penalty that our society places upon the child's free imagination and creativity. The more insecure the child's life is, the more precarious the surroundings, the more of a luxury it is to engage in a rich fantasy life, imagining things as they might be, instead of confronting the grim reality of things as they are. The inner-city child, or, for that matter, any child who must deal on a day-to-day basis with the perils of poverty, crime, and other aspects of social disorganization, cannot easily shake off this atmosphere of concrete fact so as to be able to enjoy the delights of fairy tales and the escapades of imaginary children and other imaginary creatures in imaginary environments.

In the past, we have treated the faulty inferences that have resulted from invalid thinking as just so much intellectual trash. We have failed to realize that under some circumstances it can actually be beneficial for the child to explore the results of invalid reasoning. This is not to deny that many situations call for nothing less than rigorous, logical thinking. But there are many others to which fantasy and make-believe are quite appropriate. For instance, logical fallacies can help encourage the child to consider counter-factual situations. It is logically invalid to deduce from the statement, "All onions are vegetables," that "All vegetables are onions." But if children are encouraged to contemplate what a world would be like in which all vegetables were onions, they may very well delight in thus picturing to themselves its details: one would cry when peeling carrots, smell onions every time one sliced potatoes, and so on. Obviously, this does more than liberate the children's imagination; it frees their inventiveness as well.

Helping children grow means that, at every stage, challenges appropriate to that stage have to be devised. It is not enough to challenge them to develop their logical ability alone, although such development is certainly necessary. Their growth depends upon stimulating their inventiveness and creativity as well. Unless children can imaginatively envisage how things might be, and how they themselves might be, it will be difficult for them to set goals towards which they can grow.

Personal and Interpersonal Growth

It is as yet not precisely known what effects this course may have on the children's emotions, interests, attitudes, or other aspects of their personal development. Pilot projects that have been conducted so far indicate a difference of spirit in the classroom that could very well be infectious and could translate itself into a heightened eagerness to learn and share with others, together with the development of other aspects of the individual personality. Much more investigation is needed, however, before it can be confidently asserted that the program can produce a significant increase in self-confidence, emotional maturity, and a general self-understanding.

For most children, learning to think philosophically takes place primarily in the process of interpersonal discussion, and in the reflection that follows such a discussion. Children who merely read the philosophical novel and are deprived of the opportunity to discuss their interpretations of it with their classmates and their teacher will be deprived of a wealth of meanings that the book is capable of suggesting, but which only a discussion can bring out. Most elementary school textbooks, it is true, are not thought of as vehicles for the promotion of interpersonal communication. But *Harry Stottlemeier's Discovery*, *Tony*, *Suki*, *Lisa*, and *Mark* are children's books that are to be both read *and* discussed.

The discussion, in turn, brings other advantages. In particular, it promotes children's awareness of one another's personalities, interests, values, beliefs, and biases. This increased *sensitivity* is one of the most valuable by-products of classroom communication. Unless children have some insight into the nature of the individuals with whom they share their lives, they are not likely to make sound judgments regarding them. It does no good to teach children social rules if they are so insensitive that they cannot detect when and how to use them. Unless interpersonal sensitivity is fostered and encouraged as a *prerequisite* for the child's social development, that social development will be thwarted. There can be little reason to expect sound social judgment from the child unless interpersonal insight is first cultivated, and such insight is often the product of successful philosophical dialogue.

If it should turn out, however, that sensitivity and judgment are enhanced by the program, it may well be that the program has served not simply to accelerate children's growth, but to enlarge their very *capacity* for growth. The teacher can make an indispensable contribution to this process. Any living thing goes through a process of growth, but the enlargement of the capacity for growth is something that is likely to occur only under the influence of a caring, concerned, and knowledgeable teacher. The capacity for growth will no more enlarge by itself than a ball will roll by itself up an inclined plane. Children must be treated in such a way that their powers begin to re-enforce each other, rather than counteract each other. Under proper educational conditions, this process of re-enforcement can generate in children a mutually re-enforcing set of intellectual and emotional activities that can pull them well beyond where they would have been had these factors been developed in isolation from one another.

Development of Ethical Understanding

There is a contemporary controversy about the relationship between morality and education. Members of opposing camps generally group themselves and each other in the following ways. There are those who contend that all education has a moral dimension. There are those who insist that under no circumstances should educators attempt to introduce morality into the classroom because it will inevitably, as they see it, be nothing more than indoctrination. Thirdly, there are those who maintain that a sound education can and should contain a component of moral education.

When problems of morality and education are thus formulated, we are not able to take a position among them. Each of these groups presupposes that morality consists of moral principles and rules; most of their disagreements can be traced to disagreements about which rules should be taught, or whether they should be taught at all. In our view, a philosophical approach to ethics is one that stresses the *method* of ethical inquiry rather than the particular moral rules of particular adults. The teacher of philosophy assumes that getting children to reason logically about matters to which logic applies will be genuinely helpful for the solution of human problems, including moral ones. The teacher of philosophy likewise believes that without awareness of the metaphysical, epistemological, aesthetic, and other aspects of human experience, ethical inquiry alone will be myopic and unsound. Again, the teacher of philosophy will be concerned to encourage students to see the importance of arriving at sound moral judgments, and this requires the development in such students of ethical sensitivity, care, and concern. Thus, as ethics is presented in the context of philosophy for children, it is concerned not to inculcate substantive moral rules, or alleged moral principles, but to acquaint the student with the *practice* of moral inquiry.

It should be evident that we stress helping children become aware of the nature of moral judgments, rather than pressuring them into making moral decisions or "advancing" to some "higher" stage of moral decision-making. From our point of view, judgment is only one aspect in the life of an ethical individual. Such judgment must be conditioned by moral awareness and moral intelligence. Moreover, the moral individual is not only one who is adept at making "right" judgments, but is equally one who knows when judgments are *not* called for and avoids making them in such situations.

Chapters 9 and 10 of this book are an extended discussion of the relationship of philosophy to moral education. Since the topic is enormous, even these chapters should be considered only as an introduction, but hopefully they will give some guidance in understanding the problems and dimensions of ethical questions.

Development of the Ability to Find Meaning in Experience

Earlier it was pointed out that many children object to their school life as "meaningless" and many individuals have this criticism to make of their lives in general. Assuming these accusations to have merit, what can be done to enable young people to discover meanings that their life experiences do contain. Notice that we do not say what can be done to "give" their lives meaning. Rather, the only meanings that children will respect are those that they can themselves derive from their own lives, not those that are given to them by others.

One way in which we discover meaning is to discover connections. A person may discover some serious medical symptoms. He says, "I don't know what they mean." But when he learns that they result from his exposure to certain poisons in the factory where he works, he says, "Oh, I see what they mean," because he sees the connection. Or, hearing a person express an opinion, other people may say, "We don't know what you mean. What is your reason for saying that?" When they are told the reason, they say, "Ah, now we understand better what you mean." Or, someone is told to make a choice when she has only one option. In effect, the choice is meaningless. Suppose now she discovers alternatives and sees the connections between them as well as the consequences that would follow from each of them. Immediately, her choice becomes meaningful. As long as one does not know the context of an episode, it may seem meaningless. Think of the way a sentence can be puzzling by itself but be very meaningful in the appropriate paragraph. So it is with experiences in life. If we can help children discover the part-whole relationships in their experience, we can help them find the meaning of those isolated experiences.

We can identify a number of ways of discovering meaning: discovering al-

ternatives; discovering impartiality; discovering consistency; discovering the
feasibility of giving reasons for beliefs; discovering comprehensiveness; discovering situations; discovering part-whole relationships.

Discovering Alternatives

How do children learn to think of "fresh alternatives?" How do they learn
that the way they now think is not the only way they *could* think?

One way they can do so is by developing the habit of always considering
the possibility that the *negative* of their idea might be correct. The child who
sees the sun rise and thinks that "the sun moves around the earth" learns to
think that "maybe the sun doesn't move around the earth"—and this long before anyone actually tells him that it does not. The child who thinks that "the
earth is flat," but is at the same time critically aware that the negative is possible, will also entertain the possibility that "the earth is not flat." Every factual
statement has a negative that could possibly be true.

Even more simple is taking the idea of something (not a statement but just
the thought of some thing or activity) and finding its negative. The negative of
"playing" is "not playing." The negative of "laughing" is "not laughing."
We can even say that the negative of "chair" is "non-chair," or that the negative of "table" is "non-table."

The child who works with these notions will begin to see that, when thoughts
and their negatives are put into order, they begin to display a pattern of alternatives. For example, suppose the child thinks of "working," and when the negative is considered, the result is "not working." But "not working" may be interpreted by the child as "playing," so now there are two thoughts the child has,
"working" and "playing." And now there are four alternatives: (1) working and playing; (2) working but not playing; (3) playing but not working;
(4) neither working nor playing. The child may now find that a similar set of
four alternatives can be developed for any pair of ideas whatsoever: milk and
fudge, or crocodiles and triangles, or icicles and dandelions.

Up to now the child may only have been vaguely aware of alternatives and
not fully appreciative of them as possibilities. Chances are, if the child thinks
of "sick" and "hungry," he is only dimly aware of "sick but not hungry,"
"hungry but not sick," and "neither sick nor hungry." So if you ask the child
is there a lot of sickness and hunger in the world today, the child could well
say yes. But if you ask about the other three *possibilities*, the child will likely
shake his head. A world from which sickness and hunger have been virtually
eliminated: *impossible*! Yet a simple demonstration in the child's own logic
would show that something may be possible, even if it is not practical or feasible or likely at this moment.

And this is what is meant by learning to discover fresh alternatives. It means considering all the possibilities. Nor do these other possibilities have to be as idealistic as in the previous example. A child who is aware that he is healthy and well-fed may never really have given much thought to what it would be like to be "well-fed but sick," or "healthy but hungry," or "hungry and sick" together. Or, if the child's family is planning a vacation trip, they may discuss whether to go by bus or train, and the child can point out that while they can go by either one, they might also go part way by each, or they may choose not to use either mode of transportation and go in some different fashion, such as by plane. What is important is to give the child practice in examining situations for *alternative* solutions that might otherwise be overlooked.

Discovering Impartiality

As adults, we certainly are aware that we are often *partial* rather than impartial. We enthusiastically root for the home team, and accuse the umpire or referee of being biased towards the other side. If an accident happens, we generally consider ourselves innocent and the other fellow guilty. In politics, it is often our candidate who can do no wrong, while his opponent is incapable of doing anything right.

Now, there is nothing wrong with such partiality in itself. Why should a mother not be partial to her own child, or a lawyer to his client, or a girl to her boyfriend? Obviously, there are situations that will call for partiality, yet there are others in which partiality is very definitely wrong. We would not want a judge who shows partiality; we find it difficult to condone the parent who favors one of his children over the others or who always makes one the scapegoat; and if someone agrees to mediate a quarrel—whether between individuals or between nations—it just will not do for that person to exhibit partiality.

So it is a question of knowing when to be partial and when to be impartial. The trouble is that partiality seems to come easily to most people, while they only learn impartiality the hard way.

There is one situation in which impartiality is particularly appropriate. It is the situation in which you are trying to understand something. You begin by trying to understand it solely in terms of your own point of view. You may pay little attention to how other people have experienced the matter. Let us say a friend tells you of a new regulation, and you get pretty worked up about it, because you are certain that it is a stupid rule. And all you want to do at first is tell everyone how you feel. But after you get the matter off your chest, you begin to listen to other people. Some may agree with you, and some may disagree. And you may begin to see that maybe your initial judgment of the new regulation was too hasty. Maybe it has certain merits you did not at first recognize. Or maybe it is even worse than you first thought it to be. But in either case, you have learned from the other people's experience. You have learned to see things from their points of view as well as your own. You have begun respecting them for their opinions as much as you respect yourself for your own. And you have begun to rise above your own original, partial estimate of the situation so as to be a more objective and impartial judge of it.

It is just this experience of impartiality that we have to make available to children. it is too much to expect them to be naturally objective and impartial, although perhaps some of them are. But they can all learn to be, and they learn a lot more quickly if we encourage them by arranging situations in which they can try to talk objectively and impartially about *their* problems.

Discovery of the usefulness of impartiality can be illustrated by referring to a situation observed not long ago in a sixth grade classroom.

Teacher:	Do Lisa and Fran have the same attitude towards Harry Stottle-meier?
A boy:	He bothers Lisa, but he doesn't bother Fran.
Teacher:	Why does he bother Lisa?
A girl:	Maybe she just doesn't like boys.
Teacher:	Why do you say that?
Girl:	I dunno. Maybe she thinks boys are always claiming to do better than girls, and she doesn't go along with that.
Boy:	Well, they *are* better than girls!
Girl:	No, they ain't, neither!
Teacher:	What do the rest of you think? Are boys better than girls? No, don't all answer at once! One at a time.
Boy:	Yeah, boys are better than girls.
Teacher:	Do you mean in everything, or just in some things?
Boy:	They're better than girls in sports.
Girl:	They're better than girls in *some* sports, maybe, but there are sports, like maybe volleyball, where we're better than they are.
Boy:	There are plenty of boys better than girls in girls' sports.
Girl:	Maybe a few of them are, but in *most* girls' sports, *most* girls are better than most boys.
Boy:	Okay, but in most *boys'* sports, most boys are better than most girls.
Teacher:	Are you saying that there are some girls who are better than most boys, even in boys' sports?
Boy:	Could be.
Girl:	So it isn't true, what you first said, that boys are better than girls!

The conversation moved along after this to other topics, but the point must have been obvious to everyone in the class. They had begun with very sweeping statements, both boys and girls making tremendous generalizations about "all boys" and "all girls." But gradually, they had to admit exceptions. And gradually each side began to take a more factual, more objective, more impartial attitude towards the relative strengths of girls and boys. They compared attitudes and opinions, they exchanged biases, but what emerged was a kind of consensus, with each child taking a more unbiased position than that with which he or she began.

Discovering Consistency

It would be very silly, you will no doubt agree, if someone were to say something like this:

> Goliath was very big
> *Israel was not very big.*
> Therefore, Goliath was bigger than Israel.

The trouble with the above reasoning is obviously that Goliath was "big" compared with other *people*, while Israel wasn't big compared with other *countries*. So "big" means something different in each case, with the result that the conclusion is false. The person speaking has used the word "big" *inconsistently*.

Or suppose someone else was silly enough to say this:

> No man lives forever.
> *But women aren't men.*
> Therefore, women live forever.

Once again, a word is being used inconsistently. First the word "men" is used to mean all human beings. Then it is used to mean just male human beings. So the reasoning is invalid and illogical, and the conclusion does not follow.

Now let us consider a different kind of inconsistency. Suppose someone makes a sweeping statement like "Everything that goes up must come down." But then he adds, "Of course, we send rockets into outer space, and they don't come back down." He probably is not aware that his second statement contradicts his first statement. And since his second statement is true, his first statement must be false. So once again we have the problem of a person who takes a position, and then does not stick to it. In effect, he too is guilty of inconsistency.

Cases such as these represent careless thinking. When we realize we have been thinking in a sloppy sort of way (and inconsistency is usually an example of mental sloppiness), we may be amused by it, or we may be ashamed of it, or both. But children should no more be encouraged to be inconsistent in their reasoning than they should be encouraged to multiply or subtract incorrectly. Indeed, how would it be if some days, when one added, say, 4 and 5, one got 9, and on other days, one got 17 or perhaps 3? Picture such a person looking after your bank account.

Children have to be encouraged to use their words carefully from a very early age. They should be made aware of how the meaning of words in a statement or paragraph can shift their meanings.

If people insist on being inconsistent, the least we can do is to ask them to explain their reasons for doing so. Maybe if they cannot find reasons for being inconsistent, they will come to think of the practice as indefensible, and will try being reasonable for a change.

Another example of inconsistency is the following, paraphrased from a news release by a noted educator:

> Although inflation has produced many serious problems in the area of higher education, there may be a silver lining to the cloud. As a result of the higher cost of education, many poorer students will not be able to go to college. But the colleges have been looking for some way to get rid of the poorer student anyhow. So maybe it will all work out for the best.

Obviously, there is a shift of meaning here from the first use of the word "poorer" meaning *economically* poorer and the second use of the word "poorer" meaning *academically* poorer. Doubtless, the person who made the statement did not consciously intend to imply that colleges should be glad to get rid of students who were not financially well-off, but that is what can be inferred from his statement just the same.

Together with verbal inconsistencies, there are also inconsistencies of words and actions and of actions alone. When a teacher tells a child that she is deeply concerned with his welfare but then ignores him, or if a person holds a door for you but at the last moment lets it go in your face, we see an inconsistency between words and actions or between actions that are at cross-purposes. These types of inconsistencies are related to the sorts of verbal inconsistencies previously mentioned. For example, they can be described by means of contradictions ("She was and was not concerned with Timmy." "Did he hold the door for you?" "Well, he did and he didn't"). By learning to recognize verbal inconsistencies children can be encouraged to perceive inconsistencies involving actions for what they are.

Of course, not all inconsistencies are troublesome or unsettling. The clown who puts one foot up on a stool only to reach down and tie his other shoe and the comedian who swears that his next story is true are experts at presenting joyful inconsistencies. And soberminded philosophers have puzzled over special kinds of inconsistencies called paradoxes ever since the beginning of philosophy. Learning to recognize inconsistencies requires a growing awareness that a demand for consistency is not *always* appropriate; this involves recognition of when being inconsistent is confusing, misleading, and even deceptive, and when it is playful or profound.

Discovering the Feasibility of Giving Reasons for Beliefs

Let us say you have been having trouble getting to school on time. Your alarm clock has been broken and your car's battery has run down. So now your principal asks you if you expect to be on time for the assembly program first thing tomorrow morning, and you reply, "I believe so." The principal surprises you by asking you *why* you think you will now be on time. You answer, "Because my clock's been fixed, and I got a new battery for my car, and I can't think of any other reason why I'd be late." You were challenged to give reasons for your belief, and you did.

Ordinarily, of course, no one challenges you to offer reasons for your beliefs. But sometimes you cannot help realizing that some belief of yours has just collapsed. Suppose that, tomorrow morning, fully believing that at last you are going to get to school on time, you discover you have a flat tire. What happens to your belief that you are going to be on time? You cannot continue to believe it, because there is no other means of transportation available. In other words, you now have *no reason* to believe that you will get to work on time, so you cannot continue to believe it. You may *hope*, of course, that just by chance someone will come along and give you a ride—but you have no reason to believe that anyone actually will.

Many of your actions and your thoughts are hinged upon your beliefs. You go to school each day in the belief that it is still there; you go home each day in the belief that *it* is still there. You would not do many of the things you now do out of habit if you did not believe things to be the way they are.

But this is all the more reason for your beliefs to be as sound as possible. And a good way to check up on their soundness is to be able to provide reasons or evidence for them. Your beliefs are the foundation of your whole outlook on life and of the way you live. Who would want the foundation of his beliefs to be shaky?

Think of it this way. If you were going to buy a house, you would certainly want to check around in the basement. It could be a very nice house, but it might rest on a weak foundation, with water seeping everywhere and bricks crumbling away. Well, the same is true of your intellectual domicile: you want it to rest on solid foundations—and it can do so only if your belief system is sound.

This is why it is helpful for children to challenge each other's ideas. Partly it is done out of playfulness; partly it is done out of competitiveness or contentiousness. (As with any game, there is always the possibility that it might get too rough for the individuals involved.) But it is a kind of dialogue that can be extremely beneficial, not just to the person asking the questions, but to the one thinking up the answers (that is, the person who is being challenged to provide reasons for believing as he does). And it is helpful to the others who listen in and take note of what is going on: it will cause them to think a little more about why *they* believe as they do.

Always remember that, while the children who do most of the talking are invoking *their* right to express themselves, the children who sit by listening intently are thereby expressing *their* right to *hear* what is going on. And if you violate the right of the speaker by silencing him or her, you equally violate the rights of the listeners to hear what the speaker had to say. But, of course, you alone, as the teacher, are the judge of what is *relevant* to the class discussion and what is not. You should not hesitate to terminate a speaker who insists upon talking about irrelevant topics.

In short, there are three clear reasons for being able to give reasons. First, it is a good thing to know your beliefs are sound and reliable, because you have to act on them, every day. If something goes wrong, you had better check out your beliefs. Second, in a discussion, your beliefs may be challenged. You will be asked to provide reasons for them. Thanks to previous discussions, you may be prepared to meet such requests. And third, you may have some good reasons for a particular belief, but they still may not be sufficient to justify your believing in that particular way. It is difficult to say just when reasons become numerous enough to be sufficient, but, obviously, the more you can find, the better.

Discovering Comprehensiveness

It is not enough for a person to have sound ideas on this subject and on that subject, a belief about this and a conviction about that, because all these little bits and pieces may not *add up* to anything. People generally *want* an organized set of beliefs and ideas for themselves, a body of thoughts and values that somehow are related and can be counted on in their future actions. So young people have to be encouraged not merely to love and respect ideas, and not merely to want their ideas to be sound and reasonable, but to see the connections *among* ideas as well—to see how ideas relate to one another, and converge upon one another and support one another. It is only in that way that a person can begin to build a network of thoughts that he will find permanently serviceable and useful.

The teacher can be particularly helpful here. He has the experience of the world that children generally lack; he knows a good deal about how things that go on in the world are related to one another. So he can guide children in this fashion by asking them if they can see the *connections* between certain ideas (where he believes he sees a connection and they do not) and by helping them relate their ideas to things that happen in their lives and to the world in which they live. He can help them, when they seem to be groping, by suggesting connections and possible implications or consequences of their ideas. He can attempt to put their thoughts into some kind of context that will make their thoughts more meaningful to them, for the more comprehensive the setting of an idea is, the richer will that idea be in meaning.

Thus, teachers will notice that children are intensely conscious of each episode in the philosophical novels as they occur, but the very intensity of that awareness may block out their recollections of earlier incidents in the book. A teacher can, through questioning, encourage them to see the connections between what went before and what came after. There is perhaps no better training that a child can have for the development of an adequate conception of self than to relate the present and the past and the future so as to see them as one continuous life.

As adults, we should try to be aware of how differently adults and children experience the world. A child usually feels the impact of a situation in its entirety, experiencing it as joyous or miserable, as friendly or hostile, as threatening or inviting. But generally, the child does not analyze such a situation very much. Adults, on the other hand, having already learned relationships and connections that exist among things, perceive separate features of situations in isolation from one another.

The adult thus tends to think that the child should perceive the way the adult does by focusing on separate details until, part by part, he has put the situation together. What the child needs to be able to do, rather, is to explore it, discover what parts it contains, disentangle them from one another, and understand their connections to one another. An adult who stresses beginning with the parts and ultimately arriving at the whole therefore runs directly contrary to the child's inclination to begin with the whole and subsequently discern its component parts.

In other words, children have a natural inclination to be speculative and comprehensive rather than analytic and sensitive to differences. The teacher cannot do better than to build upon this natural sense of wholeness that children demand, while at the same time helping them discover how it is put together.

Discovering Situations

Much is heard these days about teaching children to make decisions, for it is assumed, at least in some quarters, that children ought to be decisive, the way police captains and quarterbacks and business executives are decisive. Now, there is no doubt that in a situation that calls for a choice to be made, the child should be able to make that choice as intelligently as possible. Surely if the child has the chance to choose—among different types of play, or different books to read, or different things to explore—and does not do so, then the child is not taking full advantage of the opportunities that are present.

On the other hand, if pressed to be decisive in situations where it would be better to wait and see how things develop, or until more facts are at hand, then the child can very well end up doing more harm than good by premature decisiveness. Very often, the child is presented with illustrative situations that are so skeletal or schematic, so lacking in specifics, that it would be very difficult for anyone to make a reasonable decision on the basis of the few facts promised. Yet it is alleged that children are given practice in decision-making by being pressed to make up their minds as to what they would do in such artificial situations. But to exaggerate the importance of a decision is to exaggerate the product while neglecting the process. Children must be helped to grasp a situation in which the decision is required, and to read the character of that situation correctly. If the children have done so, the choice they have to make may be easier and will certainly be better due to their understanding of the situation's structure and requirements.

This program in philosophical thinking at times presents children with examples of moral situations. For instance, Dale has a problem as to whether or not to salute the flag, Ann treats her friend Suki as if she were an interesting object to bring home to her parents, Bill Beck throws a stone at Harry, Lisa accuses Mickey of stealing a briefcase. But it is not demanded of the children who read these problem situations that they say what they would do if they were the characters in the book. Rather, they are free to discuss, analyze, interpret, and explore the complexities of these moral dilemmas. In this fashion, the children in the classroom can become more sensitive to the subtleties and nuances of the situations they encounter in the book. And in the process, they may become more acutely aware of the moral character of situations that they encounter in their daily lives.

Philosophy is not a self-help course in decision-making. In fact, it might even make a decision harder to make by *widening* the range of alternatives from which to choose, rather than letting it stand as a decision between two courses of action.

Unless proper and adequate means for decision-making have already been developed in children, forcing a decision upon them, even an artificial or idealized one, is bound to be experienced as frustrating and perhaps even humiliating. We do not increase children's self-esteem when we force them into situations they are not prepared for; we lower it immeasurably.

What then are the *means* for the making of ethical judgments that must be developed in children? They are such things as respect for one another's point of view, the ability to identify sympathetically with other persons, the capacity to reason consistently, the capacity to imagine alternative possibilities, sensitivity to the variety of tiny but important factors that go to make up an interpersonal situation, and a feeling for the uniqueness of that particular situation and what would be right for *it*, even though roughly similar situations might have been treated differently in the past. Unless the children's development in these areas is carefully fostered and encouraged, they will find moral situations threatening and traumatic, and might well tend to avoid them.

Some devices that might prove helpful would be to let the children act out (perhaps in pantomime, so as to give it the zany quality of a silent film), situations such as these: a woman with a lot of wild children getting on a crowded bus with an irritable bus driver, or an overworked pair of counter attendants at McDonald's trying to handle a hungry bunch of vacationing school children; or a crowd's reaction to a tight-rope walker with an itch; or the family life of a teacher trying to grade papers at home while the teacher's own children tear up the house, watch television, and grumble about doing the dishes. There are countless such situations that can be improvised; what is important is for the children to identify with them and even to act them out without stressing the imperative that they make decisions. Let the decision arrive, if it must, by flowing naturally and without fuss or self-consciousness out of the situation. In short, it would be well to avoid making a big thing about decisions, and concentrate instead on preparing children for life situations by encouraging them to participate in imaginary ones where the emphasis is on getting them to perceive nuances of the situations rather than on the choices that may or may not have to be made within each situation.

Children who have developed the capacity for sizing up situations, having an insight into their character, having imagination as to what can possibly be done to improve their unsatisfactory aspects, and having the courage to act on alternatives that seem to them most reasonable and plausible do not need a course in value clarification or in decision-making, for they are already morally responsible individuals.

Discovering Part-Whole Relationships

Try to imagine yourself in the school child's situation. There are many aspects of a school day that children find intensely meaningful. Perhaps foremost among these episodes of intense significance are those in which what one does is experienced as part of a larger picture.

For example, you are acting in a play. You have only a few lines to read. But what makes your part so important to you is that you see it as a part of the play as a whole. The meaning of the lines you are to read depend completely on what is said by the other actors in the play. You realize this so intensely that you may even learn all the parts, because to do so enables you to appreciate more fully the meaning of the whole and the meaning of your part in the whole.

Say you are part of the school baseball team. You may live for the moment you come to bat. But everyone knows the difference between being out on the field all by yourself with a bat and ball—a rather empty experience—and coming up to bat during a game that is full of excitement. Every player watches what every other player does and so each player empathizes with all the other players on both teams. In coming up to bat you sense how the outfielders are "playing you" and you sense the strategy the pitcher and the catcher have devised to pitch to you. At the same time, the other players on your team are living your experience at bat as if they were in your shoes. You have learned to sense everyone else's expectations of you. You grasp your role as a batter, in terms of the meaning to everyone involved in the game and in terms of the relationship of your role to the game itself.

Or perhaps you are a member of the school orchestra. Your part in the school performance may be ever so slight, but it is indispensable. You may have but a single note to play on your instrument, but the entire piece of music would be seriously lacking if you failed to perform. So once again, each performance is appreciated by the player, by the other members of the orchestra, and by the audience as a totality in which each part is meaningful in terms of the ensemble in which it participates, and each work as an entirety derives its meaningfulness from the individual performances of which it is the composite.

Thus, there are many instances in the school day in which you learn part-whole relationships. Unfortunately, there are many other times during the ordinary school day in which what you are doing seems cut off from a larger picture, if there is one, and you do not seem to be able to understand what you are doing, or why you are doing it. In a well-integrated school day, there would be few such experiences. You would understand the relevance of each subject you take to your entire education, and you would understand each stage in the learning of each subject as necessary to the overall learning of that subject. You would appreciate the rationale behind alternating between intellectual and physical activity, between disciplined and innovative activity, between working with others and working by yourself, and between periods of action and periods of reflection.

How does the understanding of part-whole relationships contribute to the attainment of the four objectives listed at the beginning of this chapter: improvement of reasoning ability; development of creativity; personal and interpersonal growth; and development of ethical understanding?

Development of Reasoning Ability. If reasoning were taught simply as the principles and rules of logical inference, it would be an arid subject that would repel many students. If, on the other hand, the discovery of reasoning is presented in the setting of a children's novel, and if the reasoning then learned is shown to be valuable in the larger context of a person's life, the acquisition of the principles of reasoning can be much more attractive. This is not to say that learning and applying rules in a subject, simply as a kind of game that you can master, cannot be enjoyable in and of itself. But for many children it is hard to see principles of logic as a game, and as a result such children would find the study of logic quite joyless. Moreover, when children discover that reasoning learned in one class carries over to reasoning in other classes, that it is not confined to one subject area and is as useful in the playground and after school as it is in school, then the full impact of what they are doing in studying reasoning becomes very exciting.

Development of Creativity. The very definition of an aesthetic relationship is that of a relationship of parts to wholes (or of parts to other parts). To be engaged in art—to be the fabricator of a work of art—is to be engaged in the organizing of parts into wholes. It is obvious that without sensitivity to this essential character of works of art, the children's development and their creative powers can be seriously hampered. It should be emphasized that younger children, between the ages of two and seven, display an easy proficiency in handling part-whole relationships, a proficiency that unfortunately tends to disintegrate as they move into pre-adolescence. At that later point, fussiness about details leads to lack of overall organization, and a sense of proportion is often missing. One correlates this lack with the confusion in the child's mind at this time due to the loss of childhood patterns, on the one hand, and the problematic patterns of adolescence confronting that child, on the other hand. If the child's school day were replete with meaningful part-whole relationships, and if teachers in their teaching would pay particular attention to the relationship of fragments of knowledge to the larger context of the child's experience, then it is possible that the understanding of part-whole relationships would be cumulative rather than diminishing.

Personal and Interpersonal Growth. The confusion that a child feels about personal identity, life career, future life style as an adult, family expectations, peer relationships, ambivalence towards education, and so on can be dispelled only if the child is encouraged to reflect upon and analyze the basic direction of his own life. But how is this to be done? If philosophy for children were just a program in logic or critical thinking, then obviously it could not help the child dispel this confusion. But it is much more than that. It involves dialogue concerning issues and concepts of which children are struggling to make sense, coupled with an exposure to alternative views that have been created by philosophers in the past. Children are told to be natural, but what is it to be natural? They are told to be themselves, but who are they? They are encouraged to learn and respect the customs of society, but what are customs?

Children experience a need to reflect upon the key aspects of that period of life experience through which they are passing at the moment. We err in thinking that we can sweep away the child's problems simply by giving the child little recipes for expeditious social or personal behavior, when the child cannot understand the terms in the recipe. Adults offer explanations or issue injunctions to children while taking for granted that the children understand the terms and concepts involved in those explanations and injunctions. But this cannot be taken for granted. The child senses that the language and concepts adults employ in presenting a view of the world or in presenting a directive for how the child should act in that world—that such language and concepts form an intimate part of the adult world view. The philosophy of life that an older generation would like a younger generation to accept becomes suspect to that younger generation by virtue of the terms in which the philosophy of life is couched. This is why children constantly want to know what we mean when we use this term or that term: they are concerned not just with the words themselves but with the beliefs in which those terms are embedded and which they are not prepared to adopt without further explanation. Philosophy for children is serious about encouraging children to think for themselves, and it will help them discover the rudiments of their own philosophy of life. In so doing it helps children develop a more secure sense of their own identities.

Development of Ethical Understanding.   At the beginning of this section we offered illustrations of part-whole relationships involving a play, a baseball game, and a musical performance. In each of these instances there is an explicit or implicit understanding of what it means for behavior to be *right* in such contexts. The drama director will object to an actor's reading of a certain line by saying, "No, that won't do, that's not right at all!" The batting coach will explain to a rookie player the difference between the wrong and the right way to use one's body in swinging a bat. The orchestral conductor will criticize the way a group of instrumentalists have played a certain section of a piece over and over again, but then the conductor will say of a performance, "That's it, that's *right*, now you've got it." It is very instructive that everyone concerned can understand and appreciate the appropriateness of the use of the word "right" in this fashion. It is in each instance understood that what is right is not right in itself, but is right in terms of the relationship between an act and the entire context of which it is a part.

In encouraging children to develop an ethical understanding, we must help them see the relationship between what they propose to do and the situation in which they propose to do it. They should be encouraged to see that relationship as they would look at any part whose appropriateness to an entire context must be judged. Thus, children must be sensitized to the ethical aspects of situations in such a way that they begin to sense that what they are doing is appropriate or inappropriate as they prepare to act on them. Such appropriateness, as in the illustrations of the play, the baseball game, and the musical performance, can be judged "right," at least for the moment. Further consideration of consequences of a particular act (to others, to oneself, to institutions of one's society) may lead one to modify one's initial judgment. But a keen awareness of the general outlines of a moral situation, and a feeling for how a proposed action would fit into that configuration (as "rightly" or "wrongly") is the kind of awareness that must be one of the major objectives of an ethical education. Insofar as the philosophy for children program stresses the cultivation of part-whole understanding, it contributes effectively to the development of the child as an ethical individual.

6 Teaching Methodology: Value Considerations and Standards of Practice

Getting Children to Think for Themselves

Encouraging children to think philosophically is not an easy task for teachers to master. In many ways, it is more of an art than a technique, an art comparable to leading an orchestra or directing a play. And since, like any art, it takes practice, teachers should not be discouraged the first or second time they use the curriculum in the classroom.

As one goes through one of the philosophy for children curricula, one learns how important to its success is proper timing in the introduction and sequential presentation of materials. Teaching philosophy involves eliciting themes from students and then repeatedly returning to them, weaving them into the fabric of the students' discussions as the classes proceed. If one looks at the entire curriculum, one will notice that the philosophical themes introduced in one novel occur and reoccur, each time in a little more depth, breadth, and sophistication. Unlike "atomistic teaching," which introduces a segment of knowledge, drills for it until it is mastered by the students, and then moves on to something new, this "organic" approach to teaching touches lightly on philosophical concepts in the beginning and then slowly builds a deeper understanding of the same concepts as they relate to recurrent motifs.

A review of *Harry Stottlemeier's Discovery*, *Lisa*, *Suki*, *Mark*, and *Tony* shows that this approach to teaching is embedded in the novels themselves. The books are works of fiction in which the characters eke out for themselves the laws of reasoning and the discovery of alternative philosophical views that have been presented through the centuries. The method of discovery for each of the children in the novels is dialogue coupled with reflection. This dialogue with peers, with teachers, with parents, grandparents, and relatives, alternating with reflections upon what has been said, is the basic vehicle by which the characters in the stories come to learn. And it is how real students likewise come to learn—by talking and thinking things out.

This is not to imply that the role of the teacher is non-existent or minimal, that the learning occurs just by letting the children discuss the novel day after day. Nor does it imply that somehow the knowledge is already there, "in the children," as it were, so that all one need do is put pupils together in a room and it will all come out. On the contrary, it is assumed that philosophical learning occurs primarily through interaction between the children and their environment—and that environment consists primarily of the physical classroom, other children, parents, relatives, friends, people in the community, the media, and the teacher.

However, it is the teacher who, at least in the classroom, can manipulate the environment in such a way as to enhance the possibility that the children will continually grow in philosophical awareness. It is the teacher who can elicit the themes in each of the chapters in the philosophical novels, who can point out themes the students in the classroom fail to identify, who can relate the themes to the children's experience when they seem to be having trouble doing so on their own, who can manifest by everyday behavior how philosophy can make a difference in one's immediate life—how it can open up horizons that make each day more meaningful. Further, it is the teacher who, through questioning, can introduce alternative views with the aim of always enlarging the students' horizons, never letting complacency or self-righteousness take precedence. In this sense, the teacher is a gadfly, encouraging the students to take the initiative, building on what they manage to formulate, helping them question underlying assumptions of what they arrive at, and suggesting ways of arriving at more comprehensive answers. In order to be successful, the teacher must not only know philosophy, but know how to introduce this knowledge at the right time in a questioning, wondering way that supports the children in their own struggle for understanding.

Naturally, there are certain underlying assumptions about the nature of the mind and how a child learns embedded in the philosophy for children program. Rather than envisaging the mind as an empty passive vessel that must be stuffed with information or content in order to be "educated," it is assumed that children learn by being actively involved in exploration. Further, it is presumed that knowledge is not simply learned by rote but is something mastered by interacting with the environment and by solving problems important to children. The knowledge is theirs when they can show, through their discussions and through their actions, that they can apply it to what they are doing, whether it is figuring out a syllogism or dealing with an interpersonal conflict on the playground. It is not theirs if they can say the words but are unable to use the knowledge the words express. Philosophy is empty if reduced to a memorization of "who said what, and when" or "how one philosophical view compares with another" as ends in themselves. It takes on significance only when children begin to manifest the capacity to think for themselves and to figure out their own answers about life's important issues. As philosophy opens up alternative possibilities for individuals' leading qualitatively better lives—richer and more meaningful lives—it gains a growing place in the school curriculum.

So that children can come to grips with ideas and not merely with labels, no mention is made of philosophers' names in the philosophy for children program (although their ideas are certainly introduced), and the teacher would be better off not using these names in class. In due time, the children will discover whose ideas they originally were, but this should happen only after authentically grappling with the ideas in trying to make sense of their experience, in trying to enlarge their own horizons, and thus in coming to understand themselves and others in a more comprehensive way.

Conditions for Teaching Philosophical Thinking

Children cannot be expected to engage productively in philosophical discussion unless these four important conditions obtain in your classroom: commitment to philosophical inquiry; avoidance of indoctrination; respect for children's opinions; evocation of children's trust.

Commitment to Philosophical Inquiry

The philosophy for children curriculum is in no way designed to be teacher-proof. More than anything, philosophical inquiry among children is dependent on a teacher who understands children, is sensitive to philosophical issues, and is capable of manifesting in everyday behavior a deep commitment to philosophical inquiry—not as an end in itself but as a means for leading a qualitatively better life. Teachers who can model an endless quest for meaning—for more comprehensive answers in life's important issues—are the most important ingredient in the philosophy for children program. This commitment is evidenced in their integrity, their having and acting on principles, and their manifesting a consistency between what they say and what they do.

The teaching of philosophy consists in recognizing and following very closely what children are thinking, helping them to verbalize and objectify these thoughts, and then aiding the development of the tools they need to reflect upon these thoughts. But this role is impossible unless the teachers themselves are models of persons who believe that, in the end, it makes a difference to do this. The effective teacher of philosophy ultimately must communicate a passion for excellence in thinking, excellence in creating, excellence in conduct—values that students may glimpse in the process of philosophical dialogue.

Remember, the commitment you are encouraging on the child's part is commitment to *the process of inquiry itself*, whether this be logical, aesthetic, scientific, or moral inquiry. The child should eventually be able to distinguish between your idiosyncratic values and the process that you try to embody. While there will be times when you will stray, it is that process to which you will most repeatedly return.

Avoidance of Indoctrination

One goal of education is the liberation of students from unquestioning, un-critical mental habits, in order that they may better develop the ability to think for themselves, to discover their own orientation to the world, and, when ready to do so, to devise their own set of beliefs about it. We cannot expect children to respect themselves as persons unless they have learned to utilize fully the intellectual and creative powers with which they are equipped. Every child should be encouraged to develop and articulate his or her own way of looking at things. Different children have different values. But if they hold these values thoughtfully, if they have given consideration to why they feel and think the way they do, if they have given some reflection to their needs and interests and activities, this will be an indication that their philosophical discussions have been helpful for them. It does not particularly matter whether they turn out to have different ways of looking at things. It does not particularly matter that they disagree with one another or with the teacher on philosophical issues. What matters most is that they get a better understanding of what they think and why they think and feel and act the way they do, and of how it might be to reason effectively.

There is no study that can more effectively prepare the child to combat indoc-trination than philosophy. No discipline offers children the range of alterna-tives to questions of utmost importance to them, nor does any other discipline take more seriously the development of their capacity to judge for themselves. But the power and authority of philosophy carries with it great responsibility.

No course in philosophical thinking, whether for children or adults, can succeed if used as a means for implanting the teacher's values in the vulner-able minds of the children in the classroom. No matter that the teacher is con-fident his values are the "correct" ones; if this is what he is doing, it is the destruction of philosophy.

On the other hand, there are teachers who feel they must be very careful not to reveal any values of their own in their teaching. They believe that their method of teaching is and must remain "value free." But such teachers may be deceiving themselves as well as their students. for no educational process is completely value free. All teachers reveal their values in what they say and do, if only through inflections of voice, gestures or facial expressions, the way they conduct a class or give a test. Teachers of philosophical thinking must therefore beware at all times of wittingly or unwittingly encouraging children to adopt their own personal set of values uncritically. Nor can they escape the fact that children not unreasonably look up to those whose experience of the world is broader or deeper than their own. The teacher's attitudes, whatever they be, are bound to carry considerable weight with youngsters who are unsure of the significance of their own experience.

Students engaged in philosophical discussion should feel free to advocate any value position they choose, without the teacher's having to agree or disagree with each and every point. Teachers who persistently interpose their own views run the risk, if not of indoctrination, at least of creating inhibitions that will sooner or later close off discussion itself. Only when students have developed to the point where they are able to deal objectively with the teacher's opinions and not be coerced by them, can the teacher contribute his own opinions to the discussion—provided the students want to know what they are.

A question naturally arises at this point concerning the teacher's insistence that participants in philosophical discussions try to be coherent, consistent, and comprehensive in their thinking: "Aren't coherence, consistency and comprehensiveness simply replacements for the personal values that the teacher is being asked not to force upon his students?" There are two answers to this question.

The first is that coherence, consistency, and comprehensiveness are values only in the sense that they are standards for effective communication and criteria for effective inquiry. They are appropriate to *the way* a person should think, not to *what* he should think. Therefore, they are *procedural* considerations, not *substantive* ones.

Second, there are other forms of activity in which these rules are hindrances rather than aids. For example, the children may find that their play need not be consistent, that the chores they do at home need not be comprehensive, and that their poetic impulses are stifled if it is demanded that they be more coherent. In other words, coherence, comprehensiveness, and consistency are appropriate values for philosophical discussion and inquiry but not for other aspects of a person's life that include characteristics of spontaneity, randomness, or routine to which the aforementioned values are irrelevant.

This still does not, however, fully answer the question of indoctrination and philosophy. A further question may be raised: "Is it not indoctrination to teach children logic?" Our answer must be that such instruction does involve a degree of risk. Certainly there are kinds of formal logic other than the Aristotelian logic one finds in *Harry Stottlemeier's Discovery* and *Lisa*, and there are various other approaches to non-formal logic as well in these novels as well as the others. It cannot even be said that the child who learns logic will necessarily draw correct inferences, since logic apparently helps us very little to improve our psychological processes. Rather, by providing us with criteria by which to evaluate the inferences that we do make, logic helps us distinguish better from worse ways of reasoning. It may not eliminate our mistakes, but at least it helps us recognize them.

There is nothing final about logical criteria. They are like parliamentary rules of discussion that are agreed to in carrying on a debate. As you know, even a classroom discussion cannot proceed unless there are some implicit or explicit agreements as to ground rules such as "no irrelevant talk will be permitted," "no filibustering," "no use of force," and the like. Similarly, logic sets ground rules for rational dialogue.

Teaching logic is not a form of indoctrination, inasmuch as logic is employed as an instrument for appraising the inferences we draw. We recognize that the grammar of a particular language is a device by means of which it is possible to distinguish speaking well from speaking badly. It is no more indoctrination to insist that children be logical in their thinking than to insist that they be grammatical in their speech. Moreover, as we have already pointed out, there will be, on occasion, considerable value in forms of reasoning generally thought of as invalid. Just as a novelist may have excellent reasons for choosing to be ungrammatical, a poet may have excellent reasons for choosing to be illogical. What the teacher must seek to convey is that *in certain contexts* and *for certain purposes*, it is beneficial to be able to speak grammatically and think logically.

The question may nevertheless be asked whether the philosophy for children program might be indoctrinational with respect to areas of philosophy other than logic. In other words, does the program contain a "hidden agenda"? Is there some underlying set of values upon which the whole program is predicated?

To respond to these questions, we must recognize that any educational program is necessarily founded upon certain explicit or implicit assumptions. We assume, for example, that the process of education has much in common with the process of inquiry. We believe that at every stage of a child's development free inquiry can be fostered in ways that will be wholesome and constructive both for the child and for society. Just how far inquiry is to be promoted for a given child at a given age is not altogether clear and to a great extent will depend upon the tact and sensitivity of the teacher. But the objective of our program for children of all ages is the liberation of those of their powers that are destructive neither of the children themselves nor of other people. Free inquiry provides an incomparable framework for such development.

Respect for Children's Opinions

Respect for children's opinions assumes that in many ways you have a philosophical view of knowledge itself. If you think you already know all the answers, if you think you have a direct line to the truth, then it will be rather hard for you to respect children's opinions (or adult opinions for that matter) should they differ from your own. However, if you realize that you are still searching for more comprehensive answers in all of the educational disciplines as well as in your own personal life, and, further, if you realize that knowledge itself is endlessly being created by human beings to explain the world they live in, then you will be more apt to listen to all people, including children, for ideas that might lead to more comprehensive and meaningful explanations than you now possess.

If one has been teaching for a while, one may have experienced the remarkable capacity for insight that children often manifest. Whether it is their lack of socialization, with all of its categorization and set ways of looking at the world, or their lack of inhibition, children often display a remarkable ability to approach problems in a fresh way. And often this insight on their part is a clue to a sounder formulation of the issues.

In addition, even if a child expresses an opinion that you are sure is not based on factual knowledge, your commitment to that child's growth should be your guide to action. Rather than "putting children down," it would be more productive to try to establish a mutual relationship of trust and empathy that might get them to admit that they do not know all the answers and that, like you, they experience the world as confusing and frustrating at times. Once this happens, you can begin the slow process of helping them to clarify their own views, getting them to see what such views imply in terms of assumptions and consequences, exposing them to alternatives, and giving them the tools they need to think for themselves about matters that concern them.

Evocation of Children's Trust

As for the matter of trust, it not only is indispensable to encouraging children to think philosophically, but is the foundation of sound teacher-student relationships. Most children are extremely sensitive to the whole spectrum of techniques that enable an adult to condescend to children and humiliate them. A slight or a "put down" will have only a momentary shock, but it leaves a scar, and that scar means that the trust essential to the learning process has been lost. Some people evoke immediate trust from others. But most of us have to work at it patiently. And there is no infallible recipe for how to do it.

We should distinguish three kinds of classroom situations. Most undesirable, of course, is the classroom in which the students are afraid to open up before the teacher because they fear the loss of affection or respect. Somehow the teacher has not communicated that he respects them for what they are, whether they agree or disagree with him.

A better situation is one in which the students feel free to discuss abstract matters, but are very careful not to say or imply anything that would challenge the values they believe the teacher to hold. Again, somehow, the teacher has communicated that his views are not to be challenged if one is to stay in his good graces. This communication (typically non-verbal) can constitute a serious impediment to the student's philosophical growth.

The optimum situation obviously is one in which the students trust the teacher sufficiently to risk criticism of the teacher's methods or values, because they know the teacher will consider such criticisms from them fairly. A teacher who respects his students is ready always to learn from them, and somehow in his behavior makes this known to them. He will be able to recognize that their sometimes critical or mischievous comments are their ways of testing him for his reactions. The teacher who is himself insecure or defensive and who finds criticism from children intolerable will quickly be spotted by the children as someone whom they are not prepared to trust. Thus it follows that a teacher who is insecure or defensive about his own opinions, who for one reason or another either holds his views rigidly or dogmatically or is defensive about his way of arriving at them, is not likely to be able to encourage children to think philosophically.

This in no way condones student disrespect. Respect is a two-way street, however, and teachers who do not respect their students, their opinions, their needs, and their interests, and who do not manifest this respect in their behavior every day in the classroom, are unrealistic if they think their students are going to respect them just because they are teachers.

Teaching Behavior Conducive to Helping Children Engage in Philosophical Thinking

Everyone is familiar with the sign THINK, and just about everyone realizes that the sign does not encourage thinking at all; if anything, it inhibits it. Ideas cannot be produced on command. What *can* be done is to create an atmosphere hospitable to good thinking, and to recognize that children have very diverse styles of mental behavior, each one of which needs nurturing in a somewhat different fashion.

In this sense, thinking is an art, and every artist proceeds somewhat differently. The teacher of any art must be able to discern the creative dispositions of the child and encourage their fulfillment. Likewise with teaching philosophy, the teacher must be prepared to nurture and cultivate a rich profusion of thinking styles, yet all the while insist that each child's thought be as clear, consistent, and comprehensive as possible so long as the *content* of the child's thought is not compromised. If teachers of philosophy would keep in mind that the proper role of the teacher is to encourage intellectual creativity as well as intellectual rigor, they will be safeguarded from concluding that all children are going to approach *Harry Stottlemeier's Discovery* or the other novels in the same way.

Surely, if you visited an art class and found all the students painting alike, you would suspect that the teacher had misunderstood the nature of art education, and instead of encouraging creativity was seeking to produce uniform works of art as well as uniform children. So it is with the teaching of philosophy. To visit a philosophy class and discover that everyone in it had developed the same point of view would suggest that something was amiss somewhere. Different people have different styles of thought; they have different life experiences, different goals and objectives, and it is plausible to expect from them a rich variety of philosophical perspectives.

It is up to the teacher to encourage just this variety of philosophical insights and approaches. What is held in common in philosophy are means rather than ends. That is, philosophy insists upon reasonable dialogue, but only as a means by which students can arrive at their own points of view and their own conclusions. Philosophy insists upon logical rigor, but only as a means of making thinking more efficient, which is quite different from having everyone's ideas conform to everyone else's.

Thus, a teacher's role is to help children master such means as the rules of logical inference and the etiquette of classroom discussion. It is not your role to dictate to children what their philosophies of life should be. In this sense, take your cue from the novels. The children in those books struggle to understand, hold their views fairly tentatively, are open to new suggestions, and are committed to the kind of communal inquiry in which individuals learn from one another as well as from their own experience. To the extent to which you can encourage your students to identify with these procedures, you will not have to worry about getting the children to think, because they will embark upon the process wholeheartedly and of their own volition.

Maintaining Relevance

Just as thinking is an art, so teaching is an art, and a considerable portion of the art of teaching relates to the teacher's awareness of what is and is not relevant to an ongoing philosophical discussion. Normally, it is not too difficult to distinguish between comments that relate to discussion and comments that are irrelevant. But there is a grey area in between, in which a teacher must exercise a considerable amount of discretion. Children in the age bracket of ten to fourteen are often prone to introducing personal experiences into the discussion, some very psychological in nature. The teacher has the option of allowing such remarks to focus the discussion on the child's personal difficulty or allowing the comment to serve as an *illustration* of a broader treatment of the issue. In the first case, the danger is clear that the discussion may become not a matter of philosophy but a matter of psychological therapy. The classroom is not the place for such therapy and neither the teacher nor the child's peers are the individuals to conduct it.

On the other hand, there is nothing wrong with a child's sharing a concern or giving an autobiographical account of some experience, where the teacher recognizes that this can be deftly directed towards an objective and impartial understanding by everyone in the class of the philosophical issues involved on which the personal account just related is able to shed light. In this case, the personal account serves to illustrate a broad philosophical issue that all the children in the class can benefit from exploring, instead of merely directing the attention of the children to the personal account itself.

Suppose a boy mentions that he has been teased by some girls. Now this can be an opportunity for the teacher to try to deal with this one specific instance—and it may turn out to be another humiliating experience for the boy. One direction that the discussion can go is into exploring why the teasing occurred—whether he deserved it, whether he did anything to the girls yesterday, and so on. Another direction that the discussion can take, if the teacher guides it carefully, is into a discussion of teasing itself; what, if anything, it accomplishes, why people tease other people, and what teasing may be a symptom of. Ultimately, the discussion can open up the broad philosophical question of what fairness is. But this will not frequently happen unless the teacher plays a guiding role, gently moving the discussion away from the specific and in the direction of the general.

Children at this age may want to share views about sex, about what is right and wrong, about their relationships with their families, and other such matters. The important thing for the teacher to realize is that these topics may well be fertile ground for a philosophical discussion, but only if the movement of the discussion is away from the intensely private and personal aspects of the account and towards the more inclusive, comprehensive, and constructive aspects of the problem. A philosophical discussion is profitable if it moves from what is to what could be, or from the special case to a broader understanding. It is not a philosophical discussion if children merely get their personal problems off their chests, or express themselves emotionally, or use the hour as an opportunity to regale one another with litanies of alleged injustices, or seek attention by telling personal anecdotes. But these accounts can be starting points for a philosophical discussion in the hands of the able teacher. It is up to the teacher to determine whether the account has philosophical implications and what the implicit philosophical themes are, and to guide the children gradually into a discussion of these themes.

When a teacher hears one child say to another "you're retarded" (or "sick," or "unfair," or "gross"), these are opportunities for seeking to discover the criteria by which we determine what is healthy, what is fair, or what is beautiful. In other words, what the teacher is trying to achieve is to get the children to make explicit, when they use such terms as "sick," "unfair," "unjust," what their *criteria* are for making such statements—what standards they use for making such observations. As the discussion begins to revolve around such criteria and standards, the teacher knows that it is on solid ground.

Ultimately, the teacher is the one who has to make the judgment as to whether a particular personal account should be capitalized upon or squelched. On the one hand, a child's wish to contribute may be repetitive, redundant, superfluous, or symptomatic of a need to dominate the discussion in an unproductive way. On the other hand, it may be something which, although anecdotal, is very rich in the implications that it suggests for a broader insight into the problems at issue for all members of the class.

The children in the classroom are likely to be very attentive to the manner in which the teacher operates in this zone of discretion—between what is clearly relevant and what is clearly irrelevant. In a very short time they will be testing and challenging to see just how personal, how anecdotal, how subjective, they can be without causing the teacher to respond negatively. If they have had experiences where the teacher has capitalized on their accounts and moved them into a philosophical discussion, they will probably want to have such experiences again. If, on the other hand, they find that the teacher will put up with aimless discussion, they will continue to ramble on pointlessly until they get bored.

Questioning

Most students are curious, and intellectually lively. The chances are that they will become increasingly less thoughtful and less reflective as they grow up. The change is so gradual, day by day, that one hardly notices the loss. Slowly the brightness fades, and the potential dribbles away. Suddenly you may begin to see that they are becoming unimaginative, unquestioning, uncritical in their behavior.

No doubt you want your students to be able to think, and to think for themselves. You want them to be rational and responsible individuals. You hope they will find their lives meaningful rather than empty. But when it comes to encouraging them to reason, when it comes to encouraging them to look for meaning in what happens to them and in what they do, you may well feel very helpless.

Children need models with which to identify. They need models of leadership if they are to see themselves as future leaders. They need models of integrity if they are to realize what it means to be honest. And they need models of intelligent adult-child conversation if they are to believe in the possibility of dialogue.

To help children learn to think for themselves, to move in the direction of becoming independent, resourceful, self-sufficient individuals, ask yourself, "What good is served by my readily providing children with answers every time they ask questions?" "What good is accomplished by their memorizing information from textbooks without trying to understand the concepts involved or the underlying presuppositions?" "Do I myself serve children as a model of an individual who constantly questions, who seeks always for more sufficient answers, who is more interested in dialogue and discovery than memorization of facts?"

In *Lisa*, we encounter a model of an adult-child conversation which can be one of mutual discovery for both adult and child, while at the same time we gain some insight into the nature of questions.

> "Dad," said Harry.
> "Mmmm," said his father.
> "Dad," Harry repeated.
> "Hmmm?" his father answered.
> "Dad, what's a question?"
> "What you're asking me."
> "Yeah. I know I'm asking you a question, but that's not the question I'm asking you."
> "What's the question you're asking me? We seem to be going round and round, like Abbott and Costello. Who's on first?"
> "Dad!"
> "What?"
> "I'm serious. What's a question?"
> "Why do you want to know?"
> "Dad, that's beside the point. What difference does it make why I want to know? I just want to know."
> "You're always asking why. Why can't I ask why?"
> "Dad, all I asked you was a simple question and you go round and round. All I was trying to find out was, what happens when we ask a question?"

The conversation proceeds guardedly and somewhat painfully on both sides. But there is a sense of progress. Eventually Harry remarks that maybe a person who asks a question has a problem. Then, pondering his own remark for a moment, he asks, "Is that what you're telling me, that we ask questions because we've got problems?"

> "Do we have problems or do the problems have us?"
> "Oh, Dad, for gosh sake, will you be serious?"
> "I am serious."

"Well, what's the connection between a question and a problem?"

"What's the connection between an iceberg and the tip of the iceberg."

"The tip of the iceberg is all you can see; the rest of it is under water."

"So isn't it possible that your question is just the tip of the problem?"

"The question's mine, but the problem's not mine?"

"Could be."

"So whose is it?"

"It doesn't have to be anybody's. Look, if you were finished with school and you weren't sure what you were going to do next, you'd be puzzled, and you'd start asking questions. But if there weren't any jobs, then that's a problem, and it's not just *your* problem. That's why I said, you wouldn't have it, but it would have you."

"So the reason I ask questions is not so much to get answers, as to get to know what the problem is?"

Mr. Stottlemeier touched Harry's head lightly with his hand.

"I couldn't have put it better myself," he said.

Now, not all children are as persistently inquisitive as is Harry Stottlemeier in this novel. But when teachers are skilled in cultivating their students' thinking through questioning themselves, the end result is children who can think for themselves about everything in their own experience. Children want to think about such things as who they are, why they are made to go to school, what their minds are, what death is, what things are right or wrong to do, and so on. So why not begin there—with their problems?

The art of questioning is very complex. Naturally, there are some questions that deserve answers. If a child asks you where the library is, you may as well tell him. But quite different is a question asking you what the meaning of a word is, when you both know that there are several dictionaries in the room. Likewise, if a child asks you a philosophical question, such as "what is fair?" and you respond by telling him how you would define it, there is a danger that you are foreclosing the very kind of inquiry that his question is intended to open up—the kind of inquiry that is the very foundation of thinking for oneself.

For an example, take this conversation overheard in a sixth-grade class in philosophy:

Teacher:	Why do you go to school?
1st student:	To get an education.
Teacher:	What is an education?
2nd student:	Having all the answers.
Teacher:	Do educated people have all the answers?
3rd student:	Sure, they do.
Teacher:	Am I educated?
1st student:	Sure.
Teacher:	Do I have all the answers?
3rd student:	I don't know. You're always asking us questions.

Teacher:	So I'm grown up and educated but I ask questions. And you're kids and you give answers, right?
2nd student:	You mean, the more educated we become, the more we ask questions instead of give answers? Is that it?
Teacher:	What do you think?

Teachers who pretend to be all-knowing do a double disservice to their students. First, by supplying them with answers that they should discover for themselves, such teachers fail to prepare their students for the day when adult support will not be present, and they will be left to their own undeveloped resources. Or, when the day comes that the model of omniscience collapses, when children find out that the teacher does not have all the answers, their security and trust may be shattered, and once again they are helpless because they have not been encouraged to develop the tools they need to find their own answers. Second, such teachers create in their pupils the model or ideal of the educated person as all-knowing, rather than as a person who is intellectually open, curious, self-critical, and willing to admit ignorance or indecision.

Further, when the teacher pretends to be all-knowing, the child comes away with the view that knowledge is answers—something outside of oneself to be memorized—rather than something to be discovered and created. Instead of involving the child in the process of knowledge-acquiring, the teacher with all the answers (or the teacher who insists on children regurgitating answers) has deprived such children of the very joy that will stand them in good stead in later years—the satisfaction of finding answers for themselves. The connection between the satisfaction and being an imaginative, curious, and intellectually lively person is very substantial.

Remember that children constantly use adults as their model of sound intellectual bearing and identify with their behavior. If you want to strengthen their curiosity, display to them the image of a mature yet questioning adult. Such an image confirms children in their freedom to explore, to ask further questions, to investigate the various alternatives available, and finally to arrive at some tentative answers. The capacity to hold one's answers as tentative rather than as dogma is something children can learn readily from you. But, if you present the image of someone who has all the answers, with the implication that these answers are the "right" answers, you present the image of someone who knows it all and thus you discourage children's exploring, questioning, and searching for more comprehensive solutions.

When you ask children "Why?" you challenge them to dig deeper into their own assumptions, to make better use of their own intellectual resources, to come up with more imaginative and creative proposals than they would have if your stance towards them were that of a supplier of facts. Even if there are situations in which giving answers is appropriate, there are ways of doing so that open up the issue more and invite children's inquiry instead of closing it off.

This characteristic of questioning, which is essential to encouraging children to think philosophically, is manifested not only in how a teacher answers children, but in the way she engages in teaching throughout the day. If the teacher encourages children to accept answers to be uncritical, to memorize facts that they do not understand, if she concentrates her energies on giving tests that do not draw upon their creativity or their active understanding, her students are likely to acquire the impression that they become more educated as they assimilate more facts. And this is hardly the best way to conceive of education.

Finally, the teacher should not be afraid to challenge those assumptions that children make when he or she even happens to agree with them, if the result promises to be a livelier attitude on the child's part towards the material. For an example, take this discussion:

Student:	When was George Washington born?
Teacher:	Why don't you look it up in the encyclopedia?
Student (a few moments later):	It says 1733.
Teacher:	Is that the correct date?
Student:	Sure it's correct. It's in the encyclopedia.
Teacher:	Was there really once a George Washington?
Student:	That's ridiculous. If there hadn't been, how could we account for all the papers signed in his name, the stories told about him by eye witnesses, the house that was his and the clothes that were his which I've seen at his home in Mt. Vernon?

The point of this dialogue is that children such as this one can be induced to come up with evidence upon which to base their belief in the existence of an historical figure like George Washington, or in historical events. They are compelled to get an insight into the nature of history. They see what it would be necessary to account for if the belief in George Washington's existence were alleged to be false. Thus, by means of a seemingly outrageous question, the teacher has moved the student from a spectator attitude towards history to a personal understanding of how to account for certain historical facts or incidents. It is this movement from spectator to participant that enables the child to take a more active role in the process of inquiry itself.

Now it is not easy to know what questions to ask when, and how to ask the right question. Moreover, it is not enough to have a few questions at hand in one's repertoire; it is equally important that they be asked in a sequence that moves the discussion towards a culmination.

In our instructional manuals, we provide numerous discussion plans that enable the teacher to lead the discussion strategically without having to wonder constantly what to say next. These discussion plans usually revolve around one of the leading ideas in the chapter and are so designed as to get the children to explore the concept in depth and to relate it to their personal experiences.

Answering

The questioning teacher, by his example, encourages children to question, but this does not preclude encouraging children to find answers. An answer is a stage of satisfaction in the process of inquiry; it is a plateau at which we are content to pause for a time in the course of our efforts to understand. Questioning and finding answers are among the rhythms of living, like working and resting, or like a bird perching for a while before it goes off on another flight. The answer a child arrives at may not be correct, but it is a resolution, even if only temporary, of the period of perplexity and uncertainty the child has been experiencing.

There is seldom justification for a teacher's actively discouraging a child from finding answers. What is more important is that children be helped to develop an openness and flexibility such that they are eager to substitute effective answers for those that no longer work. In this sense, answers are beliefs. As long as our beliefs are effective in dealing with the problems that we face in life, there is no reason for us to give them up. Even when children are exposed to conflicting evidence, there exists no urgent reason for them to give up their beliefs, although it may be time they started looking around for a more sufficient explanation.

Suppose a teacher says to a child, "The trouble is that you don't have your facts straight." The child answers, "Where do I get them?" One classmate suggests, "Go out and look around." But another classmate says, "Look them up in the encyclopedia." Now obviously a question has arisen as to what *facts* are. The teacher's role in such a discussion will be to encourage, by further questioning and clarification, the children's carrying the analysis as far as they possibly can.

Very often, however, where definitions are concerned, there may be no final answers. What is the universe? What is time? What is space? What is light? The question, "What is a fact?" is a question of this sort. It can be answered by a definition—but that definition will be opposed by a contrasting definition, and so on. The resolution children arrive at, incomplete as it may be from the teacher's perspective, should be respected and let stand for the time being. There will be time to come back at a later date and go over the problem again. While no belief need be final, the aim of discussion and inquiry generally is to move towards a tentative settlement by arriving at answers and beliefs that are serviceable and satisfying.

Listening

It is not easy to catch the significance of what people say to us if we have not developed the ability to be good listeners. For example, if a person in your school makes a remark about something that you know little about, it is likely that you will pay no attention to it. This is what psychologists call "selective inattention," and nowhere is it so prevalent as in our failure to hear the remarks of children.

For example, not long ago, in one of the experimental classes in philosophy for children, a ten-year-old compared the relationship of the body to the mind with the relationship between the "grapefruit and the taste of the grapefruit." Some adults might have judged a remark of this kind "Cute." Others might have not noticed it at all. But for a teacher who knows something about the nature of philosophical thinking, such a remark stands out as extremely perceptive and insightful, and the child should be encouraged to elaborate it. In other words, the child who makes a remark of this kind may not appreciate the possibilities inherent in his own words unless someone encourages him to articulate and develop such ideas so as to recognize the importance of having such insights. But if the teacher does not hear such remarks in the first place, then the child is not confirmed in a belief in the importance and meaningfulness of his or her own thinking, with the result that insights such as these are never developed but lost. Perhaps next time such an insight occurs, it will not be expressed.

Even if a teacher has the ability to listen to what children say, there is a very human tendency to interpret their remarks in terms of the teacher's own perspective. This interpretation can be quite different from the child's intended meaning. Thus the teacher should develop the habit of encouraging children to articulate exactly what they do mean. The teacher who is a novice at encouraging philosophical thinking among children will no doubt find much of what children say perplexing and ambiguous. The beginning teacher will be unsure whether the children's comments have philosophical importance or not. This is due partly to the teacher's expectation that children's remarks are not that philosophical, partly to the teacher's own uneasiness with the evident complexities, and partly to the teacher's own lack of prior exposure to philosophical ideas. As teachers grow in their knowledge of philosophy and at the same time grow in their ability to attend to and listen to what their pupils are saying, the process is likely to become increasingly richer for children and teachers alike.

Teachers must also develop their ability to grasp the seemingly disconnected or fragmentary remarks of children as part of an ongoing and developing classroom dialogue. In other words, the teacher has to have a sense that a
worthwhile discussion is brewing and that the talk that is underway is promising and likely to make progress with the right kind of guidance. It is only after
the teacher has had considerable experience in guiding discussions that this
capacity to surmise where a verbal interchange may lead is likely to develop.

Non-verbal Teacher-Student Communication

Obviously, a teacher does not have to wait for children to express their wondering verbally. Their faces reveal it and their conduct reveals it. Many times
what is expressed by a frown, or raised eyebrows, or a quizzical expression, is
the equivalent of the question "Why?" or a fully developed demand for reasons. The teacher must recognize that verbal language is not the only language in which children communicate: there is also the language of gesture,
the language of facial expression, the language of posture, and the language
of conduct. At the same time, of course, the teacher must realize that children
in the class will pounce upon every one of the teacher's gestures and facial expressions in an effort to discover its meaning. Therefore, there is a non-verbal
side to communication that a teacher of philosophy must take into account no
less than any other teacher.

One reason for the importance of the non-verbal element in communication
is that it can in many cases be inconsistent with the verbal aspects of one's language. The mother who addresses her child in endearing terms but conveys by
her gestures that she would not like the child to get too close is behaving am-
biguously. We all know cases when a person says "yes" when they obviously
mean "no," as well as when they say "no" and mean "yes." The teacher has
to learn not to emanate inconsistency. Very often children may stare non-com-
mittally at you when you are talking and yet you know that they know what
you mean. Or children may say that they understand, but you can see from
their faces that they do not.

Although teachers should try to make their non-verbal language and their
verbal language consistent, they should also be conscious that children themselves are often inconsistent in what they say and what they mean, and should
try to encourage them to express exactly what they do mean, at least insofar as
a learning situation is concerned. Yet communication has many purposes, and
it operates on many levels. There is no reason to eliminate its richness except
where confusion or ambiguity might cause the child some harm, or cause him
to be embarrassed or feel used. Sometimes, for example, adults tease a child
by saying something that is interpreted on one level by the child and on an-

other by the adults present. The adults then have a good laugh, but at the expense of the child, who is not sure why they are laughing but suspects it is at his or her expense.

If all goes well, children will in time come to be able to read the character of the situations in which they find themselves. This will probably involve their being able to read faces, read conduct, and read the nuances of situations themselves. The teacher should be able to set an example of someone who does not have to wait for children to express themselves to be able to sense the emotional tone of a classroom. Such a teacher is more likely to evoke the trust of pupils than a teacher who is indifferent to children's unverbalized but nevertheless manifest needs. Ideally, the teacher would then encourage the children in the class to pay attention and ultimately to learn to understand one another's suggested as well as manifest intentions.

The Teacher as the Child's Model

We often underestimate how important consistency is to children themselves. Very often the child looks for adults to do what they promise to do and to be what they claim people should be. It can be very demoralizing to children to discover that the adults they have taken as models may be consistent in their words but not in their lives. The adult as ethical model must be a model of integrity.

Children look for models that they can trust and have confidence in. But a model who is merely consistent is not sufficient to provide the adult guidance that children require. A model must be capable of giving children the benefit of adult experience when they need it. The slovenly teacher is one who never objects when children fail to make needed distinctions, or when they fail to group things that belong together. This can be an unfortunate influence on children, for it is only by teachers' showing the importance of distinctions and correct groupings, and by manifesting a love for such distinctions in their everyday behavior, that they can get children to do likewise. The teacher who hears a small child say, "Last night, I had potatoes and vegetables for dinner" or "There are Chevrolets and cars on the parkway," without questioning such groupings is failing in one of the major responsibilities of teaching. On the other hand, the teacher who sets an example of one who does make such a distinction is giving the child a model of intellectual scrupulousness that can very well have lifelong significance.

Another sense in which the teacher can serve as a model stems from the teacher's readiness to respond to the child's ideas and to communicate that such ideas are to be taken seriously. The first problem is to detect an idea as being an idea rather than just ignoring it as a somewhat unconventional way of expressing oneself. But merely to spot the idea is not enough. The teacher has to be able to help develop it. Very often children are unable to do more than simply enunciate an insight. From there on they need help in elaborating and articulating ideas of which they may have had only a glimpse.

A teacher has to be able to have a certain spirit of playfulness, and should realize that the development of ideas involves a kind of free construction of meanings, just as the child's playing with blocks is a free construction of form. One should not soberly press for immediate usefulness for such creative projects.

Another characteristic that can make one an important model for the child is the fairness that one exhibits towards the different ideas that are expressed in the class as well as one's fairness in dealing with each child as a person. A teacher's concern to develop the philosophical ability of the pupils has got to be openminded. But this can be a delicate business. First of all, there are times when one may disapprove of a child's idea because one feels sure it is wrong, but one should want to be careful not to give the child an impression that in rejecting the child's idea one is rejecting the child himself. On another occasion a teacher may feel that an idea voiced by one of the students is incorrect, yet prefer to keep silent in the hope that the classroom dialogue will gradually demonstrate to children the reasons why their ideas are unsound.

There may be times when a teacher may disagree with an idea that has been voiced and when the reasons opposing it as offered by members of the class seem insufficiently convincing. One may choose to voice one's own opinion, but make it clear to the class that it is simply another opinion to be considered in the light of the whole discussion. Obviously, one should not take the latter alternative unless one is sure that the class is mature enough to accept the idea as just another view and handle it on an equal footing with the views expressed by the class members.

7

Guiding a
Philosophical Discussion

Philosophy and the Strategies of Dialogue

Philosophy is a discipline that considers alternative ways of acting, creating, and speaking. To discover these alternatives, philosophers persistently appraise and examine their own assumptions and presuppositions, question what other people normally take for granted, and speculate imaginatively concerning ever more comprehensive frames of reference. These activities in which philosophers engage are the outgrowth of philosophical training. Philosophical education is most successful when it encourages and enables people to engage in critical questioning and inventive reflection. Given this philosophical conduct as our educational objective, our immediate problem is this: what teaching methodology will ensure the production of the finest ideas and the most relevant and sustained questioning from students?

Conditions that satisfy these requirements include a teacher who is provocative, inquisitive, impatient of mental slovenliness, and a classroom of students eager to engage in dialogue that challenges them to think and produce ideas. The minimal constituents of an adequate environment in which to encourage a child to think philosophically are a questioning teacher and a group of students prepared to discuss those things that really matter to them.

Built into the very nature of philosophy is the methodology by which it is best taught—questioning and discussion. The methodology of encouraging children to think philosophically is exhibited in the discovery approach exemplified by the novels in the philosophy for children program. The teacher is an authority figure primarily in the sense of being the arbiter of the discussion process. But in addition to being a referee, the teacher should be viewed as a facilitator whose task is to stimulate children to reason about their own problems through classroom discussions.

It would be very unfortunate if the teacher in this program were to feel that there is a specific amount of content that must be covered every day, that must be extracted from each episode and eventually mastered by the students. On the contrary, a successful class is usually one in which students enter into an animated discussion that deals with something or other in the book, although

102

the conversation may range far afield from the initial logic. Such discussions are capable of creating lasting impressions on children.

The amount of information or knowledge children acquire is less essential to their philosophical education than the development of their intellectual judgment. It is less important that children remember certain data than that they learn to think effectively. It is here that "every difference makes a difference." That is, any difference, no matter how slight, in children's modes of thinking can conceivably modify their entire thought processes. For example, a child may, until this year, have been operating on the assumption that things are pretty much what they seem to be, and suddenly he or she discovers that some things are quite different from what they seem to be. The discovery that looks can be deceiving is capable of changing that child's whole life.

Since the stress in the philosophy for children program is on the *process* of discussion, and is not aimed at achieving one specific conclusion, teachers do not need to present themselves to their students as possessing a great store of information. It is better to appear to the class as a questioner who is interested in stimulating and facilitating the discussion. A teacher need not claim to be infallibly right or wrong. But the teacher may very well express interest in differences among points of view, or in confirmations or contradictions of particular opinions. It has been observed that in such an atmosphere of intellectual give-and-take, students hitherto withdrawn or reserved begin to put forth their opinions because they realize that, in such an atmosphere, each point of view will be respected and taken seriously. Such children are willing to take their chances with the ensuing discussion, and to develop reasons for their opinions.

Although one doesn't *teach* philosophical topics to children, it is possible to elicit from them the wondering and questioning characteristic of philosophical behavior at any age. Gradually the children in the classroom begin to discover that a philosophical discussion has a different style from any other type of discussion. It is not just a matter of getting things off their chests, or being able to indulge in self-expression. They begin to realize that they are able to compare notes, experiences, and perspectives with one another. Gradually they perceive pieces beginning to fit together into an objective picture of the way things might be. They begin to understand the importance of recognizing other people's points of view, and of giving reasons for their own opinions. There emerges a sense of the value of impartiality, and a need to think problems through rather than be satisfied with superficial or glib expressions of opinion.

Although philosophy for children may include some rigorous aspects such as the rules and principles of logic, you need not be perturbed if the discussion goes off in any meaningful direction the children care to take it, although, of course, you should always exercise judgment as to the relevance of the discussion and as to whether the length of time devoted to any particular discussion is or is not disproportionate. Moreover, there is a big difference between a "bull session" and a philosophical discussion. A philosophical discussion is cumulative; it grows or develops, and through it the participants may discover endlessly new horizons. The art of the teacher here consists in skillfully eliciting comments from the children in such a way as to keep the discussion building, while yet involving the greatest possible participation from the class. The teacher's role throughout the discussion is one of a talented questioner. With an eye to encouraging convergent (and sometimes divergent) lines of discussion, with a recognition that a dialogue is often open-ended and somewhat unstructured, the teacher will recognize opportunities for the children to explore new vistas, just as there will be opportunities to indicate how ideas can fit together and reinforce each other.

Under suitable circumstances, a room full of children will pounce on an idea in the way a litter of kittens will pounce on a ball of yarn thrown in their direction. The children will kick the idea around until it has been developed, elaborated upon, and even in some instances applied to life situations, although the latter is seldom achieved without the teacher's artful guidance. Yet, when the discussion is finished, they may make such remarks as "time to get back to our school work," as if what they had been doing all along was not school, or learning, or discovery of their own intellectual prowess. They may take philosophy to be nothing more than fun and games, not realizing that it may be as intellectually formative as anything they might encounter in their school experience.

Guiding a Classroom Discussion

A thoughtful discussion is no easy achievement. It takes practice. It requires the development of habits of listening and reflecting. It means that those who express themselves during a discussion must try to organize their thoughts so as not to ramble on pointlessly. Very young children may either wish to talk all at once or not talk at all. It takes time for them to learn sequential procedures that a good discussion requires.

One of the reasons that the process of discussion is so difficult for children to learn is that they are so frequently lacking in models of good discussion with which they can identify. If neither the home nor the school offers them examples of thoughtful discussion—whether of adults with children, or even of adults with adults—then each generation of children must in effect invent the whole process of discussion by itself, because no one ever shows it how. In short, it is useful to have an established tradition of discussion that each child can automatically assimilate and identify with and engage in if dialogue is to enter meaningfully into the educational process.

One of the merits of the novels of the philosophy for children program is that they offer models of dialogue, both of children with one another and of children with adults. They are models that are non-authoritarian and anti-indoctrinational, that respect the values of inquiry and reasoning, encourage the development of alternative modes of thought and imagination, and sketch out what it might be like to live and participate in a small community where children have their own interests yet respect each other as people and are capable at times of engaging in cooperative inquiry for no other reason than that it is satisfying to do so.

Perhaps one of the most distinctive features of the philosophy for children program is that it suggests how children are able to learn from one another. This is a problem that is encountered today at every level of education: there are students in colleges, secondary schools, and elementary schools who try to "make it on their own" without really seeking to learn from one another or to assimilate the life experience of their peers even when, through discussion, it might be readily available to them.

While some children speak up readily enough but fail to listen to one another, others listen intently, follow the line of the discussion, and may then respond to it by making a contribution that goes beyond, rather than merely repeats, what has been said. The teacher should, of course, be aware of the possibility that the child who does not always listen may be developing a very unusual set of ideas, and needs to disregard the conversation for a while in order to do so. (The harm some children do to themselves by not listening is therefore likely to be considerably less than the harm other children do to themselves when, having failed to listen, they are constantly forced to cover the same ground that others have already gone over.) On the other hand, there are children who seldom speak up, but who listen intently and constructively to the class discussion. They are alert and involved, even though they fail to join in the discussion.

A discussion should build by way of its own dynamics. Like children in a playground building a pyramid by standing on one another, a discussion builds upon the contributions of each of its members. In asking questions, the teacher is not merely trying to elicit answers already known. Encouraging philosophical thinking is a matter of getting children to reflect in fresh ways, to consider alternative methods of thinking and acting, to deliberate creatively and imaginatively. The teacher cannot possibly know in advance the answers that children are going to come up with. In fact, it is just this element of surprise that has always been so refreshing about teaching philosophical thinking: one never is quite sure what thought will surface next.

It is, of course, important to keep the discussion going. As the children hear about each other's experiences and begin to learn from each other, they begin to appreciate one another's points of view and to respect one another's values. But when it appears that the discussion of one of the leading ideas of the episodes has ceased to be productive, the teacher must be prepared to direct the discussion tactfully to another topic.

The Role of Ideas in a Philosophical Dialogue

You may well be wondering what is distinctive about a philosophical discussion. In what ways may a philosophical discussion be contrasted with other kinds of discussions? Here we may distinguish philosophical discussion from discussions of two other types: scientific and religious.

Scientific Discussions

A scientific discussion is generally concerned with matters of fact, and with theories about matters of fact. The questions raised in a scientific discussion are in principle answerable questions. They can be answered by discovering relevant evidence, or by consulting acknowledged scientific authorities, or by making appropriate observations, or by citing pertinent laws of nature, or by conducting relevant experiments. Discussions in a science class can be very intense and very lively, especially if there is some disagreement as to how certain evidence is to be interpreted, or as to whether a given theory explains all the relevant factual data.

By and large, the scientist is dealing with how some portion of the world is to be described and explained. Therefore, a science class may involve discussion of such questions as what are the causes of sun spots, what is the temperature of dry ice, how does the heart work, how does the blood circulate, what was the Stone Age, what causes earthquakes, and so on. In general, the issues raised by these questions can be clarified and grasped by adequate discussion and analysis of elementary scientific theories and available scientific evidence. So a scientific discussion is subject to the authority of empirical evidence, as such evidence is interpreted within the accepted framework of scientific understanding. In principle, therefore, the resolution of scientific disputes is always possible.

Discussions about Religious Beliefs

Many children in your class are already in possession of a set of religious beliefs acquired from their parents, from their religious schools, from discussion with their peers, and sometimes from their own observations. These beliefs may relate to the purpose of destiny of the world, the question of personal immortality, the existence of a God, the expectation of divine reward or punishment, and so on. These are not generally the sorts of questions that can be decided by factual evidence one way or another. In no way is it part of the role of a philosophy teacher to criticize a child's religious beliefs, or to seek to undermine them even in an indirect fashion. The teacher simply cannot infringe upon the realm of children's religious beliefs without becoming guilty of indoctrination. On the other hand, there can be no serious objection to affording the child a view of the range of alternatives from which human beings throughout the world select their beliefs. After all, if it is not indoctrination to suggest to children who profess to believe in many gods, or in none at all, that there are conceivable alternatives to their views, why should it not also be possible to suggest to those who believe in a solitary supernatural being that there are many numerical alternatives?

It is always unfortunate when a teacher, out of self-righteousness or ignorance, attempts to modify the religious beliefs of children in the classroom. Such invasion of the child's intellectual integrity represents not only a lack of respect for the child but also a misconception on the teacher's part of the nature of science, the nature of philosophy, and the nature of education. Some individuals think that children's religious beliefs are unsound in light of what we know of science and philosophy, and can be corrected with a healthy dash of scientific or philosophical information. But there are no such facts that can dispel religious beliefs one way or another. To the extent that religious beliefs are matters of faith, it is a question whether they are matters that can be resolved by either science or philosophy.

It is, of course, quite possible for children to have religious discussions, just as they may discuss their families, their friends, their fears, their joys, and other private matters among themselves. An informal religious discussion among children typically involves a comparing and contrasting of their respective feelings and thoughts about religious matters. It does not usually involve the search for *underlying assumptions*, or the analysis of the meaning of concepts, or the search for clear definitions that often characterize philosophical discussions. In other words, religious discussions usually do not explore the assumptions on which religious beliefs rest, while a philosophical discussion cannot rest content unless it does explore its own assumptions.

To repeat, teachers must be very careful that this course in philosophical thinking does not serve as a tool in their hands or in the hands of the students to disparage the religious beliefs of some of the children in the class. The course optimally should serve as a tool by means of which children can clarify and find firmer foundations *for their own beliefs*. The teacher's role is twofold. It is not to change children's beliefs but to help them find better and more sufficient reasons for believing those things *they* choose, upon reflection, to believe in. And further, it is to strengthen their understanding of the issues involved in their holding to the beliefs they do hold.

Philosophical Discussions

We have tried to show that science and religion represent very separate areas of human interest in terms of their relevance to the classroom. In other words, from an educational point of view, scientific discussions and religious discussions are separate things and should not be confused with philosophical discussions.

Philosophical discussions need not just take up where science and religion leave off. Philosophical discussions can frequently become involved in questions of science and questions of religion, as philosophical discussions may lead into any other subject. Philosophy may or may not be a party to the dispute over factual descriptions of the world of religious interpretation of reality. As an objective onlooker, a philosopher is no more party to these disputes than an umpire is one of the contestants in a game that he referees. If anything, the umpire represents the spirit of impartiality that tries to see that the game proceeds in the fairest possible fashion. In a somewhat similar fashion, philosophy is concerned to clarify meanings, uncover assumptions and presuppositions, analyze concepts, consider the validity of reasoning processes, and investigate the implications of ideas and the consequences in human life of holding certain ideas rather than others.

This is not to imply that philosophy is concerned only with the clarification of concepts: it is also a fertile source of new ideas. For wherever there is a threshold of human knowledge, those who think about that particular subject area can only grope and cast about speculatively in an effort to understand what is there. Gradually, as methods of investigation of the new subject area are developed, as methods of observation and measurement and prediction and control are perfected, the period of philosophical speculation is replaced by one of scientific understanding. In this sense, philosophy is the mother of all sciences, for as philosophical speculation becomes more rigorous and substantiated, as measurement and experimentation and verification begin to occur, philosophy turns into science. In this sense, philosophy is a source of ideas that precedes the development of every new scientific enterprise.

Now what does all this mean for the role of the teacher in guiding *philosophical* discussions? First, the teacher has to keep in mind the distinctions just made between scientific, religious, and philosophical discussions and must retain these subtle distinctions as guideposts in encouraging children to think philosophically. The teacher must be aware that what began as a philosophical discussion can easily turn into a dispute over factual information that can be settled only by looking up the empirical evidence that is available. It is the teacher's role, once the discussion has taken this turn, to suggest where the empirical evidence may be found, rather than continue along speculative lines. For example, it is not a philosophical dispute if an argument develops in a classroom over the sum of 252 and 323. It *is*, however, a philosophical question to ask, "What is addition?" or "What is a set?" It is easy enough to look up in a book the exact year when Columbus landed in the Western Hemisphere. However, this in no way settles the question of "who was the first person to discover the Western Hemisphere?" a notion that is rich in ambiguity and in need of clarification. We assume that it takes *time* for light to reach the earth from the sun. But we do not have a science of time itself, and therefore, when children ask, "What is time?" they are asking a philosophical question, and there is no reason why, through dialogue with their peers and teachers, they should not be exposed to some of the alternative views that have been offered by philosophers if these views can be phrased in terms that they can understand.

Philosophical discussions can evolve out of a great many of the demands children make for the *meaning* of an idea. It is up to the teacher to seize upon these opportunities and use them as entries into philosophical exploration. If the child wants to know what the word "authority" means, or what the word "culture" means, or what the word "world" means, or what the word "respect" means, or what the word "rights" means, the teacher can take any of these as a starting point for getting as many views out on the table as there are children in the classroom, exposing the children to additional views that have been thought up by philosophers, examining the consequences of holding one view over another, and clarifying the meaning and the underlying assumptions of each view.

How Is Philosophy Related to Science Education?

It is sometimes pointed out that scientific "facts" are often presented in the classroom as if they were final and absolute. Such an approach is contrary to the spirit of scientific inquiry, for which no fact can ever be called indubitable. To deny the student the right to doubt the outcome of a scientific inquiry is to forestall the continuation of that inquiry. On the other hand, what the instructor needs always to make clear is that the "facts" that he teaches rest upon evidence that is always retrievable or in some fashion demonstrable. It is only when science is taught in such a way as to ignore the limitations of empirical procedures that it becomes indoctrination.

Therefore, the benefit to scientific education of philosophy for children is that it encourages the critical temper of mind that all scientists rightly prize. When students question the facts that they are given in science, their behavior is totally in keeping with the spirit of the scientific enterprise. Indeed the philosophical frame of mind is essential as an antidote to scientific dogmatism, and as a source of fresh and provocative new ideas to be followed up by scientific investigations.

Many of the difficulties experienced by present-day programs in science education are due to the fact that not many young people appreciate what science is about. They find little in it to identify with; they do not understand the methodology; they have little sense of the difference between accurate and inaccurate ways of reasoning, nor do they have a general sense of the purpose of understanding things scientifically. It is difficult to see how students who have not been trained to value the difference between efficient reasoning and sloppy reasoning can function effectively with scientific materials. It is hard to see how students who have not been trained to draw proper inferences from what they perceive or from verbal formulations can ever be trained to engage in scientific experimentation.

In brief, we are suggesting that approaches to science education that should provide the student with a preliminary orientation towards the scientific enterprise itself should provide incentives that would motivate children to apply themselves to scientific pursuits, and should provide a set of working habits that would combine their creative and imaginative inclinations with their own desires to think in a disciplined and orderly way about the world. Putting philosophy in the curriculum could be a step in the direction of the achievement of these goals.

The questioning inherent to philosophy is a necessary precondition to the success of a course in science; if postponed until after instruction in science is well underway, it is often too late to maintain the high level of curiosity that successful scientific education must preserve. Philosophy for children, dealing as it does with so many of the questions that children naturally have about their own life experiences, creates conditions under which the scientific instruction they receive will continue to be relevant for them. Frequently it is the lack of such connections that endangers a more traditionally presented program. It is our thesis that philosophy can provide this continuity, and that science can be more effectively taught, in terms of the objectives of science educators themselves, when a philosophy for children program is present than when it is absent.

Fostering Philosophical Dialogue

Discussions, Good Discussions, and Philosophical Discussions

Now and then, one will hear this sort of comment during a lunch-hour conversation among teachers: "We had a good discussion in class today." Such a remark leaves one with the impression that good discussions do not happen very often. It is something like hearing the remark, "My Uncle Fud was sober last week": one is left with the impressions that the weeks Uncle Fud is not drunk are few and far between.

But we tend to think of good discussions as pretty much a matter of luck. We're grateful for the good fortune that brings us a delightful classroom dialogue as we are grateful for a pleasant day in February—but we assume that we could no more promote the one than the other.

Yet this is a decided mistake. Good discussions can definitely be promoted—and so can good *philosophical* discussions. But first we must know just what it is we are trying to achieve. We must know how to distinguish mere discussions from good discussions, and must know what is distinctive about philosophical discussions.

One can have good discussions on any topic—in contrast to discussions that are aimless or superficial. A good discussion need not involve everyone present (some people learn more by listening than by talking; they are thoroughly involved participants, even though silent). A good discussion does not necessarily take place just because many participants are engaged in verbalization. Nor can one contentedly lay claim to having had a good discussion just because the class has been polarized, or because a few participants have squared off against one another.

A good discussion occurs in any subject when the net result or outcome of the discussion is discerned as marking a definite progress as contrasted with the conditions that existed when the episode began. Perhaps it is a progress in understanding; perhaps it is progress in arriving at some kind of consensus; perhaps it is progress only in the sense of formulating the problem—but in any case, there is a sense of forward movement having taken place. Something has been accomplished; a group product has been achieved.*

In contrast, a mere discussion may evoke comments from various individuals present (one hesitates to call them "participants") but without achieving a "meeting of minds." Individuals may succeed in expressing the perspective from which they perceive the issue, but the perspectives never intersect so as to form parts of some larger frame of reference. A series of individuals may testify as to their beliefs, but they could just as well occupy independent universes for all the connection their testimonies have with one another.

Yet a mere discussion may be the soil out of which a good discussion springs, as a good discussion on any topic may be the soil out of which a philosophical discussion springs. The point is that we can tell what is a good discussion by what *emerges* as the discussion proceeds. A mere discussion is linear and episodic, like a mediocre picaresque novel in which a series of incidents is strung

*See Justus Buchler, "What is a Discussion?" *Journal of General Education*, VIII, no. 1 (Oct. 1954), 7–17.

together, yet nothing ever *builds*. On the other hand, a good discussion is cumulative; each contribution is in effect a line of force or vector that converges upon the others and is orchestrated with the others. Whether there is complete agreement or disagreement at the close of the episode is relatively unimportant; what matters is that the contributions from each participant relate to and reinforce one another, as each participant learns from what the others have said (and indeed, learns from his or her own contributions), and as each successive contribution to the discussion reflects the successive increments of understanding that that participant has amassed.

If one listens carefully to the remarks of the leader of a "brain-storming" session—or of the moderator at an ordinary discussion—and then compares these with the questions or comments of a teacher of philosophy, one cannot help being struck by the difference. The person whose only aim is to extract comments or opinions from as many people as possible will often address questions such as these to the participants:

What is your opinion on this matter:
What are your beliefs on this topic?
Do you agree with what has been said?

In other words, questions such as those just mentioned merely seek to elicit opinions, but they do not promote reasoning. Each protagonist is not encouraged to formulate his views rationally, but to spew them forth, as it were, off the top of his head.

In a philosophical discussion, on the other hand, the teacher will be found asking questions such as these:

What reasons do you have for saying that?
Why do you agree (or disagree) on that point?
How are you defining the term you just used?
What do you mean by that expression?
Is what you are saying now consistent with what you said before?
Could you clarify that remark?
When you said that, just what is implied by your remarks?
What follows from what you just said?
Is it possible you and he are contradicting each other?"
Are you sure you're not contradicting yourself?
What alternatives are there to such a formulation?

To lead a philosophical discussion, one has to develop a feeling for which sort of question is appropriate to each situation, and for the sequence in which such questions can be asked. A teacher of philosophy may pause over a certain student's comment, pursue it, explore it, while judging that the next student's comment should be allowed to stand on its own merits without further examination, because right then further analysis might be counter-productive. No recipe can be written for the perfect discussion technique, although teachers interested in finding models could do worse than read the *Dialogues* of Plato, where Socrates is portrayed as a master teacher of philosophy—that is, the master in the art of eliciting productive dialogue.

Drawing Students Out

Getting students to engage in philosophical dialogue is an art. As with any art, some knowledge is a prerequisite—in this case, the teacher should possess an understanding of when it is appropriate to intervene in the discussion and when not to. There are times when the best thing one can do to guide a discussion is to say nothing and let things happen. In fact, the goal towards which a philosophical discussion should move is one in which there is maximum *student-student* interchange, as opposed to the start of such a discussion, in which *teacher-student* interchange is at a maximum.

Eliciting Views or Opinions

We have repeatedly stressed the point that classroom discussion should begin with the interests of the students, and that having children read a story is a way of creating an experience that will mobilize and crystallize their interests. We are all familiar with the fact that our own interests tend to flag unless stimulated and directed; what is pedagogically useful in the work of art is that it animates those interests of ours that would otherwise lie dormant and inert.

Once the children have read the story, you may ask them what they found interesting in it, and as these comments are offered by the class, you may find it helpful to write them on the blackboard and check with students on the accuracy of written representations of their ideas. This series of "points of interest" then becomes the agenda for the class discussion. (Note that it is essentially the children's agenda, not the teacher's—although the teacher may find it advantageous to add to it if the pupils seem to have overlooked something the teacher thinks important.)

Now the first item on the discussion agenda is taken up. The teacher may ask for an expression of views. If such views are slow in being offered, the teacher may ask the person who suggested the item to elaborate on it, by asking such questions as:

Why did you find that particular incident interesting?
Are you familiar with incidents of this sort?
Which views do you agree with and which do you disagree with?

How did this part of the story help you understand the rest of it?
Is there anything about this episode you found puzzling?
Does this episode raise issues you think we ought to discuss?

Of course, the teacher will probably discover that there are numerous questions that are much more specific and relevant to the suggested item than the rather general questions listed above. In that case, the teacher should not hesitate to begin by asking those questions that are most immediately pertinent to the agenda item under discussion.

Helping Students Express Themselves: Clarification and Restatement

Sometimes, in the course of teaching a class, the teacher may find that students have difficulty expressing themselves. Maybe they just cannot find the right words; maybe they are shy. In any case, the teacher may want, on such occasions, to try to evoke student participation by means of helping phrases such as the following:

You appear to be saying . . . .
Could it be that . . . ?
Are you saying that . . . ?
This is what I hear you saying . . .
I get the impression that . . .
Could this be what you're saying, that . . .
As I hear you, you're saying that . . .
So as you see it . . .
Correct me if I'm wrong, but isn't this . . . ?
Well then, from your point of view . . .
As I understand you . . .
Am I correct in assuming you are saying that . . . ?
Would it be reasonable to put your position like this . . . ?
I wonder if what you're saying could be put this way . . .
Would it help if I expressed your views this way . . . ?

It will be noticed that these phrases are employed by the teacher to get the student to *clarify* what the child has said. They do not ask for the reasons or the implications of the child's remark; they are simply efforts to *restate* or to get the child to *restate* certain comments that need elucidation.

No doubt it is preferable that children clarify their own views rather than that the teacher perform this task for them. But there are times when students are stumped as to some better way of saying what they have said, and the teacher can help by offering to reformulate their remarks in some more comprehensible form.

The advantage to doing this is that it expedites discussion. The danger, clearly, is that what seems to be an innocent translation of the child's views into a formulation more readily understood is in fact an interpretation of the original view—an interpretation that can well be a *distortion* of what the child originally intended. We all have manipulative tendencies of which we may or may not be conscious, and one way in which these come out is in our efforts to get others to believe what we believe by the device of persuading them that what they are trying to say is precisely what we would like to hear them say. But a teacher's obligation is to help children express what they think, even though what they think may turn out not to be what the teacher would like them to think. If the teacher disagrees with them, there may be occasions for saying so, and for explaining why. But distorting students' views by subtle reformulation is manipulative and indoctrinational—which is another way of saying that it is inappropriate to philosophical dialogue.

Explicating Students' Views

On the other hand, the teacher may wish to do more than simply help the students clarify their views by restatement. The teacher may want to explore not merely what they say, but the *meanings* of what they say. There is a difference between asking a student, "Are you saying that . . ." and asking the same student, "Are you implying that. . . ." It is the difference between what one asserts and how that assertion is to be interpreted.

But before discussing what is involved in interpreting students' remarks, the teacher should give some attention to *explication*. Explication lies between undistorted restatement and interpretation. You explicate when you select and emphasize certain features of what a student has asserted. Or the students themselves can be encouraged to explicate what they have said. These are some of the comments that are cues for explication:

Is the point you're making that . . . ?
Which points in what you've said would you like to emphasize?
So you think the following points are important . . .
Can I sum up your argument as follows . . . ?
Could you give us a quick summary of the points you're making . . . ?
Here's what I take to be the gist of your remark . . .

Interpretation

The discussion in the classroom may now turn on the *meaning* of what someone has remarked, or on the *meaning* of a passage in what the class has read. When we unpack meanings, we are engaged in interpretation.

What you say presumably has meaning to you in your frame of reference—in your life experience. But interpretation of your remarks may differ markedly from your own interpretation of what you said. In other words, you impute one meaning to your remarks, while other persons may impute quite another.

Now, in guiding a philosophical discussion, it is quite important to be aware not only of what is being said, but of how the various members of the class interpret what is being said. There are two ways in which meanings are drawn out of what has been said by inferring what is *logically implied*, and by inference from what is *suggested* although not logically implied.

Inferring Logical Implications

By studying logic, you can learn how to tell what can be logically inferred from given statements or groups of statements. Logic will be able to tell you, for instance, that from the statement, "No dogs are reptiles," you can logically infer that no reptiles are dogs, but that you cannot logically infer from it that all dogs are vertebrates, or that no reptiles are furry.

Logic will also tell you that from two statements in the following form:

All disk jockeys are human
All humans are mortal

you can legitimately draw the inference that "All disk jockeys are mortal." Logic can tell us, in other words, what is implied by what we say, insofar as what we say can be carefully formulated and arranged to suit the rules of logic. In the course of a classroom discussion, these strict conditions often do not obtain. We can study idealized instances—like Harry, in chapter 1 of *Harry Stottlemeier's Discovery*, spotting an instance of invalid deductive inference—indeed, in that chapter, he spots no less than two such instances. In real life discussions, such possibilities of strict examination for logical inference are not too frequent. Nevertheless the mastery of logic equips the reader with powerful tools for the extraction of precise meanings from what has been read.

Inferring What Is Suggested

Interpretation is a matter of finding meaning through discovering what is suggested or implied by what someone has expressed. Note that people draw *inferences*, but expressions have *implications*. The implications of an expression are its meaningful consequences: some of these meaningful consequences are logically implied, and some are simply suggested.

For example, if a member of a class says, "Oh, no, Johnnie's not your pet at all—he just gets high grades because he's so brilliant!" the teacher would not be wrong to suspect that what has been said is ironical, and that it is being *suggested* (although it is certainly not logically implied) that Johnnie is very much teacher's pet.

Or if someone says, "Yesterday, Frank moved up to a front seat. Today, the whole front row moved to the back of the room," surely it is being suggested that the students in the front row moved away *because* Frank moved up front—yet nowhere is this logically implied.

There are also non-verbal inferences to be detected. One's reading of these must range from catching what is suggested by an innuendo or a slightly unusual emphasis to picking up gestures or facial expressions among the class and interpreting their meanings as responses to what has been said.

Since interpretation is a matter of drawing out what is suggested or implied, at times a teacher can move a discussion along by suitably interpreting what has been expressed by the students to that point. The interpretations might be introduced by phrases such as:

> From what has been said, I gather that . . .
> If I'm not mistaken, your position can be interpreted in this way . . .
> Correct me if I'm wrong, but aren't you saying, in a nutshell, that . . . ?
> As I read what you're saying, it seems to follow logically that . . .
> Are you suggesting that . . . ?
> Are you implying that . . . ?
> Would I be distorting what you're suggesting if I put it this way . . . ?
> I interpret your meaning to be as follows . . .
> Couldn't your meaning be put this way . . . ?
> Could you explain what you mean by what you just said . . . ?
> If what you're saying is correct, wouldn't it follow that . . . ?
> If what you're saying is correct, how can you explain the fact that . . . ?
> In view of what you've just expressed, don't you think that . . . ?
> In view of what you've just expressed, do you think that . . . ?
> I think what you've just said is significant or insignificant because . . .
> It seems to me the implications of what you've said are far-reaching because . . .
> Would you object to this interpretation of your remarks . . . ?

Seeking Consistency

It is useful in the course of a philosophical discussion to raise questions about consistency. (By "consistency" is meant the practice of using the same term in such a way as to have the same meaning when the term is employed several times in the same context.) You may suspect that a person is not being consistent in his presentation of his views, or you may feel that the views of several individuals in the classroom are inconsistent with one another. In either case, it would be well to explore such possibilities, using questions or comments like the following:

> Earlier, when you used the word ———, didn't you use it in quite a different sense from the way you are employing it now?
>
> Are you really disagreeing with one another—or are you saying the same thing in two different ways?
>
> It seems to me there's a direct contradiction between those two views . . .
>
> Just to elaborate on that view for a moment, wouldn't it be consistent to add that . . . ?
>
> Of course your views are consistent; but you could still be wrong because . . .

Requesting Definitions

There are times when the terms employed in a discussion get to be more confusing than illuminating. On such occasions, it may be well to pause for a definition—or else to abandon the troublesome terms altogether.

What happens, very often, is that a controversy among children can be traced back to the fact that they are using the identical term, but defining it in quite different ways. Once everyone becomes aware of this fact, they can decide whether to try to arrive at a common definition or to find alternative terms that would be more suitable.

Children may disagree over whether a movie was good or was not good, or over whether a platypus is a fish, a bird, or a mammal, and so on. In simple cases, such as the latter, it is obvious that a dictionary is the best recourse. But in other cases, the most controversial words are those that are very rich in alternative meanings. A teacher should try to get at the definitions that the pupils are implicitly employing—if such a step becomes necessary—by asking such questions as:

> When you use the word ———, what do you mean by it?
>
> Can you define the word ———, which you just used?
>
> What does the word ——— refer to?
>
> If a thing is a ———, what are its chief features?

On the whole, a teacher should be cautious about requesting definitions, because doing so runs the risk of sidetracking the discussion into *merely* a dispute over definitions. For example, a class may be discussing the problem of war, and the dialogue is progressing nicely. Then the teacher interjects the question, "What do we mean by 'war'?" It is an excellent question—but it must be asked at an appropriate moment, when the students are beginning to see the difficulties involved in the word, rather than at a moment when the dialogue is going along smoothly and productively because certain meanings of the word are being taken for granted.

On the other hand, there are discussions that seem to be unable to get off the ground unless one or more of the basic terms are defined at the very beginning. For example, a class may be talking about what happens in chapter 5 of *Harry Stottlemeier's Discovery*, and find that it is essential to come to some understanding or consensus about the meaning of the word "education." In such cases, a teacher might well begin by asking for the key word or words to be defined.

Searching for Assumptions

If one of the chief characteristics of philosophical dialogue is to discover what is *implied* (what follows from) what is said, another of the chief characteristics is the search for the assumptions underlying what is said. It is typical of philosophers to look for the presuppositions upon which every question and every assertion are based—and this quest likewise characterizes philosophical discussions—especially those that are most penetrating and profound.

Exposing assumptions does not necessarily cause students to give up those assumptions. But it may very well cause them to rethink whatever they say that is based on such assumptions.

Very often, disclosure of what a questioner presupposes reveals why the question seems unanswerable. Surely, if someone asked you how far it is from here to never-never-land, you would reject the question on various grounds, such as that it assumes that never-never-land exists, that the distance to it is measurable, that "here" is a specific location, and so on. Or, if someone asked you whether it was warmer in the winter or in the city, you would protest that the question assumed that the winter and the city could be compared in terms of temperature. Or if a question is asked, "How will the world end?" surely it is legitimate to inquire as to why the questioner is assuming that the world will end. Children can be presented with a model of critical scrutiny of questions and assertions to detect what the presuppositions are, and whether any of them are unwarranted. They can be such questions as:

Aren't you assuming that . . . ?
Doesn't what you say presuppose that . . . ?
Doesn't what you say rest on the notion that . . . ?
Is what you've just said based on your belief that . . . ?
Would you say that if you didn't also happen to believe that . . . ?

If a child asks you something like, "How are bears different from mammals?" he may be assuming that the mammal is just another species of animal. In such a case, you may be able to correct his faulty assumption. But in another instance, you may discover that his assumption is correct, but what he has inferred from it is wrong. For example, a small child might assert that trees never die. Suppose you ask him what that belief of his is based on, and he replies, "Only living things die." Now in this case, his presupposition is correct, but he has drawn a faulty inference from it, due to the fact that he has made another—and, in this case, faulty—assumption: that trees aren't living things.

Indicating Fallacies

If teachers take the lead in pointing out logical fallacies when they encounter them being made during a class discussion, they will find that the students themselves will begin to take over after a while, and will begin to correct each other in similar situations. For example, a teacher can point out fallacies such as these:

I wouldn't believe anything she has to say about history. Everyone knows her grandfather served time in jail.	Fallacy of attacking the person who makes the argument rather than the argument itself.
Sure I believe what he says about politics. After all, he's the leading hitter in the National League, isn't he?	Fallacy of appealing to an authority when the person in question is not an authority on that particular issue.
I kept thinking about his pitching a no-hitter. That's why he failed to pitch the no-hitter: I jinxed him.	Jumping to conclusion—in this case, assuming that the thought must have caused what happened (the loss of the no-hitter) just because it preceded what happened.

There are, of course, many other types of fallacies in addition to these, and one of the objectives of a course in logic is to enable one to recognize a considerable number of such fallacies. If a teacher tolerates the commission of such fallacies by students, the teacher not only encourages sloppy thinking, but also fails to teach them what poor reasons are. After all, if they cannot always find their *best* reasons, that is still no excuse for allowing them to get away with offering their worst.

Requesting Reasons

One of the dimensions of a philosophical discussion is the development of systematic presentations of ideas. For example, a theory is not usually a single concept, but a network of concepts. Similarly, what in philosophy is called an *argument* is a systematic presentation of ideas, in that it consists of a *conclusion* supported by one or more *reasons*.

Usually, children will put forth their beliefs or opinions without troubling to support them. The teacher should seek to elicit from them the reasons they are prepared to give in support of such beliefs or opinions. Gradually, other students will take over this role, and will demand reasons from their classmates. In time, many students will develop the habit of offering opinions *only* when these can be supported by reasons.

A reason may or may not be formally connected to a conclusion. For example, if a child says he does not believe there are little green men on Mars, she may offer as her reason that there is no evidence of such beings. On the other hand, she may argue (rightly or wrongly) somewhat along these lines:

Only earth inhabitants are humans.
Martians aren't earth inhabitants.
Therefore, Martians can't be humans.

This could be put into standard form as a logical argument, so that the student's reasons would serve as *premises* to support her conclusion. This class discussion would then likely shift to the controversial first premise.

In soliciting reasons for students, the questions can be fairly explicit:

What is your reason for saying that . . . ?
What makes you think that . . . ?
On what grounds do you believe that . . . ?
Can you offer an argument in support of your claim that . . . ?
Why do you say that . . . ?
Why do you believe your view is correct?
What can you say in defense of your view?
Is there anything you'd like to say in order to prove your view correct?
Would you like to tell us why you think that's so?

When one offers a reason in support of an opinion, it is generally because the reason is less controversial and more acceptable than the opinion it is meant to support. In other words, we appeal to reasons because they carry plausibility. Compare these exchanges:

Question: Why do you think potassium is a mineral?
Answer: Because my science textbook says it is.

Question: Why do you say that you don't try to get even when someone has hurt you?
Answer: Because two wrongs don't make a right.

Question: Why do you think foreigners are secretive?
Answer: Because they always talk in languages I can't understand.

Question: Shouldn't we get rid of our national anthem because it's hard to sing?
Answer: I think the reasons in favor of it—that it's beautiful and unusual— outweigh the reason you've just cited against it.

Question: Why have you stopped listening to the radio while you drink?
Answer: Because I'm tired of hearing people talk about how excessive drinking can lead to alcoholism.

Some of the reasons cited above are fairly plausible, while others are not— or are, in any case, not more plausible than the belief they are supposed to substantiate. This is why, in soliciting reasons from children, you should try to insist upon good reasons—reasons with a high degree of plausibility.

Naturally the teacher should help students distinguish between the positions they are taking and the reasons they cite in defense of such positions. But the etiquette of dialogue further requires the teacher to assist students in formulat- ing the best reasons they can for their positions, whatever the value the teacher may place upon such positions. Thus the teacher, rather than criticize a stu- dent's weakest reasons, would do well to help such a student formulate better ones. Thus, for example, a teacher may deplore the hunting of animals. Yet suppose that, in a discussion of chapter 2 of *Lisa*, a student defends hunting on the grounds that it gives hunters an invaluable opportunity to develop shooting accuracy. Surely, in a case like this, what should be done is not spend too much time considering the weakness of such an argument, for much more is to be gained by considering what better reasons for hunting might be advanced— such as that the animals are predators, or that their overpopulation is a danger— even though one may still feel that the reasons against hunting outweigh those in favor or it.

Asking Students to Say How They Know

The single question, "How do you know?" can be very useful in eliciting from children a wide range of explanations.

It may bring forth reasons for assertions, because some students interpret the question as demand for reasons. For example:

"I think it's going to rain."
"How do you know?"
"Because the weather forecast is for rain."

It may bring forth a citation of evidence for the assertion—observations or date that are offered in support of what has been stated or claimed. For example:

"I think it's going to rain."
"How do you know?"
"Well, there are those storm clouds out there to the north, the wind's beginning to rise, the barometer's dropping, and my ankle's beginning to hurt the way it always does when it's about to rain."

Or, the question, "How do you know?" can bring forth explanations that deal very literally with *how one knows*. For example:

"I think it's going to rain."
"How do you know?"
"By reflecting on the evidence, and by taking into account my past experience."

Obviously, there is a difference between asking children why they believe what they believe—in effect, asking for reasons—and asking them how they know what they know. The latter is literally a request for them to explain the process of knowing, and to say why, when they feel sure they are right, they feel the way they do.

Eliciting and Examining Alternatives

If a child were to express the view that in order to become rich, one ought to be dishonest, surely you would want to show him that there are alternatives— that many people have become wealthy without being dishonest and that many people have sought other goals in life than wealth. Eventually the choice would still be his, but at least you would have helped him see the options.

It is not infrequent for children to insist that the way they view things is the only possible way for such things to be viewed. They have not considered any alternatives because they do not think there are any alternatives to consider. This is where you can liberate them from narrow-mindedness—by suggesting that there might very well be other possibilities to explore, and by helping them to identify and examine such alternative possibilities.

Thus, if a student insists that all objects must fall to earth, a teacher might ask the members of the class if it is possible for objects not to fall to earth. If a student expresses the view that there is no such thing as personal survival after death, the teacher might want to explore what alternative possibilities there are to that view. Likewise the child who earnestly believes that everything is wonderful (no less than the child who believes that everything is dreadful) probably needs to engage in a closer consideration of the options.

You can encourage children to realize that there are alternatives to their views by means of such comments as:

There are some people who think that . . .
Would you say that any other beliefs on this subject are possible?
How else could this matter be viewed?
Does anyone else have a different view?
Suppose someone wanted to contradict your view—what position could they take?
Is your view the only one people might take on this topic?
Are there circumstances where your opinions might be incorrect?
Are there other ways of looking at this matter that might be more believable?
Are there other ways of looking at this matter that may be possible, even though false?
Is it possible that other explanations than yours are possible?
Couldn't it also be that . . . ?
What if someone were to suggest that . . . ?

It should be remembered that the purpose of opening up alternatives to children is not to confuse or bewilder them, but to liberate them from narrow-mindedness or rigidity. The purpose is not to compel them to choose other convictions than those they already have, but to equip them to discover and assess their intellectual options.

Orchestrating a Discussion

A teacher could learn all the model questions cited above, and could pose them one after another to her class, and yet a truly philosophical discussion might still elude her. For one thing, the question asked has to be precisely appropriate to the occasion. The occasion might be one that requires a clarification of some rather startling pronouncement made by one of the students that different groups within the class understand in different ways. This is not the appropriate moment to inquire into the long-range consequences of holding such a view, since the meaning of the view is not yet clear. Likewise, when the time is ripe to discuss the implications of a statement made to the class, it would be counter-productive to take up more preliminary considerations such as the definition of terms in the statement.

Knowing just which question to ask at which moment is largely a matter of classroom experience, philosophical insight, and tact. As teachers become more experienced, they develop a repertoire of questions and can quickly draw upon the appropriate one without much soul-searching or hesitation.

Moreover, the most experienced teachers are adroit at phrasing each question in a way that seems to be tailor-made for the point of the discussion that has just been arrived at. Children will quickly catch on to the fact that a teacher is using a prepared set of questions, and to canned questions they will soon begin to provide canned answers. The only recourse is to adopt a conversational style that enables a variety of questions to be posed in ways that are casual and improvisational, so that they do not seem to be mechanical interruptions in the course of the dialogue, but appear instead as welcome techniques for intensifying that dialogue. In so doing, the discussion will probably be raised to a higher level of generality. The aim should not be to make the discussion more abstract, but to make it more comprehensive. For example, a class may be discussing whether it is fair to define adulthood at different ages—one age for voting, another for theater admissions—or perhaps liquor ads for magazines but not for television. In these instances, as the discussion proceeds, a teacher may find it useful to ask, "What is fairness?" or "What is consistency?" In this manner, the students will begin to feel the profound satisfaction that can develop when they have come to grips with a subject and begin to comprehend what previously seemed baffling to them. For it is in this way that a philosophical discussion seeks to deal with what is most fundamental in human experience.

No explanation of the art of teaching philosophy can be adequate for the teacher-in-training. First, it must be admitted that philosophers themselves have never been very clear about what they do when they teach philosophy. We therefore lack a complete understanding on which an adequate explanation could be based. Second, even if we had such an explanation, it would be insufficient without a competent modelling by the philosopher coupled with the teacher's experiencing what it is to engage in philosophical dialogue. These three components—explanation, modelling, and experiencing—are indispensable in preparing teachers to teach philosophy on the elementary grade level.

The art of teaching philosophy to children is not acquired quickly. Teachers may go along for months without visible improvement in their performance and then suddenly find themselves doing it in a way that seems very natural. This experience in turn confirms the teacher's sense of the worth of the long struggle. It is also common for teachers to reach a certain plateau and then find it difficult to improve. They will be successful in eliciting children's views of their own experience, asking for alternative views, and giving illustrations. But they may not yet be proficient in moving to more philosophical levels of dialogue, such as are involved in drawing out inferences, generalizing, pointing out contradictions, asking for underlying assumptions, and stressing the need for intellectual coherence. Philosophers are experienced in devising chains of questions that will provoke their students to search for more and more comprehensive explanations of their experience. Professional philosophers are adept at responding to student comments in such a way as to commend the student for the progress he has made and yet at the same time point out the inadequacy of what the student has proposed. The philosophers may appear to the class to be perpetually dissatisfied. Whatever the student's comment may be, philosophers will be sure to discover something perplexing about it and will raise questions about just that puzzling aspect of the remark. With the subsequent student comment, the same thing will happen: what is intelligible is confirmed, but what is puzzling is noted with wonderment, and a sense of the need for further inquiry is experienced by teacher and student. In this fashion, the area of intelligibility of the topic under discussion is continually broadened, but never with the sense that all the mysteries in that area have been dispelled. A good teacher of philosophy never reaches a point where there seems no further need for wondering. The world is inexhaustibly perplexing. It is this wondering behavior that is so difficult to explain or convey by means of techniques, strategies, or recipes. Wondering cannot be feigned; it has to grow out of one's own experience. But the best way to produce that experience is for one's teacher to model it and then for one to acquire it by contagion. Once one has contracted this disease and experienced the liberation from dogma that it provides, one cannot rest until one has infected one's students with the same experience.

The philosophy classroom cannot exist on a one-dimensional plane of continuous revelation. For philosophy, new revelations generally are accompanied by a fresh sense of even profounder mysteries. If this were not so, philosophy would have died out a long time ago. It would have lacked the provocation for that wonderment with which philosophy must always begin.

The suggestions offered above regarding ways of drawing children out so as to elicit and facilitate philosophical dialogue are largely tactical. That is, their value is fairly specific. A teacher, however, must keep more general pedagogical strategies in mind, in addition to developing a repertoire of dialectical tactics.

Grouping Ideas

For example, a teacher may find it useful to keep in mind the various suggestions students have made, and to assemble these into groups or clusteres, each representing a specific position or pattern of argument. The teacher can be very helpful to the students in the class by then summing up each of these positions or arguments, for that will provide a sense of proportion or perspective which the pupils might otherwise have been incapable of attaining. Obviously, if the class discussion has polarized the class so explicitly that everyone is aware of the different positions being taken, such summarization would likely be redundant and superfluous. So it should be saved for those occasions on which it is needed.

Suggesting Possible Lines of Convergence or Divergence

As teachers become more adept at organizing discussions, they will find that their motives in asking this question or that will be determined by certain strategic considerations, such as that they would like to broaden the range of views being offered by students, or that they would like to steer some of the strands of discussion into greater convergence with one another.

To open a discussion up, and to encourage a greater divergency of views, teachers may find it useful to introduce distinctions at certain crucial points that allow for a sharpening of differences among members of the class. For example, in chapter 5 of *Harry*, Mark argues that all schools are bad. Harry, however, argues that only those schools are bad that are run by people who do not understand children, thereby offering a distinction that allows for more precise analysis than Mark's more sweeping claim. A teacher could, in like manner, seek to introduce distinctions that would increase the number of options open to the children in the classroom. Also, the teacher can introduce additional points of view into a discussion by such remarks as those just cited under the heading "Eliciting and Examining Alternatives."

At times teachers may want to show that certain views that have been expressed in class are not only different but in direct conflict with one another. To do this, they may resort to pointing out that the two views are *incompatible* because their implications eventually contradict one another. For example, suppose one person in the class asserts that "No girls are scouts," and another person asserts that "Some scouts are girls." Simply using the logic in *Harry* (in other words, by reversing the subject and predicate of the first statement), the teacher should be able to show the class that the two original statements are incompatible, because they lead to statements that are in contradiction with one another.

On other occasions, teachers will want to take the initiative in the classroom by showing *connections* that the students would not otherwise have noted. A teacher may want to point out that certain things they have thought to be distinct could quite reasonably be grouped together. Or the teacher may point out that two arguments that different members of the class have advanced are really saying pretty much the same thing—or are *convergent* upon the same general position. Thus a teacher's role may sometimes be to unify the class in spite of expressed differences, just as at other times that role may be to encourage children to appreciate making distinctions where necessary. There is no sure recipe as to which approach should be emphasized, but teachers would probably do well to consider their position as discussion leaders to be a *remedial* one, supplying that component—whether it be unity or diversity—that the discussion had signally lacked until that point.

Moving Discussions to a Higher Level of Generality

Elsewhere in this book we have referred to the tendency of children's questions to advance a discussion to a higher level of generality. Thus a child asked to add two numbers may first want an explanation of *number*, or a child asked about the size of his house may inquire in turn what *size* is.

In the novels of the philosophy for children program, there are frequent instances in which children stop to consider the concepts and terms that we use when we reflect, rather than continue to utilize such terms and concepts unreflectively. Teachers will likely find it useful to direct discussion to concepts or notions in children's ordinary language that are being taken for granted, but that are in need of analysis.

Applying
Thinking Skills to
School Experience

8 Encouraging Children to Be Logical

Logic has three meanings in philosophy for children. It means *formal logic*, with rules governing sentence structure and connections between sentences, and it also stands for *giving reasons*, which includes seeking and evaluating reasons for something said or done. Finally, logic means *acting rationally*, and concerns standards for reasonable behavior. Each of these topics is approached in a different way in philosophy for children.

Formal Logic as an Aid to Philosophical Thinking

Because the rules of formal logic govern sentences, they can be used to help develop a kind of self-awareness. They provide a means for grasping and examining one's thoughts in a structured, clear-headed way. The rules are more useful for helping children realize that they *can* think about their thoughts in an orderly fashion, and less helpful in day-to-day applications. Occasions where our thoughts actually conform to the rules are comparatively rare. It is important, then, to keep in mind that the main purpose of formal logic in philosophy for children is to help children discover that they can think about their thinking in an organized way.

Through taking part in thoughtful, reflective discussions, children gain confidence in their ability to think on their own. As a consequence, they more carefully assess things others say as well as their own remarks. These are self-reinforcing processes; once the children get going they become strikingly good at constructive philosophical thinking. But what can assist them in getting started and encourage them to go on to think for themselves? Here, formal logic lends a hand.

How Can Formal Logic Help?

If you have ever taken a logic course, you probably have some doubts about using formal logic to encourage children to think for themselves. Because formal logic is often presented in textbook fashion, with rules to memorize and apply to bookish exercises, it might seem to develop the very opposite of reflective thinking. But in philosophy for children, formal logic is presented in a novel instead of a text, and the children are especially encouraged to think up their own examples to illustrate the rules. And these two variations make all the difference.

Throughout much of *Harry* and *Lisa*, children discover and test the rules of formal logic and discover applications that show how the rules can be used. These rules are not presented in an abstract system, but are discovered individually in a broad variety of settings. Not until late in *Harry* do the children begin to see that the rules can fit together systematically, and it is half-way through *Lisa* before they discover something about how they do so. Finally, and most important, the rules are not identified as a special topic called formal logic, but instead are described as rules for thinking. Since many other styles of thinking are also exhibited in *Harry* and *Lisa*, the rules appear in a rich blend of contexts through which a child can begin to perceive limitations as well as applications for the rules. Here there is much that the teacher can contribute by pointing to the dramatic contexts in which the rules are discovered and applied and by encouraging her students to think up examples that illustrate the rules. Of course, in order to teach the rules, the teacher may need to spend some time going over examples from the novel and the manual. But the task of teaching formal logic in the fashion of philosophy for children is not completed until each child has the opportunity to come up with examples of his own for each rule. Only by taking this final step can formal logic help children discover that they can think about their *own* thinking in an organized way. The teacher may choose to flesh this out by inviting the students to invent dramatic settings for their examples, perhaps using characters from the novels.

This simple yet profound change in perspective, from using textbook rules and exercises to discussing and imitating discoveries in a philosophical novel, encourages children in the classroom to think for themselves. While to us it may not be realistic to expect a group of real children to discover rules of formal logic entirely on their own, it is vitally important that students think of those rules as something *understandable* by children—however imaginary—and that they find their own examples to illustrate the test the rules. In designing these examples, the students will be guided by the imaginary children who struggle but eventually succeed in illustrating a rule of discovering and exception. This encourages real children to think each rule to themselves; perhaps for the first time in their lives they begin to listen carefully to their own thinking. But here a word of caution is necessary.

Insofar as their examples are products of their own thinking, children are particularly vulnerable to criticism if one should misfire. A teacher must take care not to destroy by inadvertent criticism the first fruits of self-conscious, organized thinking. Before challenging a child's example, the teacher must establish a relationship of trust and mutual respect for opinions among the children in her class and between those children and herself. By first discussing the illustrations and tests of the rules provided by the imaginary children in the novels, the teacher can develop such trust and respect by handling those discussions with care.

Just as children can be sensitive to failure in their attempts to think in a structured way, they can take great delight in success. It is easy to be far too serious, too "mature" in one's expectations about responses to the study of formal logic. The realization that here is something they can definitely master, carry about in their heads, play with on their own, united with their natural fascination with language, makes formal logic utterly delightful to many children, especially when it is taught in the style of philosophy for children. And one cannot overestimate the importance for their own self-images of encouraging children to enjoy pure pleasures of the mind.

Formal logic can contribute to the development of organized thinking because its rules are rules about sentences. Acquiring and using such rules can readily encourage children to think about what they and others say. Its virtues are that its rules are clear and precise, and represent clear-headed thinking. Use of the rules can thus help foster critical thinking, but such thinking is not yet *philosophical*.

It would be a mistake to suppose that formal logic alone will promote philosophical thinking. While formal logic can serve as an effective means for helping children realize that they can think in an organized way, it gives no clues as to when thinking by the rules of formal logic is useful and appropriate and when it is simply absurd. Critical thinking only becomes philosophic thinking when it is aware of limitations to its own critical standards. And formal logic alone does not provide such insight.

Why Syllogistic?

In order that a system of formal logic be helpful in developing organized thinking, it should have rules that are easy to understand and use. Since children between the ages of ten and fourteen are usually acquainted with the main characteristics of our language, a very useful system of formal logic for such children is *syllogistic logic*. Syllogistic logic governs sentences composed of subject and predicate noun phrases. That version of syllogistic used in philosophy for children only applies to sentences that begin with either "all," "some," or "no," and use present-tense plural expressions of the verb "to be." For example, the sentence "all green dragons are fire breathers" fits these requirements: the subject and predicate noun phrases are "green dragons" and "fire breathers"; they are preceded by "all" and joined by "are."

Another example is "some race horses are fast starters," and "no cats are mice" yet another. Sentences that contradict syllogistic sentences are also covered by the rules of the system—thus "some green dragons are not fire breathers," "no race horses are fast starters," "some cats are mice," are governed by its rules. Sentences that do not directly conform, such as "first impressions are deceptive," can often be rewritten so as to fit (as with "all first impressions are deceptive experiences"). Rewriting sentences so that they conform to the rules of a logical system is called *standardization.**

While the boundaries to syllogistic logic have been drawn in different ways, there is general agreement that many sentences cannot be standardized. Sentences with singular subjects are conspicuous cases, such as "Jesse James was an outlaw." Others resisting standardization include sentences expressing relationships, such as "Ronald is to the right of Jimmy"; sentences with mixed quantifiers, such as "Everybody loves someone"; and sentences that are not descriptive, such as "Please don't stand on my foot," "I promise I'll be there," and "You can't go out today."

Along with its use of familiar language patterns, another reason for using syllogistic as the formal logic in philosophy for children is that its rules can throw light on mental procedures that have become habitual. For instance, children at an early age develop the ability to classify, but rarely do they see why classifications fit together in ways that they do. Many important sequences of classification patterns conform to the rules of syllogistic; for example, the sequence "All dogs are mammals, all beagles are dogs, therefore all beagles are mammals" fits a syllogistic rule of inference. Learning the rules of syllogistic logic can thus help children understand classification patterns, and encourage them to use classifications in ways that make sense.

A final but quite important reason for using syllogistic is that its rules are simple. They are tolerably easy to state and to remember, there are not too many of them, and they do not require prior knowledge of logic or philosophy. This reason together with those previously mentioned have heavily influenced the development of materials in philosophy for children. But this is not to say that syllogistic logic is the only way to help children realize that they can think in an organized way.

Teachers unfamiliar with formal logic may hesitate to emphasize it when teaching the novels; they should reflect on the purpose of introducing formal logic to children, and be sure that they have found alternative ways of using the novels for achieving the same results before allowing themselves to avoid syllogistic. Teachers familiar with formal logic may want to introduce more

---

*Detailed descriptions of the rules of syllogistic and of standardization are in the teacher's manuals for *Harry*, *Lisa*, and *Tony*. A summary is given at the end of Chapter 5 in the *Lisa* manual.

syllogistic rules than are provided in the novels, or to replace syllogistic with an alternative system. In either case, once they step beyond the scope of the novels they risk losing contact with the child-centered contexts the novels provide. Unless the teacher can find a secure way to avoid this consequence, it is not advisable to alter the formal logic in the novels.

Relevant Properties of Formal Systems

A system of rules of logic can help foster organized thinking because such systems have features akin to such thinking. Among the main properties of syllogistic logic are *consistency*, or the absence of contradictions; *logical consequence*, or the ways its rules describe how one sentence logically follows from other sentences; and *coherence*, or how the rules fit together as a systematic, unified whole.

Consistency

The rules of syllogistic logic do not permit a sentence and its contradictory to be asserted together. For instance, the sentence "All cats are mammals" and its contradictory, "Some cats are not mammals," are not *both* permitted under the rules. If we accept the first sentence as true, then the rules require that we do not accept the second. Likewise, if we accept "Some cats are not mammals," then the rules forbid "All cats are mammals." The rules do not tell us which sentences are true and which are false, but they do tell us that *if* we accept a sentence *then* we cannot also accept its contradictory.

The consistency of syllogistic logic is like the consistency we expect of one another in everyday life. If a person were to assert something but then deny it without explanation, others would very likely be struck by the fact that the person had contradicted himself. And, as we saw in the discussion of consistency in Chapter 4, they would then have good reason to suspect that he had not really thought about what he was saying. It is just such verbal inconsistencies that the rules of formal logic exclude and that study of those rules can help bring to light.

Logical Consequence

The rules of syllogistic govern certain patterns of formal reasoning. The relationships between sentences are instances of *logical consequence*, passages of thought where one sentence follows from others with logical certainty. A primary characteristic of such patterns of thinking is that they never lead from true sentences to false sentences.

Thinking with rules of logical consequence, children can become more aware of passages of thought. Consider the following example from chapter 5 of *Harry*:

"Look," he said, taking from his pocket the bag of candies, which was still almost full. "Suppose you didn't know what kind of candy was in this bag. And then you saw me take out three pieces of candy, and they were all brown. Would it follow that there were other pieces still in the bag that weren't brown?"

"You mean would I know what color the others were without seeing them? No, I guess I wouldn't."

"That *right!*" Harry exclaimed. "If all you know is that *some* of the candies in the bag are brown, you can't say, because some *are* brown, that some must not be!"

Harry is concerned with two passages of thought: the transition from a true "some" sentence to an "all" sentence and the transition from a true "some" sentence to a "some . . . are not" sentence. He points out that both passages violate logical consequence.

By becoming more aware of violations of logical consequence, children become more aware of passages of thought that misrepresent false sentences as though they were true. An example from *Harry*:

Lisa got on the bus in the morning to go to school, and to her delight found Fran on the same bus. The two girls chatted together for a few minutes. Then they became aware that the two men sitting in the seat in front of them were talking rather loudly, and seemed angry about something. The girls were about to decide that the men were just talking about politics, when they overheard one of the men say, "This country is really going to the dogs. And it's all because of these people who're always agitating for their civil rights. Every time I look in the paper, I read about some lawyer defending some radical. Did you ever notice how all the lawyers in this country are in favor of civil rights? And did you ever notice how all the radicals in this country are in favor of civil rights? So what more proof do you need that all lawyers are radicals?"

Fran quickly opened her notebook and wrote in it:

All lawyers are people who favor civil rights.
All radicals are people who favor civil rights.
Therefore, all lawyers are radicals.

And underneath, Fran wrote the example which she had used the other day:

All minnows are fish.
All sharks are fish.
Therefore, all minnows are sharks.

She showed her notebook to Lisa and Lisa squealed with delight: "I know, I know —I noticed the same thing. It didn't follow then that all minnows are sharks, and it doesn't follow here that all lawyers are radicals."

The scene, of course, involves fictional children. And one might want to quarrel with the generalizations presumed in the argument. But the moral should be clear. When children use syllogistic rules in the style of philosophy for children, they can become more sensitive to errant passages of thought.

Coherence

The rules of syllogistic fit together in a *coherent system*, much as the pieces of a jigsaw puzzle fit together to make a picture, or the parts of an engine work together to produce energy. Three different accounts of the coherence of syllogistic logic are presented in *Harry* and *Lisa*. The rules are described, first, as expressing mathematical relationships between sets; second, as expressing the logical meaning of "all," "some," "not," and "are"; and, finally, as describing certain ways of thinking. The first two interpretations of the rules have an important bearing on contemporary standards of formal *symbolic* logic, and could be subjects for an advanced logic course. But coherence in the third sense, as bearing on specific patterns of thinking, is directly relevant to philosophy in your classroom.

Harry and *Lisa* are studded with individual discoveries of logical rules. Although from a more advanced standpoint one can classify all these rules as syllogistic, neither the characters in the book nor the real children reading about them have the benefit of this higher perspective; to them, it is an open question whether the investigation of such rules will lead anywhere. In response to this uncertainty, the characters demand that an explanation be given for the patterns revealed by the rules.

Two examples stand out in *Lisa*. In chapter 6, Harry and Tony take three phrases and sketch out paired arrangements so as to form three successive "all" sentences. To their surprise, they soon discover that not all such combinations are consistent. After they tell Fran and Lisa about their discovery, Lisa remarks: "All you guys can show is that one arrangement works and the other doesn't—but you can't explain why, so what's the point?" In chapter 9, Tony presses for an explanation: "Heather, you said you'd tell us how you figured out the correct arrangements. I want to find out what the rules are. Aren't you gonna tell us?" These challenges to explain why certain patterns of thinking are validated by the rules while others are not are demands for coherence.

Demanding coherence does not of itself provide the sort of explanation wanted, but the way that demand is expressed reveals what coherence in this sense must be. It concerns why the rules all work together, and thus how it makes sense to think in patterns governed by those rules. To say that the rules must be coherent in this sense is to say that some such account can be given, that the rules are *worth* investigating on their own, and that their investigation will result in satisfying insights into the thinking they govern. As the rules of syllogistic are predominantly exhibited in the children's *own* patterns of thinking, this demand for coherence supports the conviction that the children's own patterns of thought are intelligible and worthy of careful attention.

Ages and Stages: Why Syllogistic between Ten and Fourteen?

Formal logic can help develop philosophical thinking when properly taught, but there are few real life situations to which its rules apply unambiguously. It is not just that a system of formal logic applies only to certain types of sentences; more importantly one rarely has *need* of its rules. The contributions of formal logic to developing organized thinking lie less in application of its rules and far more in encouraging special traits such as a sensitivity to inconsistency, a concern for logical consequence, and an awareness of whether or not one's thoughts really hold together. And these traits do apply in situations far beyond the scope of formal logic.

Given that formal logic can help develop these traits in children aged ten to fourteen, it is tempting to ask: Why these ages? The answer is simply that syllogistic has worked with children of these ages. It would be a mistake to suppose that this proves that syllogistic is the only formal logic appropriate to such children. Philosophy for children is presented in novels that contain a rich variety of philosophic themes, only one of which is formal logic. Thus, the success of using syllogistic at this age level may be better explained by reference to non-formal features of the books that happen to appeal very strongly to such children. Further, in watching videotapes and visiting classes, we have often been struck by the complexity of reasonings displayed by the children as they use passages of thought far more sophisticated than syllogistic rules. Of course, it does not follow from this that children can successfully master the more complex rules to which these passages conform, but these observations do suggest that the rules of syllogistic are not of themselves adequate to their patterns of thinking.

There have been a number of psychological studies of children's logic, most notably by Piaget. While this research has been highly suggestive for our work, it has given us no reason to presume that syllogistic is the only type of formal logic children of ten to fourteen can do. It is one thing to show that children can use this logic with profit and quite another to insist that they can work with no other.

Giving Reasons: The Good Reasons Approach

While formal logic can help children become aware that they can think in an organized way, it does not really encourage the use of structured thinking, since it is so limited to application. There is need for a second type of logic that takes into account the wide variety of situations that call for deliberate thinking. This type of logic is often called the *good reasons approach*.

In contrast to the rules of formal logic, the good reasons approach has no specific rules, but instead emphasizes *seeking reasons* in reference to a given situation and *assessing reasons* given. Since reasons that can be brought to light in a given inquiry will largely depend on its context, what will make for a reasonable search and a good reason are also context-bound. As a consequence, the good reasons approach basically relies on an intuitive sense of what can count as a good reason. This sense is best developed by exposure to a wide variety of settings that call for the good reasons approach, and the materials in the philosophy for children program—both novels and manuals— provide a very large number of such situations.

The main purpose of good reasons logic is to evaluate one's thoughts and the thoughts of others in reference to actions or events. In philosophy for children, this logic is useful for helping children discover the broad range of applications of structured, deliberate thinking. While such a discovery is bound to encourage children to use orderly thinking, the logic itself is concerned more with the variety of applications of thinking about thinking and less with how to encourage children to use such thinking.

Types of Inferences

An inquiry can concern anything at all: a source of curiosity, bother, delight, perplexity, interest, irritation, intrigue. Good reasons logic begins when there is something to inquire about. Seeking reasons involves becoming aware of perceptual, verbal, and evidential implications of the context in which the inquiry takes place, and drawing them out as passages of thought, called inferences. Here one can talk about different *types* of inferences. An inference thus provides a reason that stands in a certain relationship to the focus of inquiry. Such relationships are sometimes described as inductions, analogies, explanations, or action-guiding inferences; these are the main types, but there are many others. To examine these types in detail would require an extensive study, but a glance at their main features can help give a better impression of what good reasons logic is about.

Inductive inferences typically proceed from specifics to generalities, where the generality projects beyond the evidence base given in the specific cases. Some examples appear in chapter 5 of *Harry*. First, certain inductions are criticized.

> Maria looked thoughtful. "But people are always jumping to conclusions. If people meet one Polish person, or one Italian person, or one Jewish person, or one Black person, right away they jump to the conclusion that this is the way *all* Polish people are, or all Black people, or all Italians or Jews."
>
> "That's right," said Harry. "The only exercise some people get is jumping at conclusions."

Later Mark Jahorski cites his experiences in school, and reports from children in private and parochial schools, to support his generalization, "The schools are awful everywhere." Mark's induction is based on broader, more varied evidence than are generalizations based on an encounter with a single individual. But in both cases, there is a passage of thought from something specific to something more general.

An *analogical inference* presupposes relevant similarities between two different types of things, and concludes to a further similarity. A cluster of analogical inferences occurs in chapter 1 of *Lisa*, concerning similarities between people and animals. For instance, hunting animals is compared and contrasted with killing people—some children accept the presumption that people and animals are sufficiently similar to warrant the comparison, others reject it: "Randy shook his head vigorously. 'You just have to remember that people and animals are completely different. It doesn't matter what you do to animals, but you shouldn't do the same things to people.'" This leads to a discussion of whether animals have rights, which further explores the analogy.

Explanatory inferences reach answers to questions such as "Why did that happen?" or "Why does this take place?" They presume that nature exhibits certain regularities, and connect an event to be explained with a particular regularity. Take, for example, "Why did the light go off?" which might be explained by saying, "the circuit breaker flipped." For people familiar with connections between circuit breakers and lights, this is a reason, and in an appropriate context it can be a good one. Several explanatory inferences can be found in *Tony*.

Action-guiding inferences seek to justify what someone does. Such inferences presuppose either a system of practices, or a specific rule of conduct, or that there are special circumstances that justify violating a system of practices or a rule of conduct. A recurring theme in *Lisa* is Lisa's own search for reasons as to whether or not she ought to eat meat; this involves evaluating several action-guiding inferences. She becomes aware that her family has customarily eaten meats; this is a system of practices that can reasonably justify meat-eating, but she is not sure it is a good reason. Since Lisa accepts the analogy between animals and people mentioned above, she is deeply troubled when she realizes that animals must be killed in order to sustain meat-eating. She views this as close to a good reason for violating the system of practices, but is still troubled about what she ought to do. Finally, she hits upon the following rule of conduct: "If I really love animals, I won't eat them," which, to her way of thinking, justifies her avoidance of meat.

It is not difficult to see that evaluating inductive, analogical, explanatory, and action-guiding inferences requires organized, reflective thinking. Take, for instance, Mark's inductive inference, "the schools are awful everywhere." One can invite students to assess that inference by asking them whether they think that the evidence he cites really supports his generalization. With any inductive inference, one can invite one's pupils to compare the evidence cited with the general conclusion by encouraging them to describe circumstances in which the generalization is appropriate, and then circumstances in which it is not. Since inductive inferences characteristically project beyond available evidence, the children can discover that what counts as a good induction very much depends on the information available at the time it is made. To reach this point requires a good deal of structured thinking about inductive inferences, comparing evidence, general conclusions, and background (contextual) knowledge. This also holds true for analogical inferences, explanatory inferences, action-guiding inferences, and others.

It should be kept in mind that the good reasons approach is not taught through the use of technical expressions such as "inductive inference," "background knowledge," "analogical inference," and so on, but instead by the detailed study of realistic contexts where inductive, explanatory, action-guiding inference occur. In this way, organized thinking is tied to concrete applications. The closest the good reasons approach in philosophy for children comes to using a technical term lies in occasional use of the question: "Is that a good reason for ———?"

Characteristics of a Search for Reasons

While the good reasons approach does not have rules as formal logic does, both the search for reasons and the evaluation of reasons have certain general characteristics. The reader will benefit from comparing these characteristics of the good reasons approach with the clues to guiding a philosophical discussion given in Chapter 6.

We can list four characteristics of a search for reasons:

Impartiality.   The process of inquiry ought to be impartial, avoiding looking at the situation in question with bias or prejudice, or in ways that ignore the comments or suggestions of others. Seeking for reasons should be done in a fair manner, so that all concerned have a voice in results.

Objectivity.   The process of inquiry should be objective, avoiding preconceived versions of the results to be gained and staying with relevant implications wherever they lead. An inquiry is objective if it meets with the approval of the relevant community of inquirers, but not if it violates their sense of what counts as reasonable.

Respect for Persons.   The process of inquiry should be conducted in a style that avoids injuring or embarrassing anyone. Since each person is a source of significant reasons, any process of inquiry that places a member of the class outside the scope of the ongoing inquiry eliminates a potential source of information and inevitably distorts the process itself.

Search for Further Reasons.   The process of inquiry should be conducted in such a way as to invite other members of the community of inquirers to search for further reasons if they are not satisfied with the results. This requires that, whatever process be used, it be sufficiently open-ended so as to invite further inquiries rather than discourage them or shut them off.

Use of these characteristics presupposes that the inquirers share an intuitive sense of what is to count as reasonable. While it would be a mistake to try to formulate this too precisely, it should not be pictured as some mysterious inner feeling, but simply as a rough sense of what is reasonable and what is not. People may occasionally disagree on what is or is not a violation of one of these characteristics, but such disagreements are usually confined to borderline cases.

An example of a shared inquiry in which such a borderline case appears is in chapter 7 of *Harry*. While searching for reasons concerning whether Dale should have to salute the flag, Suki proposes that he should, because "rules are rules." Mrs. Halsey, who is moderating the discussion, accepts this as implying that if we make rules we should keep them. Mickey then responds: " 'No,' he insisted, 'rules are made to be broken. Don't you know the expression, "every rule has an exception"? Well, Dale's case is the exception! Therefore I think Dale doesn't have to salute if he doesn't want to.' " Mrs. Halsey criticizes this use of "every rule has an exception," implying that it is too idiomatic to be relevant to the purpose of the inquiry. But Tony, Sandy, and Mark then show that a case can be made for its relevance: When rules of conduct are not made by the people to whom they apply, rules can have exceptions in situations where those people do not want to obey them. This leads to an impasse, and the reader is left to speculate on whether or not "every rule has an exception" is a reason why Dale should not have to salute the flag.

The discussion is a good example of a logical inquiry, and there are several others in the novels. Together with the discussion with Mrs. Halsey mentioned above, two of the best examples of good reasons inquiry occur in the last chapter of *Harry*, with Mr. Spence, and the last chapter of *Lisa*, with Mr. Partridge. Though the children often engage in logical inquiry on their own, this is usually spaced out in separate sequences rather than concentrated in a single uninterrupted search. An example of a compact sequence is the row of discussions about doing to others as they do unto you in chapter 14 of *Lisa*.

In practice, the process of inquiry and the evaluation of reasons often combine as inquirers shift back and forth from one to the other. But it is useful to distinguish the characteristics of searching for reasons from the standards for evaluating them. The first procedure seeks reasons for something, the second evaluates results, sorting out better reasons from worse, deciding whether a given reason is a good one. There is a tendency to equate all reasons with *good* reasons, to suppose that a reason for believing or doing something cannot really *be* a reason unless it is a good one. But this ignores the fact that we sometimes do things for bad reasons (rather than no reason at all), and that we can compare reasons as better or worse.

Characteristics of Good Reasons

Good reasons logic uses the following standards for evaluating reasons:

From Fact.   A good reason is one based on facts. For instance, there is all the difference in the world between taking shelter for the reason that one has just heard a tornado warning, and doing so as a consequence of overhearing Chicken Little exclaim on a TV show that the sky is falling. Only the tornado warning is based on fact—the sighting of a nearby tornado. Facts are not always available and, where they are, may not entirely decide the point at issue, but a reason that has factual support is better than one that does not.

Relevance.   A good reason is clearly relevant to the object of inquiry. For example, while it is true that one can plunge thirty-nine floors from the top of a forty-story building without sustaining injury, this is not a good reason for jumping off if one wishes to survive. The rate of fall, target area, and nature of the human body combine to give a very good reason for not jumping. The latter are relevant to what will happen upon arrival at ground level, the lack of injury beforehand is not. While one cannot always tell whether a given reason is relevant to the point at issue, a reason that can be shown to be so related is better than one which cannot.

Support.   A good reason lends support to the object of inquiry by making it plausible, intelligible. For instance, the discovery of fifty bags of potato chips stowed in a school closet may be explained by reference to a mad hoarder who is out to beat an imaginary potato chip shortage, but the alternative explanation that there is going to be a school party lends support to the presence of all those potato chips in a way the former explanation does not, because it gives the more plausible account. A reason that makes sense of the point at issue is a better reason than one that does not.

Familiarity.   A good reason refers to something familiar when it is used to explain the object of inquiry. For example, the rapid ascent of a small child's balloon might be explained by reference to a complex equation describing how balloons intentionally disentangle their strings, but the better explanation is simply that the child let the string slip loose. Sometimes, the more familiar may actually be wrong—for instance, while the bumps you get on your skin at a horror movie are often explained by reference to the chilling effect of fear, they really are hair raisers that function as a protective mechanism (much as a cat distends its fur). But generally speaking, a reason that refers to something well-known is better than a reason that leads to obscurities.

Finality.   No reason is a good one that does not meet one or more of the above standards, and every reason must be open to evaluation by the members of the community of inquirers. There is no higher court of appeal, no higher standards in evaluating reasons.

Taken separately, each of these standards invites criticism. With a little ingenuity, one can think up a situation in which a standard will be *violated* for a good reason. To develop philosophical thinking about the standards, it is helpful to imagine such a situation for each of them. This is important, but it is also important that one not miss seeing their collective significance. By using the good reasons approach in class discussions, you will go a long way towards helping your students discover the broad range of possibilities for organized deliberate thinking.

As with the characteristics of inquiry, use of these standards presumes that the children share a rough sense of what counts as a good reason. The good reasons approach is much less a matter of presenting something new and unfamiliar and far more one of encouraging children to sort out, from among their many responses to an inquiry and its results, those which are the more useful and appropriate.

Teaching Good Reasons Logic

Children are wonderfully inquisitive. So long as their native curiosity has not been completely discouraged, when philosophy is introduced they soon develop the ability to seek reasons on their own. The main efforts in teaching good reasons logic consist of sustaining the process of inquiry and of encouraging the evaluation of reasons. Both these goals are best achieved in the context of a community of inquirers who take part in shared dialogues. The process of inquiry comes alive in the give and take of discussion; its public setting makes obvious the need for reflective thinking in order to evaluate reasons properly.

While there is no reason in principle to avoid discussing the standards for evaluating reasons and the characteristics of logical inquiry, the teacher should not expect students to make much sense of either when stated abstractly. Only as they actively take part in inquiries and evaluations can children form a basis for thinking *about* these characteristics and standards. Generally speaking, it would be a mistake to suppose that children can learn the good reasons approach by talking about it. The teacher should keep in mind that the primary goal of good reasons logic for children is to help them discover the broad range of applications of structured deliberate thinking, not that there is a topic called "good reasons logic."

Teaching good reasons logic requires using that logic while encouraging dialogues. This in turn depends on having material available that can invite such discussions, and this is just what the philosophical themes in the novels are designed to provide. By reflecting on the opinions and actions of the characters in the books, children are encouraged to draw inferences, to compare and contrast them, and so to engage in shared inquiry. To help children do this effectively, two models of inquiry are presented to the students: the illustrations of good conversations in the novels and the discussions in their own classroom.

While much already has been said in Chapter 6 about running good discussions in philosophy, some important features of encouraging dialogues are particularly relevant to teaching good reasons logic, and deserve re-emphasis.

Children are not in a position to evaluate a reason for something unless they clearly understand what it is. So, they need to learn to listen to themselves and to each other as they discuss topics at issue. They especially need to get a hold on the reasons offered, and to have time to think about those reasons in the context of inquiry. These requirements make strong demands on teaching. Encouraging children to listen to themselves requires that the teacher takes time to listen and to remember—there is no more effective way to encourage children to listen to themselves than by listening to them and remembering what they have said.

Getting children to listen to one another takes even more time and, especially, patience. They tend to revert to looking to the teacher for an evaluation of what another child is saying, and to ignore it if it does not meet with an instantaneous sign of approval. In overcoming this habit, they easily replace it with the impression that anything goes, that whatever comes to mind can and should be said, with no regard for the theme of the discussion or other members of the class. It can take a great deal of patience to weather these reactions. Here the best and strongest resource is the teacher's own memory; a teacher can make it a point to recall what went on before a digression set in, to ask how a comment bears on prior remarks, and so encourage students to stay with the subject.

Learning to listen to oneself and to others in a community of inquirers is essential to good reasons logic. Impartiality, objectivity, respect for persons, and searching for further reasons all depend upon paying careful attention to one's own thoughts as well as those of others, to developing the discipline of a well-trained ear. And use of the standards for evaluating reasons requires a real ability to listen to others as well as to oneself. More can be said about the relevance of other discussion techniques for successfully teaching good reasons logic, but the main connections between the good reasons approach and the use of such techniques should be apparent.

Both formal and good reasons logic can be used as guides to *structuring* philosophical discussions. Consistency, logical consequence, and coherence are fundamental to such discussions, as are the characteristics of inquiry. And the standards for good reasons are basic clues to evaluating the results of such discussions. The most effective way to teach these types of logic lies in consciously using their norms and standards in running discussions. "Is that consistent with what you said before?" "How does that follow from what's just been said?" "How do your comments connect with what we've been saying?" These are basic types of questions for the teacher to use, as are questions framed in terms of good reasons. In this fashion, the teacher can help her children to realize that they are quite capable of thinking about thinking in an orderly way, and to see that such thinking has a tremendous range of applications.

Acting Rationally

Formal logic shows children that they can think in a structured, clear-headed way, and the good reasons approach shows them that organized thinking has many day-to-day applications. Both kinds of logic can encourage children to use reflective thinking on their own, but neither logic has this as its main focus. For that, philosophy for children turns to the logic of acting rationally, and its guides for reasonable behavior. The main purpose of this logic is to encourage children to use reflective thinking actively in their lives. To see just how this logic is designed to fulfill this function, we need to take a concentrated look at the material used in teaching philosophy to children.

Role Models: Styles of Thinking

Among the main themes of *Harry* and *Lisa*, sharply reiterated in the arguments in the closing chapters of *Harry*, is the view that only some people think in patterns conforming to the rules of syllogistic logic, and that such rules are appropriate only to certain types of thinking. Both books present, in explicit contrast, a broad variety of other sorts of thinking. This plurality of styles of thinking is exhibited in two crisscrossing ways. First, the individual children each display a predominant style of thought. Second, each child occasionally uses a different style. Thus, while one type dominates for each child, what is characteristic of one is also exhibited now and then by others. The result is a complex matrix of types of thinking, such that for certain strands formal logic is appropriate, for others obviously not so, while the rest provide applications of good reasons logic. This is the philosophic core of logic for children, and warrants detailed attention.

A survey of *Harry*, for example, shows that at least eighty-six different kinds of mental acts are attributed to the children in the book. These range from being suddenly aware that one is being looked at, to sharing a special insight with a friend; from wondering whether one's grandfather will keep a promise to buy a football, to constructing a rule of formal logic. Those most commonly displayed (used by the same child in at least five different situations) include thinking something to oneself, thinking about oneself, remembering, being uncertain, using a rule of formal logic, consciously expressing an opinion, devising an example for a proposed rule, trying to figure something out, wondering (whether, why, how, what), and making a decision.

Among the major characters, certain kinds of mental acts, especially logical ones, recur. These predispositions to think in certain ways make up the different styles of thinking; one such style tends to be formally deductive, others include variants of the good reasons approach. Those that predominate are wondering (Harry Stottlemeier), thinking in formal logical patterns (Tony Melillo), intuitive or hunch-like thinking (Lisa Terry), seeking and enjoying explanations (Fran Wood), being sensitive to the feelings of others (Anne Torgerson), and thinking creatively (Mickey Minkowski). While this is only a partial list of types of mental acts and associated styles of thinking illustrated in *Harry*, one can already see that they constitute a very broad network. Mental acts and styles of thinking are both strictly attributed to individuals; of hundreds of references to mental acts, only four refer a mental act to children as a group (mainly, as a class in school). This concreteness and specificity strongly contribute to the reader's awareness of the plurality of styles indicated.

The diversity of styles of thinking is further illustrated by occasional overlaps. For example, Lisa characteristically reaches conclusions by means of hunches and sudden insights while Harry's inferences are generally thought out, yet both make snap judgments that turn out to be faulty. They differ again in that Lisa promptly expresses hers, while Harry keeps his to himself until he is led to revise them in the face of new evidence. Likewise, Harry shares with Anne an ability to have insight into others, yet for Harry this depends largely upon verbal clues while Anne's are visual. Thus, while Lisa and Harry do differ, they are similar in some respects, and so too are Harry and Anne. The lack of any overt contrast between Lisa and Anne shows that the matrix of kinds of thinking is not fully articulated, thus leaving room for the reader to add in his or her own ideas on similarities and differences among the characters and their thinking styles.

Each style of thinking represents a model of reasonable behavior. In effect the many characters in the book directly model rational actions for the readers. This is not to say that children are encouraged simply to mimic the characters in the book; rather, the characters are designed to show the readers how the active use of reflective thinking can make a difference in what one says and does. The imaginary characters are only partially defined role models—as noted above, not all contrasts and similarities are articulated in the books. Just as the real children will flesh out these characters in their imaginations, so too do they interweave their own thinking processes and types of mental acts with those of the characters. In this way, the lines between fictional characters and living children blur. As the living children step more and more into the stories, they are thereby encouraged to think and act rationally and to develop their own styles of thinking akin to those of the characters, similar in some respects, differing in others.

Guides for Reasonable Behavior

While neither formal logic nor the good reasons approach alone are designed to encourage children to use reflective thinking actively, their use by the characters does serve this purpose. Neither logic is presented as an abstract topic; both are entwined with the characters' own thinking styles. Thus, when the characters speak about what we would call formal logic or the good reasons approach, they simply refer to thinking, recognizing and respecting the thinking of others, and trying to think well.

To see how formal logic and the good reasons approach serve as guides for reflective thinking and acting, one should look to the dramatic settings of which the books are composed. There are many instances; a few examples from *Harry* will serve as illustrations.

In chapter 16, two patterns of logical consequence in formal logic, together with two patterns of erroneous thinking, are identified by the children. The formal patterns are *modus ponens*, which has the following patterns (where P and Q are symbols for sentences):

| Suppose | If P then Q | is *true*. |
| And that | P | is *true*. |

| *Therefore* | Q | *must be true*. |

and *modus tollens* (P and Q are symbols for sentences):

| Suppose | If P then Q | is *true*. |
| And that | Q | is *false*. |

| *Therefore* | P | *must be false*. |

The erroneous patterns are *affirming the consequent* (P and Q are symbols for sentences):

| Suppose | If P then Q | is *true*. |
| And that | Q | is *true*. |

Thinking that therefore P must be true—but nothing really follows.

and *denying the antecedent* (P and Q are symbols for sentences):

| Suppose | If P then Q | is *true*. |
| And that | P | is *false*. |

Thinking that therefore Q must be false—but nothing really follows.

As the children are working out these patterns, it is announced that one student (Jane Starr) has accused another (Sandy Mendoza) of stealing a briefcase containing a wallet. Through Jane's subsequent responses to questions, together with his own testimony, Harry establishes that although the briefcase was recovered well outside the room, Jane still had it there at 2 P.M., and that Sandy Mendoza had not left the room between 2 and 2:45, when Jane first noticed it was missing. Harry then reasons, using modus tollens: "Now, if Sandy has taken the briefcase then it would still be here in the room. But it wasn't found in the room. Therefore, Sandy didn't take the briefcase." Lisa then remarks that she believes another student, Mickey Minkowski, took the briefcase. This idea is described as a hunch, and she tries to justify it by claiming that hiding the briefcase where it was found is "just the sort of thing Mickey would do." Tony Melillo next shows this to be a case of erroneously affirming the consequent: "If it was Mickey who took the briefcase, then he would have hidden it behind the water fountain. Second part true: *the briefcase was hidden behind the water fountain.* But what follows? Nothing. We already agreed that just because the second part is true, you can't prove that the first part is also true." Sandy drags Mickey onto the scene, insisting that Mickey admit to having taken and hidden the briefcase.

Here we see both illustrations of rules of formal logic and a juxtaposition of discursive thinking with intuitive thought. When the children discussing the rules first learn that Jane has accused Sandy, they are told that Sandy has denied taking the briefcase, that although he has admitted to having teased her earlier that he would take it, he had not actually done so. Jane's accusation is thus similar to Lisa's accusation of Mickey, and we have the following outline of contrasts: Jane's hunch (incorrect) versus Harry's use of the modus tollens rule (relevant to who did it), Lisa's hunch (correct) versus Tony's pointing out an error of affirming the consequent (not relevant to who did it). The episode closes with a hint of the good reasons approach. Lisa admits that her idea was just a feeling, a kind of hunch, and a teacher replies: "Yes, Lisa, you made a shrewd guess. And as it happened, you were right. But if you'd been wrong, another innocent person, like Sandy, would have suffered. You weren't actually wrong to have tried guessing who might have done it. But guessing isn't a substitute for careful investigation." An *accusation*, of course, may well be supported by reasons other than deductive ones; Jane had some reason to suspect Sandy, and Lisa's hunch had inductive support.

Another example occurs in chapters 2 and 3 of *Harry*. Tony Melillo is unhappy; in response to Harry's questions, Tony says that his father takes it for granted that he will grow up to be an engineer like him and that, when Tony suggests he might do something else when he grows up, his father gets angry. Harry asks Tony why his father believes that he will be an engineer, and Tony replies: "Because I always get good grades in math. He says to me, 'all engineers are good in math, and you're good in math, so figure it out for yourself.'" Harry realizes that concluding from this that Tony is to be an engineer violates a previously discovered rule of formal logic: "Your father said, 'all engineers are good in math,' right? But that's one of those sentences which can't be turned around. So it doesn't follow that all people who are good in math are engineers." Later, in chapter 3, in a conversation with his father, Tony repeats Harry's conclusion. Challenged to explain it, Tony momentarily forgets Harry's account, is confused and afraid, but then recalls the rule. When his father questions the rule, Tony admits that he cannot explain why it works. His father then draws a diagram of concentric circles for the sentence "all engineers are people who are good in math." As a result, Tony concludes that "that's the reason we can't turn sentences 'all' around. . . . Because you can put a small group of people or things into a larger group, but you can't put a larger group into a smaller group."

This use and justification of a rule of formal logic at first seems rather straightforward, but a closer examination shows a wider, less simple context than first appears. In one sense, Tony's thinking obviously improves. He learns to spot a fallacy and, in the process, successfully overcomes some fears and confusions. But, from a broader perspective, this improvement may have limitations. Tony is happy with his father's explanation of the rule of reversal, and does not question his father's rule of interpretation. The advance in his thinking is confined to replacing a confusing and uncomfortably distorted situation with a pleasing, rule-governed one—he shows no sensitivity to potential limits of rule-governed thought. For example, insofar as his confusions and discomforts stem from his father's pressures on him to become an engineer, he has not yet met this source of difficulties; if anything, he has resolved one point of confusion in a style no doubt quite similar to his father's own, and in that sense is now all the more like him than before. Tony's discomforts when confronted with suggestions that he should grow up to be like his father thus remain untouched by this rule of formal logic and its interpretation, and the two contrasting modes of thought remain at odds—semi-articulate though highly developed feelings versus rule-governed discursive thoughts.

There are many more examples. In *Harry* alone, eighteen rules of formal logic are discovered and used. And instances of the good reasons approach make up an immense variety of comparisons and contrasts between verbal thinking that is structured by principles of formal logic and verbal thinking that can be judged by good reasons standards. There remain the many mental acts and related styles of thinking, verbal and nonverbal, that use neither formal deductions nor good reasons thinking.*

Conclusion

The basic purpose of each book in the philosophy for children program is to provide its readers with a means for paying attention to their own thoughts and to ways that their thoughts and reflections can function in their lives. The novels approach that purpose through a discovery of rule-governed thinking and by illustrations of a variety of non-formal types of thought. The logical rules are not simply stated for the reader to learn; instead, the books provide illustrations of rules and of search techniques so that their readers are encouraged to use such rules on their own.

*An earlier version of portions of the foregoing material appeared in *Teaching Philosophy*, Vol. I, no. 4 (Winter 1976). Reprinted with permission.

Rule-governed thinking is exemplified by the discovery and development of formal logic. But there is far more to reflective thinking than formal logic alone. As there are explicit rules of formal logic, so too can one speak of implicit good reasons procedures that bear on matters such as the pursuit of inquiry, listening to others and thinking out what they have to say, and thinking for oneself.

Together with the discovery that certain kinds of thinking are rule-governed, children should also be made aware of contrasting modes of thought such as imagining, dreaming, pretending, in which logical rules play little or no part. Through coming to appreciate and enjoy this broad variety of kinds of thinking, they can then realize that while their thinking often has logical form (and occasionally fails to when it should), much of it does not and need not. This is the key to how logic can be introduced and developed for children— never as a barren set of formulas, but always in contexts of reflective thinking, especially in efforts to think more clearly about thinking itself.

9 Can Moral Education Be Divorced from Philosophical Inquiry?

The Presumption of Rationality

Presumptions are common in every domain of human activity. In the law, it is presumed that persons are innocent until they can be proven guilty. In scientific inquiry, it is presumed that events are caused, even when evidence of such causes is lacking, or when explanations can be offered only on a statistical basis.

Likewise with ethical inquiry. The variable factor that distinguishes older from younger persons is experience, and it would be shocking if we were to · level accusations against young children for doing things that, due to a mere lack of information, they did not know were inadvisable or prohibited. To blame a toddler for playing with matches when the child as yet knows nothing of what matches can do and is unaware that playing with them is prohibited is just this sort of misplaced judicativeness.

On the other hand, we very often excuse children from the obligation to use their reason, on the grounds that they are too young. When we do this, however, we do them no favor. And, indeed, the situation is much worse, for what we are doing, when we fail to presume that the child is a rational being even when our relationship with him is a moral one, is a censurable act of moral disrespect.

There need be nothing inappropriate in the psychologist's presumption that children act but do not reason. But it is especially important that such a presumption be excluded when considering the child in a moral education setting. Piaget may maintain* that "childish thought is devoid of logical necessity and genuine implication; it is nearer to action than ours, and consists simply of mentally pictured manual operations, which, like the vagaries of movement, follow each other without any necessary connexion" (pp. 145–146). Piaget refers to a "pseudo reasoning" on the child's part, which "consists in a series of immediate judgments following one another in freedom

---

*Jean Piaget, in collaboration with Miles E. Cartalis and others, *Judgment and Reasoning in the Child*, trans. Marjorie Warden (London: Routledge and Kegan Paul, 1928).

from all logic" (p. 90). Indeed, Piaget implies that the same pseudo reasoning may be characteristic of adults: "it will perhaps one day be the task of child logic to explain that of adults," rather than "reconstruct the thought of the child on the pattern of adult mentality" (p. 91).

Thus, Piaget is at liberty to hypothesize that all human reasoning, and not just the child's, "consists in a series of attitudes which bring each other into play according to psychological laws . . . and not in a string of concepts which imply one another logically" (p. 91). But once this hypothesis is carried over into the sphere of moral experience, the presumption of rationality must be abandoned, and with it must be jettisoned any hope of successful moral evaluation. For if the children are deemed incapable of principled moral behavior, incapable of having reasons for what they do, incapable of rational dialogue about their conduct, incapable of employing patterns of logcal inference, then they must be treated as no different from the lower animals, or even as mere things.

One may or may not, as a scientist, be a strict determinist. But as a moral educator, one does not have such a luxury of choice. The presumption that the child is incapable of reasoned, principled behavior rules out the possibility of treating that child as a moral being, and therefore destroys any possibility that such treatment can be either moral or educational. This is why stage theory and philosophy are incompatible: there can be no legitimate philosophical discussion in which one party considers the other inferior, not simply as a matter of prejudice, but as a matter of principle.

Setting the Stage for Moral Growth

Few teachers today are unaware of the expectation of parents and society that education, in addition to developing basic skills, also expand the moral dimension of the child's personality. But, to do this, a teacher must become a substitute parent, and of course it is no easier for a teacher to be a surrogate parent than it is for a parent to be a surrogate teacher. In brief, the question of how a teacher is to encourage students to be moral is one of the most perplexing issues in modern education.

Educational theorists have presented the teacher with so broad a spectrum of alternative theories of the moral nature of the child that the extreme views virtually cancel each other out. On the one hand, the child is viewed as a little savage who must be tamed and domesticated; on the other hand, children are seen as little angels with impulses already moral and virtuous, so that all that is necessary is to provide the right environment for them to be themselves. A more reasonable view is that native to the child are innumerable dispositions that, if encouraged, could lead to *any* kind of human behavior, and often do.

What is important is that the environment in which the child grows up should be such as to screen out those forms of conduct that do not contribute to growth, while encouraging those that do. This is not the same as the romantic view that holds that all one has to do is to provide the right environment and let children be their "naturally good" selves. In other words, a teacher has a responsibility for screening out those forms of behavior in pupils that are obviously self-destructive, and for screening in those forms that are self-constructive. The teacher may have to decide on the basis of knowledge of individual children just which features of conduct need to be encouraged or discouraged in each individual case. One child may need to be drawn out; another may need to develop more self-control. But the object is to liberate the child's creative powers of thinking and acting and making by developing his or her capabilities in ways that reinforce and strengthen each other rather than block each other or cancel each other out.

Each child is an individual and at the same time each child is part of the class. The teacher must forget neither of these facts. But they are not separate facts. As an individual the child is distinctive, and can develop his or her unique powers in terms of the roles to be played in the group. The individual distinctiveness will reveal itself in the difference that he or she makes in the classroom, and *every child in the classroom should make a difference*. Thus, in a sense, the teacher's role is to ensure that each child feels that he or she has the capacity to make a difference and each day acts on that presupposition. Teachers must ask themselves regarding each child in the classroom: "Would the absence of this child make a distinguishable difference in the classroom?" If the answer is "no," then something is definitely wrong with the way that the teacher has conceived his teaching role in relation to that child. To the extent that he has not encouraged that child to be an active seeker of his or her own uniqueness, an active harmonizer of his or her own powers, an active creator of his or her own contributions to the class group, as a teacher he has fallen short of success.

It may seem harsh to place so much responsibility on the teacher's shoulders, but children cannot be expected to develop a sense of responsibility unless the adults that they are surrounded by, and whom they seek to emulate as models, likewise accept responsibility for what happens in the classroom. In this regard, it is worthwhile to distinguish those things that are responsible merely in the sense of being *causes* from what is responsible in the sense of being *accountable*. Thus, the child's organic impulses and native dispositions play a causal role in his conduct but they cannot be held accountable for his behavior. The child is, of course, accountable for controlling those impulses.

On the other hand, the school environment over which society has control, an environment that encourages or discourages those dispositions, is something for which society can very much be held accountable. To this extent, the moral development of children can be estimated only in relationship to the accountability of the society in which the children find themselves. A society that does not value a school environment conducive to moral growth (and often this is expressed just in terms of the amount of money that it is willing to invest in education) is a society that should openly accept its share of blame for the amoral conduct of its children.

Instead of relying on a child's home environment, a setting that might or might not be conducive to moral behavior, the teacher must focus on the kind of environment that can be created in the classroom. The teacher's responsibility, as has been said, is for screening in those kinds of dispositions that lead to children's growth, and for fostering interaction between the individual child and the classroom environment as a whole. (That environment includes the teacher as well as the other children.) It is a truism that a child in the classroom who has been treated in the past with condescension and contempt is now likely to treat himself or herself with disrespect. Those who treated this child in this fashion are of course accountable for having done so. But the teacher in whose classroom this child is found is accountable for seeing to it that the child find an environment that accords respect and support, so as to counteract the treatment of which he or she was a victim in the past. Another child may display a lack of imagination or curiosity, again as a result of a deadening environment or regimen either at home or in school. The responsibility of the teacher is to see to it that an environment is created for this child that is challenging on a daily basis so as to overcome the numbness and apathy resulting from his former environment. Still another child, perhaps as a result of the home environment where he or she is often the object of aggression, may resort to very aggressive behaviors towards others. It is the teacher's responsibility to make sure that this child is placed in such a setting that there is no need for him or her to engage in aggressive behavior in order to protect or to restore damaged integrity.

It is proverbial that "the child who disturbs others is a disturbed child." But this is inadequate because it diagnoses *the child* as pathological, rather than *the situation* that produces the behavior. Thus, once the teacher begins to assume responsibility for actively creating environments that are supportive, and that lend themselves to the building of self-respect and self-mastery, a most essential step has been taken towards engaging in moral education. Unless an environment is created that is conducive to mutual trust and respect for each individual in the classroom, no educational program, neither philosophy for children nor any other, is going to make much of a difference in helping children to become moral individuals.

Socialization and Autonomy in Moral Education

Very often, it is taken for granted that children are complex, difficult, unruly, and amoral. One then infers that the child is responsible for the problematic character of moral education, rather than acknowledge that the problem of moral education is complicated by one's own presuppositions about it. But it should be evident that if we better understood just how much autonomy we are willing to accord the child and just how much control we are willing to retain and relinquish—if we better understood and were more honest with ourselves about what kinds of persons we want our children to be, and what rights they have in exercising choice as to the kinds of persons they want to be—the moral development of children would be considerably less perplexing.

It is not uncommon to pose the problem of children's moral development in this fashion: either moral education must be construed as a way of getting children to conform to the values and practices of the society in which they find themselves, or education is a way of liberating children from those very values and practices so that they can become free and autonomous individuals. Such a formulation of the problem is most unfortunate, because it commits education to the kind of ideological controversy from which education itself should rescue human beings. So to pose the problem of moral growth is to gloss over the many non-constructive dispositions and proclivities of any individual, and to gloss over the many supportive and beneficial aspects of human society. Putting these value labels on society and on the individual is counterproductive, if our objective is to encourage children to judge for themselves. To think of human individuals as innately good or bad or of society as innately good or bad is to foreclose all possibility of determining through inquiry what is responsible for each situation as it stands, and how it can be improved. To the extent that any dogmatic statement about society or the nature of the individual cuts off inquiry, man is reduced to a passive unresponsible spectator rather than an active, involved, and responsible shaper of the society in which he lives.

Moral eduation worthy of the name necessarily involves acquainting children with what society expects of them. Moreover, it involves enabling children to develop the tools they need in order to assess such expectations critically. As with the parent-child relationship, the society-child relationship is fraught with mutual duties and reciprocal rights. It is not education to present these in a one-sided fashion. Some of us tend to think of institutions as themselves repressive and that in a better world we would not suffer from institutions at all. But this is a serious misreading of the situation. It is not a question of whether or not to have institutions, but rather whether the institutions we have are to be organized in a rational and participatory fashion. When they are not, it is correct to say that the individual is at their mercy. When they are, they cease to be coercive and become constructive instruments for the achievement of individual concerns and objectives.

Acquainting children with the conduct that society expects of them is only part, although a very important part, of a responsible moral education. It is also necessary that children be equipped to think for themselves, so that they can creatively renew the society in which they live when the situation demands it, as well as for the sake of their own creative growth.

When we say that education of necessity must enable children to develop the tools they need in order to assess society's expectations of them in a critical fashion, we do not mean to imply that the teacher's role is nothing more than the fostering of critical judgments on the part of students. The objective is not to form a classroom of critics, but rather to develop human beings who have the capacity to appraise the world and themselves objectively, as well as the capacity to express themselves fluently and creatively. The forming of a critical attitude is only part of the teacher's role. Students must come to realize that although being able to stand back and look objectively at the institutions around them is essential, it is not enough. If one is disposed to be critical, one must also try to propose something new and better. This is why dialogue in the classroom is helpful: it brings out the positive and constructive ideas that children are capable of generating as well as their negative ones. A teacher must be able to applaud creative insight when encountering it just as a teacher has to be able to applaud instances of logical reasoning.

Criticism can often be the springboard for the teacher to initiate philosophical discussion. For example, in *Harry Stottlemeier's Discovery*, when Mark begins criticizing all schools as bad, he launches a discussion regarding the aims of education in terms of which his classmates are then able to judge whether the schools are or are not capable of achieving those aims. The discussion culminates in their devising alternative ways of running schools so that the aims of education might be better met.

A child in the classroom might begin not with a criticism but with an imaginative alternative proposal that suggests how things could be, but that unfortunately lacks any indication of how it is to be put into practice. Rather than concentrate on the ineffectiveness of such an idea, the teacher should encourage the other children in the classroom to suggest specific ways in which the idea might be put into practice.

But what of ideas—creative as they might be—that the teacher judges to be destructive? For example, suppose a child should suggest "Let's get rid of minority X as a first step to a better society." As always, the best source of the answer to such ideas should be the other children in the classroom. If the idea is genuinely unconstructive, then the critical abilities of the other children should spot the deficiencies of the idea and point them out. But suppose they do not? Should the teacher intervene? Well, the teacher always has the right to intervene and state his or her own opinion if the circumstances warrant it. What is obnoxious is the teacher introducing his or her own opinion before the children have had a chance to respond to the original proposal, thus foreclosing genuine consideration of alternatives. On the other hand, if the teacher feels that the children have been able to develop their own ideas and can hold them in a strong and confident fashion, then that teacher should not feel hesitant about introducing his or her own ideas, where the children themselves have failed to bring forth such a point of view. The children should understand that the teacher has temporarily abandoned the role of moderator in order to assume that of co-participant.

Now let us push the matter a step further. What if, after presenting a point of view, the teacher gets this response. "Well, that's only one point of view and we don't buy it!" It is here that philosophy is unique. Since it is inherently a process of dialogue, it is not under any obligation to come to a particular conclusion at a particular time. The teacher's response could be, "Well, let's talk about it some more tomorrow." Or, "I'll take your views into serious consideration and we can talk about it again."

The substance of what we have been saying is that it is unconstructive for the teacher to put himself or herself in the role of bringing about the child's submission to social values, or to assume the role of encouraging the child's individuality to give way to mindless non-conformity in the area of moral education or any other area. The teacher is a *mediator* between society and the child, not an arbitrator. It is not the teacher's role to adjust the child to society but to educate children in such a fashion that they can eventually shape the society in a way that is more responsive to individual concerns. It is important that educators recognize the plasticity of society as well as that of individuals and the necessity for community self-renewal, if society is to continue in a participatory fashion. Nothing so guarantees the inflexibility of society with respect to individual creativity as the teaching of children that society is inflexible with respect to individual creativity.

Dangerous Dichotomies in Moral Education

Teachers today are bewildered by the overwhelming array of alternatives in moral education. There are purely cognitive approaches that portray morality as efficient reasoning. Others construe morality as obedience and acceptance of discipline, thereby making it a matter, not of intellectual reasoning, but of character. Still others interpret the child as being naturally virtuous, so that good behavior will naturally ensue if only the emotions are unthwarted and unrepressed and sensitivity to others heightened. What bewilders a teacher is that, based on experience in the classroom, it is evident that each of these positions has a degree of validity. There is an element of reasoning in moral education, as there is an element of character-building, and as there is an element of emotional liberation and sensitivity training. The problem is not to devise a program that would do any of these things but to do all of them.

If morality were simply a matter of knowing rules and obeying them, then moral education would consist in developing in children a conscientiousness that would permit them to carry out these rules in a happy, unquestioning fashion. But morality is not so simple. It is not clear that there are rules for every situation, nor is it clear that it contributes to children's development that they should accept uncritically those rules that might apply. Consequently, the child must be equipped to cope with situations lacking clear guidelines, situations that nevertheless require that one make choices and that one accept responsibility for the choices one makes.

We have been stressing that, in the area of moral education, the teacher must do much more than acquaint the child with the predominant values and morals of that society. The teacher must involve children in a process that will ensure that they learn to think for themselves, that they be trained to read the cues and signs of other people's interests in situations in which they are involved, and that they become aware of their own emotional needs. We do children a disservice if we hold them responsible for behaving in a particular way in a particular situation when we have given them no practice whatsoever that would develop their capacity to deal appropriately with such a situation when it comes up. This is one reason why programs in moral education that emphasize moral *thinking* are insufficient. They fail to develop the patterns of constructive *conduct* that make moral behavior something children can readily engage in when the need arises for them to do so. Unless such patterns are developed beforehand, each new moral confrontation becomes traumatic for children, because they have not been given preparation in moral practice. Moral education is not just helping children to *know* what to do; they have to be shown how to *do*, and be given practice in *doing* the things they may choose to do in a moral situation. Without such doing, moral education breaks down. Nowhere so much as in moral education is the bond between theory and practice, knowing and doing so, so important—yet nowhere is it so often disregarded.

Children find themselves in various situations during the course of a day. Some of these situations call for action: some do not. But children can hardly know what actions or decisions are called for or appropriate unless they have developed an awareness of the dimensions of each situation, its complexity and its various nuances and subtleties. If children can become aware of the requirements a situation places upon them and the opportunities it offers them, they can respond to it appropriately and effectively. We therefore emphasize the importance of calling children's attention to what is involved in the various life situations they face, as a prerequisite to their intelligent response. Once they grasp the meaning of a situation, they will better know what they want to do.

But we can hardly expect children to carry out their responses effectively if they have not been able to prepare themselves through various forms of moral practice. We can hardly expect children to be tactful in moral situations where tact is called for, if they are unfamiliar with tactful performance. There are situations that call for a young person to encourage another child, to console another child, to express gratitude, to advise, to reconcile. Yet children can be mute and inarticulate and passive with such demands upon them, because they have had no practice in performing in these ways, or even in imagining how they might perform. Exercises in moral practice are therefore important supplements to sensitizing the child to the moral aspects of situations.

But it is not enough to criticize the dichotomy between thinking and doing and to recognize the need for both in an effective program of moral education. It is equally necessary to insist upon the indissoluble bond between thinking and feeling. There is little value in instructing a child in what would be universally right to do in a given situation when the child does not care about anyone, let alone everyone. It is hard to see how a child who is not interested in other people's feelings would have any sympathy with their needs, or how one who is not in the habit of putting himself in other people's places would be the least bit interested in acting in accordance with moral rules even if they were known and accepted. Moreover, the feelings necessary to moral conduct are not restricted to particular sympathies for this person or that person, since it is equally indispensable that one be sensitive to the entire situation of which one is a part. Such sensitivity may require the most delicate awareness and capacity of discrimination. It involves an ability to appreciate what a situation requires and what might be appropriate to those requirements. It requires the capacity for considering as fully as possible the consequences of one's behavior. Often, what we condemn as immoral behavior may simply be the result of a certain insensitivity to the character of the situation in which one finds oneself and one's lack of capacity for seeing oneself in relationship to the whole. The morally inconsiderate person is often one who has failed to take all things into consideration before acting. The tactlessness of a child in the classroom is often due simply to a lack of a sense of proportion, in which individual needs and feelings that should be placed in the context of the needs and feelings of everyone are instead accorded absolute priority.

Now the teacher may ask, "How can I develop this kind of tact and sensitivity in my pupils?" Here is where the heightening of aesthetic perception can lead to a greater moral awareness and sense of proportion. For example, a child may have difficulty picking up cues about what is going on in a meeting, or he might be incapable of seeing how his talents and insights can play a contributory rather than monopolistic role in a certain group. He still continues to view his relations in an egocentric rather than social sense. Instead of endlessly moralizing about the need to develop sensitivity, empathy, a feeling for "what is going on," without giving the child any definite tools to develop these traits, involvement in the type of dance activities called kinetics, or the type of musical activity (chime activities, choral activities, group work of one kind or another) that calls for listening to the notes of others and then attempting to play an appropriate sound, often results in the child's beginning to develop the necessary sense of proportion that he might be lacking.

An assumption frequently made is that the child's intellect is educable but his feelings are not. Human emotions are assumed to be primitive and irrational. One can tame and domesticate them, but one cannot cultivate and refine them, much less use them in cognitive enterprises. They are simply brute forces, and one must use all the wiles and stratagems of one's intellect in order to discipline and control them. This is a very curious view of human emotions. If our desires and feelings were not educable, we would never want better food, better friends, better art, better literature, better communities. The theory of the ineducability of human feelings and desires flies in the face of the fact that people do learn to desire more knowingly and more reasonably. Instead of always pitting intelligence over and against feelings, an educator should focus upon making desires more intelligent and intellectual experiences more emotional.

To separate the affective and cognitive in moral education is treacherous and is to misunderstand the nature of learning. Our own conception of intelligence is not a "mentalistic" one. We do not see intelligence as something that takes place in the "mind." Rather, intelligence can be displayed in any form of human behavior, in one's acts, in one's artistic creations, and in one's reflections or verbalizations as well.

Today, when a teacher hears the word "affective," all sorts of things are suggested. In the realm of affective education, expressing one's feelings, getting things off one's chest, baring one's soul, letting off steam, all seem to be part of the picture. Such an approach implies a patronizing view of human emotions. The image is of a person building up too much emotional pressure and then finding release in some harmless escape. In this way, the emotions are dispersed and the force that they might have provided for the child's constructive activities is lost.

On the other hand, an alternative and equally mischievous view regarding affective education is that the affective is superior to the cognitive and should be the primary focus of all education, including moral or value education. Such a view has no more to recommend it than the polar opposite just discussed. The school that fails to sharpen children's cognitive skills condemns such children to be helpless to deal with those aspects of life situations that call for rational analysis. The result is a fatuous dwelling upon affective behavior, with no development of the skills essential to making a difference in one's society or to making an imprint on one's world. If we fail to develop their cognitive skills it is paradoxical of us to hold children morally responsible for their behavior.

Another dichotomy that is an underlying assumption of many moral education programs is the dichotomy between fact and value. This assumption has often led teachers to believe that somehow value education can be treated as a self-sufficient and autonomous discipline, separated from the different subject areas of the curriculum, and that it is valid to separate "facts" from "values" as though they were two different things, facts being "objective" and values being "subjective."

Thus, we have a time during the days when we explore and clarify our values (a personal subjective enterprise) and other times when we explore and clarify facts (an objective social enterprise). But the teacher who is compelled to deal with values by themselves in this detached fashion often finds that it is an area of curiously bloodless abstractions or, even worse, an endless discussion of children's demands for "what we want" and "what we desire" rather than of "what matters are really of importance to us."

While we urge that children be given practice in reading aright the individual character and significance of the individual situations in which they happen to find themselves, in no way do we assert that moral values are merely subjective, or merely relative in the sense that any response is as right as any other for a given situation. We deplore the fashionable doctrine that, in matters of value, "everything is relative; what may be right for you may be wrong for me, and that's the end of it!" To assert this is equivalent to saying that anything goes.

Our stress upon logic and inquiry is meant to counter this subjectivism by giving children some of the tools that they can use to analyze the situations in which they find themselves so as to come to sound and reliable conclusions. Children who have the opportunity to discuss their feelings with one another can proceed to analyze those feelings and understand them more objectively. As they develop habits of thinking carefully and critically, they reach out more systematically for factual evidence, and begin to consider alternative ways of acting, rather than merely basing their judgments upon hearsay, first impressions, or "subjective feelings."

To assume that facts and values are separate is treacherous in its implications for moral education. Given this separation, it is easy to suppose that one can change one's values without a change in the facts of one's situation. But this is an illusion. It is futile for a teacher consciously engaged in moral education to hunt for certain disembodied entities called "values," or to encourage children to eke out such entities on their own when, in fact, all that is meant by the term "value" is *a matter that is or should be of importance to the child*. All too often, children encouraged to clarify their values end up talking about their feelings and wants, rather than assessing the *objective worth* of what their feelings and wants are about. For example, children might say that they feel much more positive about being on the playground than about being in school. What a philosophical discussion should bring out is what the objective differences are between playgrounds and schools, so that children can assess the importance of each and under which circumstances one is to be preferred to the other. Values should not be identified as a person's desires but as those things that after reflection and inquiry are found to be matters of importance. Thus the process of inquiry moves from a subjective to an objective orientation.

In the perspective of perceptual observation, this round bit of copper is identifiable as a "fact": in the perspective of economic matters, this same thing is the least valuable of our coins—and is therefore an economic "value." That you are now reading this page is a fact. That you find it worthwhile to do so makes reading the page not just a fact but a matter of value. The existence of the apples you consider purchasing is a fact, but the store identifies them as "fancy," and thereby cites their grade of "value." So fact and value are nothing but the same thing viewed in different *perspectives*.

For purposes of analysis, we can isolate an order of "facts," and likewise, for purposes of analysis, we can isolate an order of "value," but matters that concern us are always at the intersection of those orders. There are not two different things, "facts" and "values": there are simply matters that are simultaneously factual and valuational. This is essential for a teacher to understand, because it is the teacher's responsibility to see to it that children do not disconnect moral ideals from moral behavior. This separation often occurs when children are encouraged to talk about values as if they were independent and self-sufficient entities divorced from the world of fact, instead of talking about courageous behavior, fair behavior, respectful behavior, right behavior, and just behavior in particular situations.

On the other hand, we should not assume that children are incapable of talking *about* morality. That children can analyze moral issues does not exclude their discussing abstract ethical concepts such as "fairness" or "rightness," since children are able to function on a theoretical as well as on a practical level.

What to Do to Help the Child Know What to Do

The teacher's role is not that of a supplier of values or morals, but that of a facilitator and clarifier of the valuing process. The child who comes to realize the uniqueness of many moral situations will be able to discover that no moral rule can be uniformly helpful in determining what to do. Insofar as previous educational experiences have challenged this child to improvise and invent where rules have been lacking, such ingenuity will stand him or her in good stead. The appropriateness of children's actions, however, is to a great degree dependent on their understanding of and personal commitment to the valuing process itself. Thus, the fact that a child might have to come up with a new solution in a particular moral situation in no way excuses that child from being concerned about his or her motives, society's expectations, or the probable consequences of the action.

The teacher, in the role of facilitator and clarifier of the valuing process, must introduce children to certain criteria by which to judge whether or not an action is moral. Such criteria can enable children to reflect on: how this action affects them; how it affects the structure of their habits and character; how it affects the direction of their lives; how it affects the other people around them; and how it affects the institutions of the society of which they are a part. These measures or criteria become the guideposts that the teacher can use to steer the children towards some kind of cumulative understanding of the nature of particular actions.

It is always important, however, to keep in mind that moral situations are not necessarily routines to which routine solutions apply and that moral criteria must be re-evaluated constantly and reconstructed to make them relevant to the times. It is this openness with regard to criteria and moral actions themselves that sets the "philosophically-oriented" teacher apart. The realization that often situations are opportunities for innovation (and such innovation could well involve going beyond the call of duty rather than merely living up to it) must always be kept in mind. Thus, it follows that the teacher should concentrate on helping children engage in moral reasoning for themselves and not merely pass along to those children the values of society or the teacher's own values.

We do not mean to say that every personal, moral situation is unique. Situations can have much in common, and, when they do, rules that have generally worked in like cases can be expected to work again. What we *are* saying is that the child should be equipped to distinguish like from unlike situations, usual from unique situations, typical from atypical situations. The child should be prepared to confront the different or unprecedented courageously, resourcefully, and imaginatively, rather than try to impose upon the unusual situation a rule that is doomed to fail.

So long as the child cannot distinguish similar situations (to which rules based on past experience may apply) from dissimilar situations (which require that unique solutions be devised), the whole question of the role of rules in moral behavior is moot. The sensitive discrimination of similarities and dissimilarities among situations is of fundamental importance to the child's moral development. The child must be able to take into account a large number of subtle and complex features of situations—their metaphysical, aesthetic, and epistemological as well as their moral aspects—that are present whenever we compare or contrast such situations with one another. We cannot expect to encourage children to respect persons unless we acquaint them with the full implications of the concept of a person, and this requires philosophy. Nor can children be expected to develop an ecological love of nature without some philosophical understanding of what "nature" is. The same is true of such terms as "society," "thing," "wealth," "truth," and countless other terms and phrases which we constantly employ, but of which the child generally has only the most diffuse understanding. Comprehensiveness is what philosophy in its broad sense tries to provide. More than anything else it is comprehensiveness that moral education—in the traditional sense of rule-inculcation or in the conventional sense of "decision-making" or "value-clarification"—cannot provide.

Imagination and Moral Education

To many people moral reasoning is confined to logical reasoning, that is, to drawing conclusions from premises or from factual evidence. But moral reasoning should not be so narrowly defined. The rule of imagination in moral reasoning is of utmost importance.

Of course, this would hardly be so if the solution to moral problems could be worked out in a purely mechanical fashion as one might pose an arithmetical question to a computer and have it display an answer. Very often, wrongdoing is not the result of someone's malice, but merely of that person's inability to imagine a constructive or creative approach to a predicament. For example, two decades ago the spread of polio had reached serious proportions and there was considerable panic among parents. When it was announced that a polio vaccine had been invented there was widespread relief. But the Department of Health, Education and Welfare promptly provoked a blast of criticism by confessing that it had ordered only a relatively small number of doses. The secretary of HEW responded: "Who would have thought that the public demand for polio vaccine would be so extensive?" For an official in a position of responsibility to make such a remark would seem to represent a failure of moral imagination, to say the least.

Moral problems are a sub-class of human problems in general. It takes imagination to envisage the various ways in which an existing unsatisfactory situation might be transformed. One has to be able to visualize what would happen if this were to be done or if that were to be done, or if nothing were to be done at all. In other words, imagination is needed to anticipate the goals and objectives that a moral individual or a moral community might seek.

At the same time, it takes imagination to review the alternative ways in which each of these goals might be achieved. What steps would have to be taken? What materials would have to be employed? Who would have to be involved? What must be done first, and then secondly, and so on? And what would happen as a result of the employment of each of these alternatives? It takes a vivid imagination to rehearse all these possibilities. But in so far as morality is the planning of conduct, then it exhibits very much the same characteristics as any kind of successful planning does. One cannot plan without imagination. One cannot plan a business venture without imagination and one cannot plan one's conduct, if it is to be successful, without imagination. Now it is evident that the kind of conduct we prefer children to engage in is the kind we should encourage them to practice. Likewise, it seems plausible to expect that exercise in moral imagination could very well develop a readiness in the child for dealing imaginatively and creatively with situations that otherwise the child might find perplexing and bewildering.

Exercises in moral imagination consist of two major varieties; first, there are those that involve consideration of different types of means-end relations, and, secondly, there are those that involve different types of part-whole relations. Getting children to practice breaking down a problematic situation into its parts, then imagining how it could be transformed into an improved alternative, is a combination of both of these varieties. Children have to be encouraged to exercise imagination with regard to each of the facets of solving moral problems.

Imagining Means-End Connections

Such practice in moral imagination of the means-end variety can be formulated in a cooperative fashion: for example, one might engage the class in an exercise such as this:

1. Imagine someplace you would like to visit. Write it down and exchange papers with your neighbor. Now let your neighbor write down all the things he or she can think of which you would have to do in order to get to the place you want to go, while you write down all the things your neighbor would have to do in order to get to the place he or she wants to go.

Suppose, for example, your neighbor says she would like to visit her grandparents in a city that is 3,000 miles away, and would like to stay there for a week.

You might write something beginning like this:

First of all, you want to arrange transportation. You may want to go by airplane. So you have to get tickets. Find out how much they will be. Do you have money to buy them? If not, maybe you will have to use a cheaper means of transportation.

Next, you will have to decide what you will need to wear at your grandparents'. You will have to have some kind of luggage to take it in, too. You will have to prepare your clothes, etc., etc.

2. Perform the same exercise, only imagining the following:
   a. What you would like to be someday.
   b. What you would like to do tomorrow.
   c. The kind of "best friend" you'd like to have.
   d. What kind of community you would like to live in.

3. Are there things you have now that you wouldn't want to change at all? Name some of them.
   *a.*_____
   *b.*_____
   *c.*_____

In the first part of this illustration, children are encouraged to think of where they might wish to go as an imaginary exercise. They are then made to see by their neighbors that such wishes are ends that require means for their implementation, and the neighbors spell out these needs. How well the neighbor does in this task will again depend upon a capacity to visualize and anticipate the practical aspects of getting something done. Thus, this is an exercise in encouraging children to specify an imaginary end and then requiring them to cooperate in the imaginative construction of the means of achieving such ends.

Imagining Part-Whole Connections

Similarly, moral imagination requires encouraging children to consider how wholes can be broken down into parts, and how parts can be used to build imaginary wholes. Of course, if the teacher does not know how to do this, it will be impossible to transmit the art to a child. For example, suppose you are considering admonishing a child who has been disruptive by sending him to the principal or counselor. A segmental view of this situation would involve your merely directing this admonition to the child. But you can hardly neglect consideration of the larger context of your actions, namely how will this action be viewed by the class as a whole and how consistent will it be with the remainder of your behavior towards that class? Thus, your action is not just between you and the disruptive child but involves the totality of interrelationships in the classroom.

An example of the part-whole exercise in moral imagination might be the following:

Suppose someone has suggested to you (as editor of the school newspaper) that you run a contest to see who is the prettiest girl in school. You decide to talk this over with the editors of the newspaper, and one of the editors points out that this would probably get people to read the newspaper, and that's good. But another editor asks what the effect of this will be on the school community as a whole. Your class can take it from there. The questions that it can raise include: What is meant by pretty? Why is the contest limited to girls? How do the losers feel when the contest is over? Is it worth having a contest when so many people might feel badly? Is the kind of competition that is encouraged by this sort of thing healthy? In other words, one tries to see a particular activity as a part of a larger frame of reference.

We talked earlier about the necessity for creating an environment of trust, mutual respect and cooperation in the classroom as a precondition of any meaningful moral education. But what kind of activities can you as a teacher come up with that will involve all the children in your class, each in a different or unique way, in a cooperative enterprise that, in turn, can begin to create this kind of mutually respectful environment? To conceive of the class as a community, the teacher has to be prepared to imagine various divisions of labor within the class that will offer individual children distinctive roles in that community. You have to see the parts within the whole, just as you have to be able to construct a whole out of the parts.

Needless to say, one of the most useful ways of stimulating a child's moral imagination is to place him in situations that call for innovative conduct, although they are not specifically moral. Discovery-type situations in science classes are of this character, but even more helpful are dramatic or dance situations in which inventiveness on the part of each participant is encouraged. A ballet, for example, where one of the dancers comes up with a novel movement can excite the entire group to respond, each in his own way, although what they do does not have to be lacking in composition or coordination.

Every time a child paints there is the need to work from parts to wholes and to analyze wholes into parts. The same is true with writing a poem or any other instance of artistic creation. What the teacher concerned about moral imagination must be prepared to do is to help the children relate these instances to one another. The teacher can point out that the heroic deed discussed in a literature or history class was creative, an act that took the same kind of imagination as a remarkable innovation in one of the arts. We are not all called upon to be heroes, just as few people are great artists, but every moral problem presents a need for some degree of imagination if its reconstruction is to be effective for all concerned.

The Role of Models in Moral Imagination

One of the virtues of the philosophy for children program is that the novels the children read, such as *Harry* and *Lisa* are in effect model communities of children. They are not so idealized that children reading them cannot identify with the characters, while at the same time they provide models of intelligent discussion among children as well as between children and adults.

The novels also provide models of inquiry, models of cooperation, and models of caring, sensitive individuals. What this does for the student is demonstrate the feasibility of such an ideal children's community, where the participants are intellectually and emotionally wholesome, lively, and actively involved. A student having no inkling of the possibility of ever interacting with such comrades in such a situation is deterred from using his own powers of reflection, cooperation, and discussion. One reason why children are often taciturn or reticent, even to the point of being withdrawn, is perhaps that they cannot see the feasibility of using their powers in a constructive fashion. They are often creatures of fear, anxiety, and pessimism.

A model community, even though fictional, converts such fears into hope. It lets the child know of the imaginative possibility of a world where people relate to each other in a way that evokes the creative possibilities of each individual. The model therefore stimulates children's moral imaginations. They may never have known what they wanted or what they sought. The model helps them understand their own needs, their own desires. They begin to see that this is *how things could be*. And they can begin thinking seriously of alternative means that can be explored and examined in an effort to achieve something like the ideal that they have now glimpsed.

The ideal, however, is not held up for the child to imitate in a docile or uncreative fashion. A young artist wishing to be like Rembrandt would not think that his life task would be the slavish copying of Rembrandt's paintings, but would seek to be true to his own situation the way Rembrandt was true to his. To emulate a model is not to imitate it or copy it but to use the model and allow it to stimulate those feelings of hope, courage, and belief in oneself that might enable one to live as effectively in one's own unique and creative way as the children in the novel live in theirs. So models are enormously useful for the stimulating of moral imagination in the child, which in turn liberates those constructive feelings and energies that can be converted into moral activity.

Where to Begin

Perhaps a word should be said about "moralizing." To help children develop morally does not require that, at every possible moment, one point out to students the moral implications of what they are doing. Children have every justification for finding such behavior on the teacher's part difficult to tolerate. From an educational point of view, it is counterproductive, for it sets up a situation in which the child recognizes a patronizing and condescending attitude towards his or her own moral capacities. The child's strategy of self-defense is to seek ways to challenge or test the teacher's interpretation of the situation and the battle is on.

In order for a moral education program to be adequate, it must enable the child to think reasonably, develop patterns of constructive action, become aware of personal feelings and the feelings of others, develop sensitivity to interpersonal contexts, and acquire a sense of proportion regarding his or her own needs and aspirations vis-à-vis those of others. Obviously, this is a huge task for any teacher. The teacher may well throw up both hands and say, "This is more than I can do. How can I even begin to go about it?"

The teacher can begin by helping children develop habits of logical and critical thinking, by encouraging them to engage in philosophical dialogue where they can discuss their opinions and feelings with others and at the same time learn about other people's values and points of view, and by giving them the opportunity to engage in individual and collaborative inquiry where they can appreciate the values of objectivity, impartiality, and comprehensiveness, values that are indigenous to the philosophical enterprise. By encouraging children to engage in moral practices, by allowing them more and more responsibility in the classroom, on the playground, and in the schools as a whole, coupled with exposure to all other aspects of philosophy, we can help them to begin gradually to make sense of the moral dimensions of their world.

How much autonomy should a child be given? Neither more nor less than what he or she can handle at a given moment. It is up to the teacher constantly to assess and reassess what children are capable of handling, thereby providing an opportunity for them to test and retest their capacities. The word "responsibility" often has an unpleasant connotation for children, because they associate it with their liability to being blamed if they do not do what they are supposed to do. This is a most unfortunate interpretation, because it is only insofar as children are given more and more resposibility for dealing with the conduct of their lives that they acquire any modicum of freedom. The child who thinks of freedom as the opposite of responsibility has bought the same misconception that his parents may have accepted: that freedom is merely getting away with not doing what one is supposed to do. This interpretation, characteristic of immature individuals, equates freedom with license. The misguided child thinks of freedom as not doing what grownups want rather than seeing that freedom resides in doing what one *upon adequate reflection and inquiry* desires to do in a particular situation. Children can seldom realize this, however, unless they are given more and more opportunities to have some say over their own behavior, and to have some input into the decision-making processes of the group to which they belong.

Thus, "children's rights" from the viewpoint of the child, means the child's right to say, "I want more and more responsibility, as I am able to handle it with regard to my own conduct. To deny me the opportunity to discover what is appropriate conduct, to deny me the opportunity to be responsible for myself, is to keep me a perpetual child, dependent on others for setting up the laws and rules of my behavior. It is to deny me that experiential foundation of freedom and responsibility that is essential if I am ever to think for myself with regard to morality." Obviously the role of the teacher is to gauge the rate and timing of the child's acquisition of this enlarging capacity for assuming responsibility.

Why Moral Education Cannot Be Divorced from Philosophical Education

Now it may be asked, "What has all of this to do with philosophy for children? How will philosophy for children accomplish this moral education? How is it different from other methodologies now available to teachers?" In the first place, philosophy provides a regimen for thinking, so that the logical aspects of the moral situation can be dealt with by the child who has learned how to unravel the logical aspects of a situation and can see the need for objectivity, consistency, and comprehensiveness in his or her own approach to such situations.

Second, philosophy involves a persistent search for both theoretical and practical alternatives, with the result that the encounter with philosophy generally leads the child to a more open and more flexible attitude towards the possibilities in a given situation.

Third, philosophy insists upon awareness of the complexity and multi-dimensionality of human existence, and systematically tries to point out this multi-dimensionality to children so that they can begin to develop a sense of proportion about their own experience. It stresses the fact that a problem situation is seldom merely a moral situation, but has metaphysical, aesthetic, epistemological, and other aspects. Consequently, as the child comes to engage more and more frequently in the practice of considering life situations fully and exhaustively,—that is, taking into account their many dimensions instead of treating them superficially—he or she becomes more and more sensitive to the complexity of such situations and the need to take into account as many of their dimensions as possible.

Fourth, philosophy for children involves not just reasoning about moral behavior but also the devising of opportunities to practice being moral. This contrasts with programs that stress decision-making or the making of choices by the child, in that it seeks to prepare children for moral life by developing those competencies that they need in order to do what they choose to do. The exercises in moral practice that form an integral component of the philosophy for children program give children an opportunity to act out how they would engage in forms of behavior that often have a moral dimension, such as consoling, caring, advising, honoring, sharing, and the like. We cannot expect children to be considerate if we do not give them opportunities to learn what "being considerate" is through allowing them to practice engaging in such conduct. Exercises in moral practice are primarily designed to involve the child in doing. We can exhort the child to care and to be considerate, and we can even show the logic of this behavior, but it will avail us very little if the child does not know what actions are consonant with care and concern. Moreover, it is not that such actions emerge naturally from a caring and concerned individual, but rather that the voluntary performance of such actions tends to develop care and concern in such individuals as perform these actions.

This is a very important insight for the implications it sheds on the role of the teacher in the classroom. Rather than talking about considerateness, caring, or any other moral virtue, it follows that the teacher's role is to set up situations in which children can actively partake of such experiences as will reveal to them what considerateness, caring, and other moral characteristics are in the light of their own experience, and what people do who have such feelings, for morality consists not in the feelings themselves but in the conduct that is conjoined to such feelings.

Fifth, we said that a sufficient moral education program would have to develop in the child an awareness of the feelings of others. Philosophy can never be separated from dialogue because philosophy inherently involves questioning, and questioning is an aspect of dialogue. When philosophy for children enters the classroom, the classroom becomes an open forum for all sorts of ideas. But it is not just a brainstorming session where all ideas can be thrown out uncritically. Philosophical discussion leads to acquaintance with the wide diversity of points of views to be found in any group, and with the equally broad set of differences among opinions and beliefs. Since offering opinions in a classroom discussion do not pose the demand for competence that is posed when the teacher asks for a correct answer to a question, children find the exchange of opinions and the disclosure of differences in perspective inviting and reassuring rather than threatening.

Once this reassurance has been established, however, the teacher must assume responsibility for introducing the criteria of a philosophical discussion, (that is, impartiality, comprehensiveness, and consistency) and for making sure that the discussion itself builds and "makes a difference" for the children. Students will become rightfully impatient if too great a degree of irrelevance is tolerated. Similarly, if the discussion does not seem to have a cumulative development, students will become fatigued by it. Moreover, the teacher has to be aware that a discussion leader has to be extremely careful, should it be appropriate to endorse a particular opinion voiced by a student, not to close off further discussion and inquiry by such partisanship.

It is the teacher's role to encourage consistency in the presentations of the students, although such encouragement may take different forms. For example, in one case it might be necessary to point out to a student that what he or she is saying does not follow from what was said before by the same student. In another case, where the student's intent was evident but the presentation fumbling, the teacher may offer to restate the position in a more coherent fashion. In short, philosophical discussion, by making children aware of one another's beliefs and points of view, and by subjecting such beliefs and opinions to philosophical criteria, leads children to become conscious of one another as thinking and feeling individuals. Without such dialogue, children may sit side by side in classrooms for years without encountering one another as individuals who are like themselves, striving to make sense of their own experience. One unfortunate consequence of this is that the child often comes to an erroneous conception of knowledge itself, thinking of it as a merely private matter. In contrast, philosophical dialogue leads children to realize that the acquisition of understanding is more often than not a *cooperative* achievement.

Sixth, philosophy for children introduces the novel as the vehicle of moral education, as well as of education in metaphysics, logic, aesthetics, and epistemology. The novel as a philosophy text affords an *indirect* mode of communication that, in a sense, safeguards the freedom of the child. Children are less inhibited when they feel that they, their family experiences, and their personal life experiences are not the focus of classroom attention. With the distance that the fictional technique permits, children are left free to interpret and eventually decide for themselves which philosophicl views make the most sense to them, without the dread that they may fail to come up with the morally "right" answer, or that the discussion process is part of a manipulative diagnosis or a phase of a therapy session by an amateur therapist.

A sufficient moral education program must insist upon the development of both cognitive and affective capacities without making the one superior to the other. Instead of conflicting, thought and feeling can be induced to reinforce one another. Using the novel as a vehicle for exposing the students to philosophical ideas and concepts has the advantage of demonstrating the affective and cognitive dimensions of life interwoven at every moment. These ideas are then discussed in the classroom, in the context of the children's own responses to them. The progressive elaboration of ideas in the classroom dialogue continues to interweave the cognitive and affective strands of experience. For example, mastery of the logic component of the philosophy program has its affective as well as cognitive rewards: it increases children's self-confidence and ability to make sense of their experience. In areas where ideas presented in the program are highly controversial (for example, the aims of education), children begin to discover their own points of view as they listen to other people express their opinions. They also discover how ideas, when passionately expressed from one's own point of view, can vehemently attract or repel listeners.

Children slowly begin to discover that as they are able to distinguish sound and unsound ideas, a growing taste for sound ones and a distaste for unsound ones begin to emerge. That is to say, children's feelings come to be enlisted in the pursuit of intellectual understanding. In time, children come to develop a stronger desire for the more warranted assertions than for the less, for the more beautiful rather than the less, and for that which is better in conduct rather than worse. One can say at such a point that the individual has grown to have enlightened feelings and intelligent desires. Thus, the ideal curriculum in moral education would introduce to the child every philosophical concept illustrated or embodied in some affectively charged activity, and conversely would endeavor to impart to every such activity and mode of feeling an appropriate cognitive content.

With the introduction of strictly affective techniques into the classroom in the past decade, we have observed that children often are very reluctant to "bare their souls," as it were, in the public context of the classroom, nor should they have to. Often children feel under a great deal of pressure to talk about their emotions when they do not want to, for fear of being thought "up tight." If the child is reticent, the teacher may feel a need to press harder, thereby assuming the role of therapist to which the teacher is ill suited. In the end, the process can be counterproductive.

On the other hand, when children find themselves reading a novel about other children, they can feel more at ease in discussing the affective aspects of the novelistic character's life experiences, because such affective aspects are integrated with the cognitive searchings of these fictional characters for ways of reasoning that will help them make sense of their world. As these reasoning rules are mastered, the children in the story begin to feel more self-confident and capable of expressing themselves, their ideas, and their feelings.

Then, as open dialogue ensues in the classroom, the teacher will probably find that the students will reveal increasing confidence in themselves and trust in their classmates. This trust and sense of mastery can fuse, and the philosophical discussion can proceed confidently to move from the children in the novel to personal interpretations and applications should the children in the classroom feel a need and a desire to do so. Although it is the teacher's role to encourage children to see the connections between the theoretical concepts introduced and practical life problems, it is never justifiable to pry or to force any child to talk about personal emotions or personal life experiences in the context of a philosophy course.

In addition to providing an indirect mode of communication, the philosophical novel can also serve various other purposes. It can act as a model of philosophical dialogue for the children in the classroom. It can also act as a springboard for the discovery process. That is, it can hint at philosophical ideas that can then be elaborated on and developed into substantial philosophical concepts through classroom dialogue and activity. It can enable children to learn the difference between logical and illogical thinking in a relatively painless fashion, and attempt to indicate to children when logical thought is appropriate and when non-logical thought might be preferable. Another essential function that the philosophical novel can perform lies in its attempt to *sensitize* children to the complexity and ambiguity of moral situations and, at times, to the necessity of inventing or creating appropriate moral conduct. This is a role to which the novel is particularly suited. We might all admit that often we learn more about how to act and how to judge the appropriateness or morality of actions from reading and discussing novels than from reading and discussing books on moral philosophy. The novel is a form well suited to crystallizing the multi-dimensionality and complexity of moral situations and moral choices, as well as for revealing the consequences of those choices. It is in this fashion that the novel provides a vehicle for the development of moral sensitivity. To the extent that children become involved in the plot and critically reflect upon the actions of the characters, taking into account the complexity of the situations in which they find themselves and the consequences of their actions, to that extent they are involved in a process that can result in a heightened moral sensitivity—that is, a heightened sense of appropriateness with regard to human actions. Further, the novel, as such, can often facilitate discussion among children as well as between children and teacher. It thus can become a vehicle for transforming the traditional dynamics of the classroom into a situation in which the children begin to realize that they have as much to learn from one another as from the teacher, and the teacher can discover how much can be learned from sharing the children's perspectives.

There are a number of educational approaches today that seek to promote classroom discussions (particularly in the area of moral education) and this of course includes the philosophy for children approach. The eagerness of children to engage in examination of their common problems makes it possible for such discussions to develop very easily and naturally, once an atmosphere of trust and mutual respect has been created. There might be little to distinguish a classroom engaged in a philosophy for children program from a classroom engaged in other moral education programs. The observer would see children expressing their thoughts or feelings, sometimes with deep conviction, sometimes merely in an effort to please the teacher or in an effort to conform to the thoughts expressed by their peers. But a more experienced observer might note two important differences. First, the philosophy for children approach deliberately seeks to keep the moral dimension within the larger context of the child's life and to balance it with discussions of other philosophical subject areas—metaphysical, aesthetic, logical, epistemological, and so on. This is not to diminish the importance of the moral in children's eyes, but to strengthen their awareness of the other domains, so that such heightened awareness can then inform, enrich, and humanize the insights they may develop with respect to moral issues. Second, the experienced observer would discern the constant employment by children, in their discussion of the philosophical text, of logical techniques that are conducive to more efficient and critical thinking. It is the teacher's role as the program develops to explain these logical techniques and then supply the children with exercises that help them not only to master the techniques but to apply them to situations that have meaning for them. As both teacher and children begin to understand and utilize these logical techniques, classroom discussions tend to display objective progress rather than relativity or stasis.

The philosophical novel itself provides a vehicle for demonstrating that each child has his or her own style of thought and conduct. The children in the novels can act as models that reinforce the notion that children are not merely little blobs, but that each child, whether in the novel or in real life, is a person who is beginning to work out and put together a style of life and a basic direction to that life. This is essential in the education of every child, because once the child can perceive what the basic direction of his or her own life is, then that becomes the basic criterion against which he measures the choices he makes in particular situations. The child who lacks a sense of direction will treat every situation on an *ad hoc* basis. This is mindless empiricism at its worst. When children's conduct is steered along the lines of the basic directions they are finding for their lives, their achievements build on one another, become cumulative, and are capable of helping children grow. Moral education involves helping them assemble and rally their energies and abilities, and directing them along the lines in which they themselves choose to develop. A sound moral education must provide strategies that the teacher can demonstrate to children so as to help them discern the innumerable connections that exist between themselves and their peers, between themselves and grownups, and between themselves and the customs and institutions amidst which they must live. Without awareness of such connections, children cannot be expected to understand the moral dimension of human experience, and to act effectively upon such understanding.

The Relationship between Logic and Morality

The reader of *Lisa* will readily recognize not only that the book is about reasoning and morality, but that it is very much concerned with the *interrelationship* of logic and morality. In the first chapter, we find Lisa noting that she loves roast chicken, and that she loves animals as well. But now she glimpses a problem: if she really loves animals, is it consistent for her to eat chicken? It is not a question here of her duties to other people; it is simply a question of the consistency she would like in her own life—among her own thoughts, and between her thoughts and her actions.

Later, the children in the book begin to complain about an invasion of their privacy of discussion, when they realize that they learned of this through accidentally overhearing the principal's conversation. Once again the problem of consistency confronts them. How can they demand privacy for themselves but deny it to others?

On another occasion, Lisa wonders how it is that Millie thinks it all right for men to marry women younger than themselves, but not for women to marry men younger than themselves—to Lisa, Millie's position seems inconsistent.

Still another instance—the children tell the principal that if he genuinely believes in education, then he will encourage them to think for themselves. But, they tell him, he is not encouraging them to think for themselves. So he must not really believe in education.

The case of Lisa finding a discrepancy between loving pets and loving to eat animals points up an important but often neglected consideration—that a crucial aspect of morality may be not so much one's values taken individually as the relationships that obtain *among* them. Lisa's affection for pets in no way obliges other people to like pets. Lisa's loving roast chicken in no way obliges other people to love eating chicken. But, Lisa suspects, she cannot live comfortably with herself while holding incompatible values. If she really loved animals, it seems to her she would not eat them. But she eats them. So, she is forced to conclude, she must not really love them. The moral issue here is not one thing or the other, but the connection between them.

The person who has been taught that morality is concerned simply with the particular values that one holds on particular issues will likely fail to see much significance in the point here. Either lying is right or it is not, he will say. Either stealing is right, or it is not. But these are flagrant cases, lurid cases, about which we have intense anxiety, and it is very difficult for us to discuss them reasonably. Consequently we may find it very difficult to explain to a child just why we believe that not lying is right, or why not stealing is right. Focusing on the act alone is like looking at something through the wrong end of the telescope: suddenly it looks too large, out of all proportion, and we can no longer see it in context. When we focus just on the act of lying itself, without envisaging it in its connections with other acts and beliefs, when we consider the act as isolated and out of context, we suddenly find we are talking about an abstraction. Yet we feel so strongly about it that we cannot think of any other way to deal with it but to insist upon its wrongness more and more vehemently. Unfortunately, this gets us nowhere with the child we are trying to educate morally.

Nothing is easier than to disregard the connections among our values, but in so doing we disregard the basic structure of morality. As Harry Stottlemeier and his father note in one of their discussions, it is possible to take a large-scale social event culminating in some atrocity, and dismember it, isolating into discrete, simple, and morally neutral acts all that preceded it and contributed to it. By breaking a large-scale moral fact into these tiny splinters or fragments, we effectively de-moralize our world. Looking at each action individually, detached from the connections that would reveal its deeper meanings, we see nothing in each such act to condemn or to praise. We refuse to look at how it paves the way for the atrocity it leads to, and we exonerate it from all responsibility. Needless to say, the same demoralization process can occur with regard to actions that contribute to magnificent, heroic events, when viewed as mere aggregates of disconnected "morally neutral" human actions.

When children want to know about morality, we find it very difficult to answer them effectively, because the matter seems both vast and elusive. We are at a loss for an authority to cite whose credentials they cannot question, and we are likewise at a loss for *unquestionable* ethical principles. Involving their consciences seems not to get us very far, and conducting sessions in "value clarification" seems to succeed only in demonstrating our moral wasteland.

Nor can we think of good reasons to offer for being honest, respectful of others, and so on, without such reasons sounding shallow and superficial. Yet we are sure that there must be a better justification than the one we eventually settle on.

Lisa wonders how it is she hates lies, when she cannot recall a single instance in which her parents told her it was wrong to lie. But a child whose life has *integrity*—that is, whose thoughts and actions are consistent with one another, will resist performing an action incompatible with the rest of that child's life, and in fact will be shocked and disgusted by that which is so out of line with that child's normal practices. She will no more need parental injunctions to avoid telling lies than she will need to be warned repeatedly not to cut herself when handling a bread knife.

We see this in the learning of grammar. Children learn the rules of grammar and the practice of those rules, until such rules and practice become "second nature." One does not have to think of whether this or that one is about to say is grammatically correct or not because one habitually practices correct grammar and deplores grammatical slovenliness. And yet, when occasions arise on which there are good reasons for violating such grammatical rules, one may easily proceed to do so, for the rules are not rigid and inflexible. So too with moral practice: it should develop consistently and form an integral whole in the case of each individual. For such morality to be effective, the unwarranted violation of that whole, of that consistency and that integrity, should be looked upon by the individual himself as a self-destructive violation of his own integrity, and therefore wrong.

Children who come to value their own integrity, and who practice honesty as a consistent portion of such integrity, feel lying to be a rupture of the self, and avoid it much more assiduously than they would if it were simply a matter of fairness (although it may be that too). And children who have learned what reasoning is, so that they can distinguish sound from sloppy reasoning, are not so likely to be deceived as to what is or is not compatible with their own integrity, or with the basic direction of their lives. It is for this reason that the learning of reasoning is essential to morality. It is not that children who study reasoning are then able to use their logical skills to settle their quarrels with one another and with their parents, although this may occasionally happen. But what is likely is that such children then have criteria with which to assess what is relevant and what is irrelevant to their interests. They can better judge what fits into the basic scheme of their lives and what fails to fit in.

We wish to repeat this so as to leave no doubt as to our emphasis upon the point. We do not encourage the teaching of reasoning to children because we believe that moral problems are simply disguised logical problems, which will yield promptly to logical analysis. Such is the glib premise of cognitivists, and we cannot accept it. But we do think it important for adults to encourage children to develop a consistent texture to the fabric of their lives, and they cannot tell what we mean by this until they can appreciate what it is for ideas to be inconsistent with one another, or incompatible, or contradictory. A child can have a life of integrity without learning logic, of course, but logic helps one appreciate the difference between that which integrates one's life and that which disintegrates it.

We are saying then that children whose lives display wholeness and coherence and integrity are children to whom the distastefulness of say, a lie, will come as no surprise, insofar as it represents a dismemberment of that integrity. Children whose habits and beliefs have been coherently integrated are the best guardians of their own virtue. If, then, we value virtue in children, we should do everything possible to encourage the development of the integrity of their selves.

At the same time, it must be emphasized that the child who is committed to the practice of honesty will shun lying not only as inconsistent with that practice, but as inharmonious with the whole or integrity of that child's life. In this sense, awareness of part-whole relationships is as truly disciplinary in moral education as is awareness of logical consistency. To Lisa, telling a lie would be repugnant, in view of her practice of honesty, in somewhat the same sense that it would be repugnant for her to wear dress gloves with her denims.

Thus the integrity of one's self is based upon an integrity of praxis—one's thoughts consistent with one's actions, and one's individual acts in line with or compatible with the whole character of one's conduct. Unless such praxis has been established day by day, bit by bit, lesson by lesson, moment by moment, into a tough, closely knit texture, the individual lacks a strong moral base. Such practice is not reducible to a "good reason" for telling the truth, not hurting others, and so on. Good reasons are far too inadequate to convey the force of such practice. Good reasons are more likely to come in on those occasions in which overriding situational pressures—something of an emergency—requires that we diverge from what we normally do— and with good reason. It is the exception that good reasons typically justify, not the rule, for the rule is not reducible to a single principle or set of principles. It is the living warp and woof of the interwoven thoughts and actions of the child's life.

The development by the child of such practice is an achievement of momentous importance. Once we fully realize how difficult it is to accomplish, we can have little patience with the superficial slogans that are being offered everywhere in the name of moral education—"letting kids talk it out," "getting kids to see that there's really only one moral value—justice," "laying it on the line to kids—telling them the rules and walloping them if they disobey"—and so on.

To be effective, ethical education must be enormously patient, persistent, and scrupulous; it must be carried on in a manner that is truly caring and benevolent, consistent rather than ambivalent, and concerned that children should be helped to think, feel, act, and create for themselves. So far, our civilization has devised only one instrument that has even remotely approached serving as such an aegis, and that is the family. Today, with the family under enormous pressure, with its function in doubt and its structure changing, there are efforts to shift its moral function to other agencies, and in particular to the school. Insofar as the school accepts this shift of responsibility, it should be fully aware of what it is taking on. The parent-child ratio was not one adult to twenty-five children—it was between two adults to three children and two adults to seven children. This gave the family an opportunity to concentrate on moral education at virtually any moment of the day. And if parents have not always been intelligent, they have at least, more often than not, been concerned. If schools now presume to enter the ethical education domain, they must be prepared to enter it on a systematic and scrupulously careful basis—in terms, that is to say, of a commitment from kindergarten to grade 12, and with a view to the entirety of the school day, not just a moment during each day devoted to moral inspiration. Such a commitment will in turn require an obligation to neutrality and non-indoctrination on the one hand, and to strengthening the child's efforts at logical, creative, and moral practice on the other. We see philosophy for children as the opening wedge of that commitment.

A final word of caution regarding the relationship of logic to moral education. We have stressed the importance of consistency between one's beliefs and one's actions, as well as among one's beliefs and among one's actions. We have argued that the logic component of the philosophy for children program can be helpful in arousing in children an awareness of the criteria for such consistency, so as to mold more consistent habits and dispositions. And we have contended that the philosophy for children program alerts children to the importance of good reasons in justifying their beliefs, and in justifying departures from patterns of conduct they might normally have adopted.

But there is always the danger that one or another of these elements will be taken out of context and overemphasized. We see a role for logic to play in helping children sort out and understand their own activities, even to the point of recognizing how some of the things they do can undermine their intentions and actions in other respects. But this is not to conceive of logic as a technique for decision-making, as if one need only feed the data into the mechanism and the right answers will automatically pop out. To do so is seriously misleading. Some years ago, for example, we held a series of discussions with some high school students about the usefulness of philosophy, and, in the course of one of the discussions, we presented a perhaps overly rosy view of the possible benefits of logical reasoning. As it happened, the students were at that moment engaged in a heated debate over the policy to be adopted with regard to the presence or absence of drugs at the annual class encampment. To our surprise, there was an attempt to press the syllogism into service, as though *it* alone could demonstrate conclusively that certain policies were the right ones. When we endeavored to point out that one could examine the logic of any argument, but that logic *alone* would not solve their problem, the students were rather miffed, as if they had first been oversold and then betrayed.

You should try to avoid similar misunderstandings among your own students —and you can take the most effective step towards this end by being clear in your own mind about the limited usefulness of any one of the components of the philosophy for children program in the absence of the program as a whole. Logic is only one part of philosophy, as moral education is only one aspect of education. A teacher should keep in mind not just the relation of logic to ethics, but the relation of philosophy in its entirety to the total educational process— just as the teacher should keep in mind what that total educational process can do for the whole of the child's life.

The Improvement of Moral Judgment

The problem of how to improve the moral judgment of the young is as complex as any that a society must cope with. That parents should normally have the responsibility for dealing with the problem is of course part of the burden they assume in choosing to be parents. But teachers can rightly be apprehensive about being asked to assume even a portion of such a burden.

Of course, there is no lack of advice. There are experts aplenty when it comes to specifying ways of making children moral. There are those who would indoctrinate and those who would not, those who hold that there are moral principles and those who hold that there are not, those who favor the development of "moral feelings," "moral character," "moral intuition," "moral sense," and those who decry such efforts as useless. Teachers thus find themselves in a most uncomfortable situation, with social pressure being exerted on them to guide the development of moral judgments among their students, while the pedagogy that would supposedly enable them to perform such guidance turns out in fact to be a chaos of conflicting theories and pseudo-theories.

Moreover, while none of the proposed approaches for developing excellence of moral judgment among children has appeared persuasive to the bulk of those concerned, neither has any of these approaches been shown to be totally unworthy of consideration for at least one or another aspect of the matter. It has not been shown, for example, that habit formation is irrelevant, that rules and principles are irrelevant, that aesthetic considerations are irrelevant, that logic is irrelevant, that affective components are irrelevant, and so on. Nor is it likely that any such demonstration of irrelevance will be forthcoming.

Consequently, teachers are left with the task of deciding which of these many approaches to employ or emphasize, and in what fashion. It should be evident that teachers are going to need a good deal more guidance than they have heretofore been given, if they are to deal effectively with a problem as vast and as bewildering as is involved when a moral dimension is explicitly introduced into the educational process. The philosophy for children approach, in this respect, can be helpful.

To interpret the ethical component of philosophy for children as merely an effort to strengthen children's cognitive powers or *reason* (so that their reason can dominate their emotions) would be to distort our approach enormously. Even if we were to hold (which we most certainly do not) that reason is somehow civilized while human emotions are somehow primitive and barbaric, the notion that reason is some kind of equipment by which emotions can be tamed and dominated is virtually worthless. The image of the rational thinker coolly keeping his head and making perfect deductions while emotions swirl all about him is a vestige of a psychology that should have been recognized as obsolete long ago.*

One of the most perceptive of classic philosophers put the matter quite succinctly when he observed that it is not by reason that a passion can be con-

---

*It may be noted here that while *psychologies* come into being and die out as they are replaced by superior psychological theories, the same cannot be said of philosophies in general, or of ethical philosophies in particular. Psychologies come and go—philosophies remain as permanently possible frameworks of interpretation. The ethical theories of Kant and Bentham, for example, appear several thousand years after the ethical theory of Aristotle, but one cannot say that the later theories are necessarily better than the earlier one. Scientific theories, on the other hand, do succeed each other and replace each other whenever the later can demonstrate its superiority to the earlier. It is therefore a matter of some oddity that some psychologists who are now beginning to tread upon the terrain of ethics naively assume that ethics must be developmental in the way that their own psychological theories are successive and developmental. They even invent elaborate, self-certifying theories of "moral development," in which they demonstrate that children naturally grow up to have moral notions much like those advocated by the psychologists themselves. One can obviously amass considerable evidence in support of such a contention; as a theory of value it is manifestly of little worth, and, at each of the so-called "stages," there exists the possibility of mature ethical conduct side by side with less responsible types of conduct. Yet all these are lumped together as if they were indistinguishable. Thus, for example, the proponents of stage theory offer us no effective means of distinguishing between such conduct as selfishness and self-love, although the moral value to be imputed to such conduct differs enormously. As a result, the net pedagogical effect of stage theory is to confuse and misguide teachers rather than illuminate them as to the proper role they may assume in moral guidance of their students.

quered, but by another and still stronger passion. From this it follows that what should be encouraged in children—if we wish to help them control their inclinations to irrationality—is their impulse to rationality, their natural love of meaning, their desire for understanding, their feeling for wholeness, and their passion for investigating the endless byways of their own consciousness. The current flurry of interest among philosophers in the notion of "rational passions" is a healthy antidote to the morbid and futile effort to strengthen the intellect at the emotions' expense.

Indeed, nothing would seem to be more evident than the educability of the emotions—yet few things are so hotly disputed. It would appear that the first order of business in moral education would attend precisely to this point, for if passions are susceptible to cultivation so as to become more rational, then this should indeed be the primary objective of moral education, rather than child-obedience training in respect for so-called "universal moral truths," or teaching children something so indefeasibly cerebral and cognitive as "critical thinking."

That our feelings and desires and appetites do in fact become more sensitive, more knowing, more selective—in short, more judicious—would seem to be difficult to deny. It is not our "minds" that compel our always raw, untutored desires to prefer better works of art, better friends, better jobs, nobler deeds—it is rather the growing judiciousness of our desires themselves. If we would have children prefer noble actions to ignoble ones, we would do well to devote ourselves to the cultivation of their developing tastes and preferences, and to the guidance of their budding appetites and desires, instead of merely belaboring them with moral advice. If we can help children desire more intelligently, have more cultivated tastes and appetites as well as more rational preferences, we will accomplish far more towards making them moral beings than if we merely equip them with a smattering of logic, exhort them to love or respect one another, and induce in them a docile attitude towards our favorite doctrines and ideologies.

The cultivation of children's moral dispositions and the improvement of their moral judgment should be an expected result of our provoking them in a variety of ingenious and surprising ways to the exercise of such of their natural powers as taste, discrimination, reflection, and analysis in the countless forms and phases of making, saying, and doing. But teachers nonetheless need to have spelled out for them the basic distinction between what it is appropriate for them to do and what it is proper for them to refrain from doing with respect to advancing the moral growth of the student. It is particularly useful, in this respect, for teachers to grasp the distinction between the procedural and the substantive, and so to exhibit that grasp that their students will likewise acquire it and utilize it in their own deliberations.

We have elsewhere noted the particular usefulness of the distinction between substantive and procedural considerations with respect to classroom instruction. The teacher, we have pointed out, should normally be neutral when moderating discussions among students about specific substantive issues in which value questions predominate. But the teacher in such discussions should definitely be partial to and insistent upon the rules of procedure by which the discussion is carried on. Should these rules happen to become themselves the substance of the discussion, then the teacher should endeavor once again to assume a neutral attitude towards them. For example, the teacher may make a practice of limiting the amount of time allowed for an individual student's contribution to a discussion. But this practice may be criticized by the class, and become a matter for philosophical discussion—in which case, it would seem, the time limitation should be suspended until the issue is resolved.

We have also observed elsewhere that it is unrealistic to expect judicious moral conduct from children who are uncaring or morally unconcerned. Now the primary focus of care in a person exercising moral judgment is on procedural rather than on substantive matters. Moral judgment is careful, scrupulous judgment—its opposite is carelessness, a lack of attention to procedures because procedures are considered unimportant. Adequate moral judgment therefore manifests itself in care for the procedural principles of inquiry, rather than in insistence upon the rightness of this or that substantive principle of morality. There is an enormous difference between allegiance to, say, *justice* as a substantive principle of moral conduct, and allegiance to fair, nondiscriminatory procedures in the resolution of disputes. Unless there is care for the means or instruments necessary for the implementation of justice, we can rest assured that justice will not be implemented. Nor is it fair of us to hold children responsible, when we have never shown them how to be attentive towards the procedures that moral conduct involves.

But if care and concern for procedures are among the objectives of philosophy for children, then it is obvious that the objectives of the program are not limited to purely cognitive matters. Care and concern are primarily affective and character dependent. They are, moreover, quite evidently the result of continual practice and habit-formation. There is in all education a balance between discovery and instruction, freedom and discipline, order and innovation, practice and creativity, and to these there must be added the balance between procedure and substance. It is far better to be clear about the domain of the teacher's neutrality and the domain of unneutrality, about the region of student independence and the region of routine learning, than to be permanently confused about the differences between these contexts, and about the criteria for distinguishing between them.

What philosophy for children can best do is improve moral judgment by developing in children the techniques involved in the making of such judgments, and by developing in them at the same time the love of and the care for such techniques. The capacity of the average person to be consistently judicious in moral matters is highly precarious. Our critical dispositions are easily deflected by self-interest, and our foresight regarding the untoward consequences of our actions is readily blinded by wishful thinking. It is indeed remarkable how persons of character, normally scrupulous in adhering to proper procedures of moral inquiry, can casually ignore considerations of the greatest gravity for other persons involved, should their own advancement be at stake. It is not so much callousness as fecklessness that marks the morally injudicious person— not inconsiderateness towards persons so much as disrespect for procedures. We can inveigh endlessly to such individuals about the need for interpersonal respect, but such exhortations are likely to be no more relevant today than the edifying essays of our more puritanical ancestors.

Indeed, attention to procedure, which becomes part and parcel of the child's character, will do more to develop that child's moral judgment than all the edifying discourses ever written. But at the same time, we must bear in mind that the infinitely varied nuances and subtleties of human intercourse cannot be conveyed didactically. Only literature has shown the delicacy and flexibility needed to penetrate and communicate the many-layered multiplicity of human relationships. Consequently, the improvement of moral judgment will require for its effectiveness the construction of a special body of literary works that will embody and display the modes of moral awareness, the nature of moral integrity, the techniques of moral inquiry, and the alternative structures of ethical understanding. Philosophy for children, to be an effective curriculum for ethical education, must consequently stress the conjoint employment of literary texts, together with philosophical procedures aimed at developing logical proficiency, aesthetic sensitivity, epistemological insight, and metaphysical comprehension. Children who are about such procedures are children whose moral judgment is most likely to be improved in the course of their education.

10 Philosophical Themes in Ethical Inquiry for Children

Junior high school is neither the earliest point at which children can be introduced to ethical inquiry nor is it the latest. But it is a point at which such inquiry can be pursued in a considerably more systematic way than it could have been in earlier childhood. Partly this is because children in junior high school have a greater command of logical reasoning and partly it is because they have a greater concern with interpersonal and social aspects of life.

Before turning our attention to a particular ethical inquiry curriculum, let us consider what is involved in encouraging children to engage in ethical inquiry. The branch of philosophy that attempts to understand moral conduct is called ethics. It represents objective and dispassionate inquiry into moral problems and moral situations. Its aim is never to indoctrinate, but rather to help individuals more clearly understand what their moral possibilities are within a given situation.

Ethical inquiry should not be equated with "values clarification," "decision-making" or the moral dilemma–stage theory programs. Although it is true that these programs call attention to activities with which moral inquiry is concerned, it would be a serious mistake to reduce ethical inquiry to any one of these activities. Children should be aided in understanding their wants, needs, and desires, but this is not the whole of moral education. And although children should be helped by giving them practice in dealing with possible moral problems, moral education must be much more than this. Further, to reduce moral education to decision-making is rather like saying that farming can be equated with harvesting, when in fact the farmer's primary concern is with plowing, cultivating the soil, watering, and a myriad of other activities in preparation for the harvest activities without which there would be no harvest.

A second moral education minimally involves helping children understand such matters as the nature of criteria and how they function; the discovery of underlying assumptions; the process of reasoning; the giving of good reasons; detecting the moral character of situations; the relative importance of and proportion between parts and wholes; discerning the interests of the community

188

in which one finds oneself; the need to take all relative factors into account; the need to weigh consequences; the importance of neither overestimating nor underestimating the role of the self in a moral situation; the importance of sizing up one's own and other people's intentions; the anticipation of possible harm, both to others and to oneself, as the result of one's actions; and the importance of preventing moral crises before they occur. These are some of the things that comprise a sound moral education. Apparently, there is no short course that can develop all these characteristics in a child, any more than a farmer can find major shortcuts in growing corn. The process of preparation is a time-consuming one, one that requires continuity from year to year, and reinforcement each year of what had been learned the year before. It requires, moreover, an able teacher committed to dialogue and open inquiry.

While philosophy concerns itself with many things, there are three about which philosophy is most insistent: we must learn to think as clearly and logically as possible; we must show the relevance of such thinking to the problems that confront us; and we must think in ways that search out fresh alternatives and that open up new options. If we apply these dicta to the moral education of children, it is evident that children must learn how to think (and to think about thinking) as clearly, logically, and effectively as possible. Then they must learn to identify and think about moral issues, such reflection being ethical inquiry proper. The aim of ethical inquiry is not to teach children certain particular values; it is rather an open-ended, sustained consideration of the values, standards, and practices by which we live, discussed openly and publicly so as to take all points of view and all facts into account. It is the assumption of ethical inquiry that such discussion and reflection, taking place in an atmosphere of mutual trust, confidence, and impartiality, can do more to foster moral responsibility and moral intelligence in children than any system that merely acquaints them with "the rules" and then insists that they "do their duty."

In Chapter 9, we took the position that moral education could not be divorced from philosophical inquiry. We will not present a case in point by considering a particular ethical inquiry curriculum—one designed specifically for junior high school students. We will draw our examples from *Lisa* and the instructional manual that complements it, *Ethical Inquiry*.

Lisa is a novel in which children in a classroom community of inquiry struggle to develop techniques of reasoning that will enable them to demonstrate and defend their moral values. While they make considerable progress, they are frustrated to discover that the logical deductions they work out are contingent upon the truth of their premises. This leads the children, who are already impressed with the importance of consistency, to turn their attention to the problem of truth. The book, therefore, deals with the tension between these two major philosophical concerns: the need for consistency and the need for true premises as these apply to ethical reasoning.

The logic in *Lisa* presupposes familiarity with the sequence of logical ideas introduced in the curriculum for grades 5–6. In *Lisa*, however, the logic is now applied more concretely and specifically to moral situations in which the children in the book find themselves involved.

In helping children engage in ethical inquiry, it is important to work as much as possible with the language they themselves use and in the contexts in which they customarily use it. Such a structure must be emphasized because all terms of ethical inquiry (for example, *right*, *fair*, *just*) are "value laden," that is to say, they are permeated with the values derived from the approach of the person using those terms. Thus, when adults use moral terms, such terms carry with them adult values. Likewise, if the ethical inquiry of children is to be portrayed with integrity, then the terms children use have to be presented as imbued with children's values. We must ask ourselves, then, how children conceive of fairness, or rightness, or goodness, and we must pay particular attention to how they employ these terms, and to the contexts in which they employ them. It is true that children seldom *define* their terms, but they intimate their meanings nonetheless, and a careful listener can piece together the implied value-perspectives in the process of trying to understand the philosophical underpinnings of children's ideas. Thus, for example, instead of trying to reconcile the children's use of the term "right" in *Lisa* with ordinary adult usage, or with philosophical usage, it would be preferable to understand its use in this novel as consonant with the meanings intimated by the language of children themselves.

There are some major philosophical themes that run throughout *Lisa*. They are not necessarily the basic themes that underlie all ethical inquiry; a different novel dealing with ethical inquiry might treat a number of different philosophical issues. But in this particular novel twelve themes are of paramount importance: the relation of logic to ethics; consistency; the right and the fair; perfect and right; free will and determinism; natural; change and growth; truth; caring; standards and rules; questions and answers; and thinking and thinking for oneself in ethical inquiry.

The Relation of Logic to Ethics

Moral education can be a very risky venture. The dangers that ordinarily accrue to the taking of extreme positions are here magnified many times. Different people see morality differently. There are those for whom moral conduct is not a matter of thoughtfulness or reflection at all; they see it as a matter of conscience or duty or love. On the other hand, there are those who adopt logic with a vengeance, and seek to make all moral decisions into a mere matter of deducing conclusions from premises. A teacher who adopts the first position, that moral education is a matter of conscience, duty, or love, will find that she has little to *educate* with—she can only indoctrinate, offer examples, or preach. Of these various stances, only modelling—offering examples—is a legitimate part of education, since to educate is to help children by equipping them with the procedures that will enable them most effectively to explore and understand the subject matter under discussion, to the end that they can think for themselves about the issues that that subject presupposes. Those who indoctrinate are not really interested in open, public discussion or in helping children discover their own answers; those who indoctrinate already know the answers and they want children to believe as they do.

The teacher who attempts to solve ethical problems by means of logical demonstration may have some plausibility, for it will be found that all such problems have some aspects that yield to logical analysis. Unfortunately, these logical aspects are far from being the whole of most moral problems. Logical demonstrations, consequently, deal effectively with certain aspects of the matter but leave the remainder untouched. We would certainly not want to deny that logic has value for ethical inquiry; but one cannot read *Lisa* carefully without recognizing that sense of despondency that the children have throughout the book as they realize that logic in and of itself is not enough when doing moral inquiry.

Then, a teacher might ask, why is there so much logic in the book? Do I and my students have to go through the process of mastering it just to find out that it is useless? The fact is that discussions in ethics, as much as any other discussions, must be careful, scrupulous, rigorous, and disciplined. Those who wish to state a case must marshal their argument in a efficient and coherent fashion. They must demonstrate clear understanding of their assumptions and a clear understanding of how to move logically from those assumptions to their conclusions. There is no discipline, other than logic, that can teach people how to do these things effectively. Just because logic will not give you the ethical solution you seek does not mean that you can dispense with it altogether. It remains one of the most powerful tools in the hands of those who would like reason to prevail among human beings and who would like to see the establishment of a rational society. If we had no logic, such goals would not be meaningful.

Consistency

Throughout both *Harry* and *Lisa*, but particularly in the first several chapters of *Lisa*, there is an emphasis upon consistency as a basic criterion of all reasoning. Consistency is generally considered a fundamental characteristic of all discourse and communication. Even those who wish to write disparagingly of consistency find themselves constrained to presuppose it in their writing.

As important as consistency is, you will note that the children in *Lisa* before long begin to recognize its complexity. For example, they condone Mark's behavior when he tells the truth about his sister's whereabouts, although shortly before he had answered the same question in a very misleading way. The children perceive that in one situation an honest answer was called for, whereas, in the other, an honest answer would have been inappropriate since it would have resulted in possible harm to his sister. The question then arises whether Mark has in fact been guilty of inconsistency. We would suggest that he has been no more inconsistent than a doctor who decides that one case warrants an operation and another does not. The question is: what does the doctor take into account when he makes these different decisions? In both cases, he holds himself scrupulously to the notion of correct medical procedure. If an operation is indicated in one case but not in the other, the doctor realizes that this is no cause for alarm at all and that he has in no way violated proper medical practice in coming to these two opposed recommendations. Likewise, the children in the episode with Mark and Maria are not disturbed that when they have taken everything into account, including the motives of the people who want to know about Maria's whereabouts and the consequences that both honest and dishonest answers would bring about, that Mark acted in the way he did. They have confidence in their procedures, which are the procedures of ethical inquiry.

The procedures of ethical inquiry should not be confused with what some people think of as absolute moral principles—for example, that one should always do what would be appropriate for all people to do in similar circumstances, or that one should always seek in one's conduct the greatest happiness for the greatest number. These "principles" can function as useful generalizations from past experience; as such, they can be helpful as possible guides to future conduct. But they are not unfailingly reliable. What the children in *Harry* and *Lisa* exemplify is a commitment to the search for ethical understanding. They do not seem to exhibit a conscious allegiance to such notions as duty or love or justice, although they may behave dutifully, lovingly, and justly. What guides them in their quest is not a set of ideal values but a commitment to the procedures of ethical inquiry.

The role of a classroom teacher is to help the students understand more clearly what this commitment involves and what ethical inquiry involves. Further, to the extent that a teacher can encourage them to practice this inquiry in their everyday life, she successfully achieves the main aim of the program.

Children are very ready to recognize that special cases require special solutions. They will insist vehemently that teachers should treat all students alike and yet, if a child with a disability is part of the class and therefore gets different treatment, they can understand and accept it, because the different treatment is justified by the differences in the children's situations. This obviously requires that children possess the capacity to perceive similarities and differences. If the child's disability is not perceived, then the teacher's actions appear unfair. Thus, another objective of this course is to help children read situations accurately so that they are aware of relevant similarities and differences. One of the objectives of a moral education program is to help children perceive situations accurately and to make sound moral judgments. For example, if a teacher were to ask the children in her class if cruelty is wrong, possibly they would all agree, although such agreement may not be very important. If they were presented with a situation in which one student was punished and claimed that he was being treated cruelly, however, the question would then be whether what happened to the child was in fact an instance of cruelty. Logic would help us to see

All cruelty is wrong.
This is a case of cruelty.
Therefore, this case is wrong.

We may all accept the first premise just as we may accept the premise that all love is good, all justice is good, and so on. But the real heart of ethics is in trying to determine the factual second premise. Was this *in fact* an instance of cruelty? If so, it was wrong. But, in fact, was it? And here only sensitivity in our judgment—only the ability to perceive and read the situation in all its complexity—can help us. You need the syllogism to get from the particular judgment to the conclusion, but the syllogism is only a tool. Without the ability to read the situation, you have nothing. The heart of the issue is in the *perception* of that second premise. And the perception takes time to develop. The novel aims to help, the dialogue with one's classmates helps, the role of the teacher in encouraging children to master the procedures of ethical inquiry helps, and attention to the everyday practice of the children in their school situation helps.

The Right and the Fair

Earlier we observed that our treatment of such notions as right and fair are rooted in what is intimated by children's everyday language. In the case of fairness, children's usage does not seem very dissimilar from adult usage. When Lisa and her friends talk about what is fair, they seem to mean that people in similar situations should be treated similarly and, to the extent that the situation is different, to that extent their treatment should be different. Thus there are times when it is quite relevant to ask, "What if everyone were to act that way?" Such a question assumes a basic similarity among people and their situations. If this assumption holds, then it is quite appropriate to raise the key questions of fairness. "What if everyone were to act that way?" and "What if everyone were to be treated that way?"

But as Lisa very early points out, not all situations are such that their similarity can be presupposed. There are matters of one's personal life or life style in which we assume that we are free to express our individuality as we please. In these matters, what we do neither harms nor places an obligation upon others, and what others do neither harms nor places an obligation upon us. In matters of life style, it is our own decision whether we want to be conformists or nonconformists. What criteria guide us in the making of such judgments? If it is not fairness, what can it be? The term that Lisa and her friends make use of is the term "right." They apply it very broadly so that it often encompasses nonmoral usages, as well as moral ones: a dress is not "right" for Lisa and Marty maintains that he alone can decide the "right" girl for him. "Right" is being used here to mean compatible with one's life style. What is right is what fits harmoniously into the totality of one's existence. Lisa raises the question: "What is right for *me*?" not merely "what is right?" just as the children in the novel will raise the question, "What is the difference between thinking and thinking *for oneself*?" The children in *Lisa* do not take for granted that thinking for oneself is identical with thinking. Likewise, they do not take for granted that what is right is identical with what is fair.*

Perfect and Right

When Lisa and her friends use the word "perfect," they assume an understanding of the way they employ the word "right." An individual act is right when it fits harmoniously into a person's life style, that is, that area of our lives with regard to which we are free to make our own decisions without being concerned as to whether or not they are fair to others. A situation in which *everything* were right would be perfect. Children do not often use words like wholeness, gestalt, completeness, fulfillment, totality, and other

*If you are curious as to the philosophical thinking to which the usage of Lisa and her friends corresponds (although not utilizing the same terminology), we would suggest you consult John Stuart Mill's *On Liberty*, in which a very sharp distinction is drawn between those obligations we have to society and the freedom we have in our own personal lives to judge what is right for ourselves. A more difficult but still relevant and useful source would be *The Ground and Nature of the Right* by C. I. Lewis. Also, for a more general approach to the theory of ethical inquiry, we suggest John Dewey's *Theory of the Moral Life*. (For more on the distinction between right and fair as it relates to *harm* in *Lisa*, see chapter 4, leading idea 12, of the manual.)

similar adult phrases that imply the desirability of unifying the various strands of one's experience into a seamless whole. The fact that children lack the varied vocabulary of adults does not mean that they are insensitive to the many ways in which experience can fall short of harmony and completeness.

Children can be acutely aware of the shortcomings of a picnic or the shortcomings of a birthday party, and might say, "it's just not right," or some other expression meaning that in some respect it fell short of conpleteness. Many children are disturbed by the fragmentation in their lives. Thus one of the aims of the philosophy for children program is to help children see connections between various parts of their lives, and to find ways of bringing these strands into harmony. Lisa's father points this out when he says, "Sometimes when we can't find the right connections, we have to make them."

Free Will and Determinism

The topic of free will versus determinism is probably one that seldom arises in the ordinary experience of elementary school children. As they approach adolescence and are increasingly concerned with the development of their own individuality, however, the question of just how free and just how determined they are begins to manifest itself in their concern over just what is in their power and what is not. This distinction can have far-reaching consequences for one's ethical outlook. That which is not in my power, I cannot change, and I bear no responsibility for. It is especially beyond my power to affect it if it is completely determined. On the other hand, that which is within my power, I *am* responsible for. I can modify it, alter it, change it—but then I must accept whatever credit or blame may accrue as a result of what I have done. We often say to children, "Don't cry over spilt milk," meaning that it is not in their power to change the past. What is done is done, so accept it and work from here. Gradually the child begins to realize that there is a world that goes on around him and independently of him, a world in which things happen that are beyond his or anyone's power to change. On the other hand, he also begins to realize that there are things within his power to affect, and it is here that the conception of "right" plays an important role. Children become concerned with the question of what behavior is right for them. Just as they are becoming aware that some actions are right, they are becoming aware that some actions of theirs are *voluntary* and that there are at least some aspects of their lives in which they are free of external coercion. This is as yet a very crude notion of freedom for the adolescent and has a long way to develop. Freedom at this time is "where I am free from external control." Only gradually will the children begin to develop a more sophisticated notion of freedom in which their freedom resides not merely in that area that is out of the reach of others, but in their use of their powers to affect the lives of others in a way that would be creative and liberating for all.

In teaching this program, one of your goals should be to help children move from this very crude notion of freedom that begins to dawn on them in early adolescence to a more enlightened conception that includes not only their own autonomy but deliberation with others as well. One does not help children achieve this by telling them about it. Rather, one must involve them in a process that of its very nature moves them from one conception of freedom to another.

The methodology of doing philosophy is such a process. One can observe the transition simply by watching the growth of dialogue in the classroom. It is normal to expect in the beginning that the students will participate as individuals, each wanting to speak his or her idea and probably doing very little listening. As they see it, they are exercising their freedom, their right to say what they think. Their focus in all likelihood is on what they say. As the course proceeds, they should begin to shift the focus from themselves and their ideas to building cooperatively on the ideas of all the members of the classroom.

This is an observable change that you can even measure. But the more important changes will be invisible. Development of greater tolerance, clarity in their thinking, development of heightened attention and keener perception, better organization of their values and ideas, greater sensitivity to meanings of personal experiences and the world around them, a sense of the preciousness of other people, an understanding of social institutions and how they operate—all of these deepenings occur sometimes with very little measurable indication. The only sign is often the *quality* of the dialogue, the *quality* of the maturity that is beginning to manifest itself.

Natural

Another theme that runs throughout *Lisa* is the theme that is expressed in the question, "What is natural?" On the one hand, young adolescents are becoming very keenly aware of convention, of the pressures to conform to etiquette, to social disciplines of one form or another. On the other hand, they are becoming aware of their own biological drives and needs, which at times come to be very much in conflict with convention. The growth of the self is associated with the Romantic aura in which one persuades oneself that, to be true to oneself, one must be natural, whereas to assent to convention or custom or tradition is to yield to artifice and inauthenticity. Thus "the natural" becomes a touchstone in a period of very great turmoil. Children who are not yet sure of the precise role they would like to play in life are experimenting by playing many roles and trying out many different possible forms of behavior. They dream of different occupations, different lives, to the point where they are no longer sure who they are, and as a result one of the major preoccupations of adolescents is with the question of their own sincerity. "Who is the real me? Am I being true to myself? What is natural for me to do? become the important questions in their lives.

On the one hand, we appeal to the natural as that which is healthy and sound. (Millie, for example, is very concerned that her grandmother's marrying a man fifteen years younger than herself is not natural.) On the other hand, what is natural is suspect to the adolescent. Our natural drives and natural appetites are things we might become frightened of and we start thinking about the need for control, maybe even suppression. In this sense, the natural in oneself is identified as something frightening. Either way, the natural becomes a focus of adolescent concern. It is for this reason that the theme runs through *Lisa*. One of the aims of the program is to encourage children to consider the natural in a way that creates enough of a distance so that the child is enabled to discuss and probe the issue in an objective, rational, and communal fashion.

Change and Growth

Students should be alerted to the question of whether characters in both *Harry* and *Lisa* give evidence of growth. Certainly they change, but mere change is not growth. The weather changes every day or every week but one could hardly say that the weather exhibits any kind of progress or improvement. Seasons change, but they do not grow. Growth is *cumulative*. There is *progressive enlargement*. Even the snowball rolling down the hill grows. But it only grows quantitatively, not qualitatively. It grows mechanically, not organically. Growth in a human being would involve maturation, ripening, deepening of understanding, greater richness of modes of experiencing the world. In the cases of Millie, Harry, and Lisa, growth is very marked. But what about some of the other characters? What about Fran and Mark? What about Mr. Stottlemeier or Mrs. Terry? What about Mr. Partridge? Or Mr. Spence? (Obviously, growth is not limited just to children.)

Students, however, may point out that growth is not necessarily an unmixed blessing—there can be growth of pollution, there can be growth of crime, and there can be growth of many other things that we consider very bad. To this a teacher can reply that, as they themselves mature, their capacity of judgment improves, and they can more and more readily distinguish an improvement from a mere increase. The teacher can ask the students questions designed to help them see the difference between something that is merely bigger and something that is better. Is a higher-paying job necessarily a better job? Is a bigger house necessarily a better house? Is a bigger country necessarily a better country? Are you happier going ten miles an hour or five miles an hour? Is it better to swallow a drop of poison or a gallon of poison? As children develop clearer perceptions of what is involved in ethical inquiry, they are better able to deal with questions of this sort and they will be able to see that, while growth is a powerful concept and very valuable for many purposes, it itself, like any other individual concept, cannot be accepted uncritically.

Truth

From its very beginning, philosophy has been depicted as a quest or a search. Philosophers have pictured themselves as seekers of wisdom or as lovers of wisdom—but always as undogmatic, especially when it comes to the question of the nature of truth. Philosophers are particularly puzzled by the problem of truth, because, even if they were to come up with a theory of truth, they are not quite sure by what means they could tell if it were true. To use their own theory and their own criteria would seem to be circular. This does not mean that philosophers do not believe in truth. It merely means that they find the notion a very perplexing one, and will sometimes seek to substitute for the word "truth" phrases that appear to them more manageable, such as "warranted assertion," "reliable statement," "verifiable description," and so on. Even philosophers for whom truth has become an unattainable ideal may continue to find it a useful notion, just as mariners who know they will never reach the North Star continue to guide themselves by it in their navigation.

Likewise, the problem of truth haunts the children in *Harry* and *Lisa*. In the very first chapter of *Harry*, they find themselves enmeshed in the problem because Harry proclaims that, "if you take a true sentence and turn it around, it becomes false." Even if we gently correct Harry on this point and argue that *in most cases* turning a sentence that begins with "all" around will cause it to become false, for there are certain exceptional cases where it remains true, we can do so only by ourselves assuming that there are such things as truth and falsity.

Although the urgency of the issue subsides in the succeeding chapters of *Harry*, the problem surfaces again in the second half of *Lisa*. But now the matter has become far more pointed and urgent. The children realize that their entire enterprise is now hanging precariously in the balance. The procedures of inference that they have discovered work with false sentences as well as with true ones. (Indeed, from a false sentence it is apparent that *anything* can be inferred.) Thus, logic by itself is empty. It needs to be supplemented by criteria for distinguishing truth from falsity. Hence, in the last five chapters of *Lisa*, the children turn their attention to the problem of truth.

Naturally, the problem of truth is not solved in those last five chapters. But the children do come up with a number of approaches to the problem of truth, and these are gradually refined into several more explicit theories of truth. At the end of the book it remains uncertain whether any, all, or perhaps none of these theories can claim the title of being the true theory of truth. The children offer them to one another as plausible candidates, and students can reflect upon these theories to determine their plausibility for themselves.

Caring

Caring is more of an implicit than explicit theme that runs through *Harry* and *Lisa*. The children exhibit it more than they talk about it. The theme of caring can be traced on a number of levels in both novels. On one level, it reveals itself in the continuity of dialogue in which the children continually discuss issues of mutual importance while retaining respect for one another's points of view. This is not typical of people who are uncaring. As the children discover one another's perspectives and share in one another's experiences, they come to care about one another's values and to appreciate each other's uniqueness. Thus they construct through dialogue a small community whose commitment is to inquiry and whose members are caring participants in that community.

On the second level, the children in *Harry* and *Lisa* are caring in the sense that they engage seriously in philosophical inquiry. They are concerned with outcomes: what they are doing is not merely a game to them. It is something meaningful and important, and they exhibit their seriousness in the way they go about their probing. Children in a classroom are not likely to begin a course in philosophy with this same degree of seriousness. There are those among them who might tend to be cynical or superficial or facetious and use the philosophy sessions as a chance to show off or treat it as a game. But if the sessions are productive, these immature kinds of conduct will tend to diminish. The more meaning that emerges out of these discussions for the students, the more they will manifest a serious attitude to the inquiry itself.

Until that happens, they are not doing philosophy. However, it works two ways. Students will care about philosophy if the teacher cares enough about them to make it relevant to their lives. Thus, in the beginning, the teacher should try to get a sense of the students' interests and try to deal with issues that will be meaningful to them.

On still another level, the theme of caring reveals itself in the attention that the children give to the procedures of philosophical inquiry itself and the rigor that these procedures involve. They are not satisfied with mental slovenliness, and gradually develop a sense of revulsion for sloppiness in reasoning. In part, this is because they are good craftsmen and they love the tools with which they work, as a carpenter loves his saw and hammer. But it is also because they appreciate the methodology of inquiry. You see the same concern with methodology in the practitioners of the law in any society. They are not so much concerned about this verdict or that verdict as they are about due process and the improvement of due process. They care about law as an institution, as a set of procedures that represents a common public methodology for dealing with problems. In their own modest way, the children in *Lisa* are trying to do the same thing. They are trying to devise a methodology for dealing with ethical problems, one that will be open, public, and rational. Essentially what distinguishes them as morally responsible individuals is their care for the procedure, and their genuine concern to put it into practice.

Standards and Rules

Whether it is in a game of baseball or in a game for making up sentences that they themselves have devised or in a philosophical discussion at home over the dinner table, the children in *Lisa* are shown dealing with or talking about the problem of rules. To many people, rules are not a problem; they see rules as permanent, universal, and not to be broken. But the children in the novel are not so sure this is so. Can we always be sure that the rules given us are the best rules for dealing with the issue at hand? The children in *Lisa* are not disrespectful of authority when they raise a question as to the status of rules; it is simply that they feel more inclined to go along with rules that they understand rather than with rules they do not understand, and they see no harm in asking for explanations.

The struggle to understand the nature of rules in *Lisa* is only partially successful. The children do not make as much progress with it as they do in the other areas they explore. At times, as in the baseball game and in the "It Figures" game, they glimpse the possibility that rules are simply conventions—stipulations that are socially agreed upon for the common good. At other times, they simply perceive that some rules are generalizations based upon experience. (The burnt child who shuns the fire does so on the basis of a practical rule derived from experience.) At still other times they see rules as traditional recipes for conduct that may or may not prove successful in a given situation (for example, the rules of etiquette).

The most explicit discussion of rules occurs when the Jahorski family contrasts rules with standards in chapter 10, where it is remarked by one of the family that "rules tell you how to act . . . , a standard is a measure you use when you judge." In other words, one obeys a rule but one does not obey a standard. A standard is a criterion by means of which one can distinguish one kind of thing from another or tell the better from the worse. As children become practiced in distinguishing rules from standards, they will begin to realize that rules too must be judged, and that we judge them by certain standards. These standards in turn must be appraised by still other criteria. There is not necessarily any ultimate standard or criterion. But understanding of the process of judgment is something that the children in *Lisa* seek, because it is a process, they think, that will be easier to live with if they understand it than if they do not.

No mention is made of the term "principles" in *Lisa*. This does not mean that the children are unconcerned with moral principles, but rather that they do not identify them in so many words. They are very much interested in such questions as what is fair, what is right, what is true, but in a very concrete way. They treat them as questions to be discussed and inquired into within the context of particular situations, not as ultimate or absolute values divorced from their everyday experience. Thus, instead of focusing on abstract principles such as justice or goodness or beauty, they seem more concerned with direct experiences in the form of making, saying, and doing. This is not to say that the principles do not enter into their thinking. But they enter in as guiding ideals in their everyday behavior.

Questions and Answers

Questioning is a type of behavior that is often found in classrooms. Sometimes it is engaged in only by teachers, sometimes only by students and sometimes by both. If we examine questioning more closely, we find that it comprises a fairly large family with many distinct varieties, of which we can distinguish a few.

Sometimes questions are purely rhetorical ("Why did Napoleon want to be emperor? I'll tell you why Napoleon wanted to be emperor!") The person who asks such a question has no intention of waiting for your answer since he is already prepared to tell you the answer he has in mind. It is a device to pique the curiosity of the listener in the inquiry.

Another well-known form of questioning involves the asking of so-called "leading questions." These are often put in negative form, such as "wouldn't it be a good idea if we all settled down and did our exercises now?" or "It's time for a break, isn't it?" The leading question sets the stage in such a way as to direct the listener to come out with some information that is needed for the discussion to get started. For example, a teacher might begin one of the sessions asking the children, "Now you'd agree that Lisa and her mother have not seen eye to eye throughout the whole book, wouldn't you?" This is a leading question, but it may serve as an efficient way of initiating a discussion of eliciting the grounds of agreement with which the discussion can begin. The leading question is pernicious where it cuts off inquiry, but it can be useful where it is used to *initiate* a discussion.

Leading questions can be sharply distinguished from searching questions. Rhetorical and leading questions are those to which the questioner already knows the answer, or a least thinks he does. In the case of searching questions, the questioner himself does not know the answer to his own question, but raises it anyhow in order to provoke discussion or to see where such discussion may lead. The questioner may be aware that there are certain conventional or well-accepted answers to his question, but he may have doubts about such answers, and may want to elicit the underlying assumptions that such conventional answers rest upon. The purpose of his questioning is therefore exploratory.

Exploratory questions may lead to the discovery that the conventional answers were right after all. Or they may lead to the discovery that the whole issue is in need of reformulation—that the very terms in which we have been thinking need to be redefined. Or, finally, exploratory questions may uncover far-reaching problematical situations that might have been undetected had not the searching question thrown light on what had long been concealed because everyone had taken it for granted.

An illustration of the searching kind of thought that leads to a redefinition of terms can be found in chapter 14 of *Harry*, where Fran, very much aware of how people conventionally employ the word "savages," contrasts the way people economize (produce and distribute goods) in different parts of the world, and offers this as proof that the conventional understanding of the word "savages" is unenlightening. Likewise, in chapter 9, when Mr. Partridge refers to Mr. Spence as "a credit to his race," Fran calls attention to the disparaging suggestion implicit in the phrase. In these instances, what Fran is doing is calling for a fresh look at the way we define the terms we use.

In Harry's discussions with his father, there is further probing of the nature of questioning. They conclude that raising a question may be something like finding the tip of an iceberg: one becomes aware that there is a great deal more beneath the surface of what one has discovered. Raising a question about why Mr. Terry died in chapter 9 of *Lisa* leads to a discussion of the relationship between illness and unemployment. That, in turn, leads to a discussion of the nature of unemployment in modern industrial society. So the original question triggers an inquiry into underlying socio-economic problems that are responsible for day-to-day events in our lives.

You will by now have noticed that the stress in this course is on questions rather than answers. It is not that answering is unimportant, but that the kind of answering a teacher wants to promote is the kind that both moves the dialogue or inquiry along and at the same time provokes still further dialogue. In philosophy, a teacher is not looking for terminal answers. If anything, he should be wary of them. Like a terminal illness, a terminal answer gives you no options. Supposing you were to say, "Everything is known." Immediately I would have to shrug and say, "There is no reason to find out anything for myself. Just tell me and I'll memorize it." Methodologically, your answer, "everything is known," has shut off further inquiry. A good answer is instead like a candle in the dark. It provides both light and mystery. It should, of course, illuminate, while at the same time reveal the contours of the unknown so that the listener can surmise that there is much more to be investigated and learned.

Thinking and Thinking for Oneself in Ethical Inquiry

Suppose you are a student and you go to science class and you are taught about color, and how color is a function of light vibrations, and how different frequencies of light vibrations produce different color experiences. In another portion of the science course you study sounds and their relation to air vibrations. Such understanding is valuable, but it is quite different from what you do in an art class, where you learn to paint using color, or in a music class, where you learn to play music by arranging sounds. The artist makes visual judgments; the composer makes auditory judgments and as they proceed in their creative endeavors, they generate complex works of art, such as paintings or sonatas. Obviously, there is a great deal of difference between the physicist concerned with the science of color and the artist who thinks in terms of colors in order to create a colorful work of art. Likewise, there is an important difference between an objective understanding of sound and the personal selection of sound through a series of choices so as to compose a work of music.

In the same fashion, it is possible to contrast thinking and thinking for oneself. We can study the processes of thinking in a detached, impersonal, and objective fashion. We can consider the criteria of good thinking (as established by logic), and apply these to any form of discourse. But it is quite another matter to reflect upon and bring to utterance our own personal perspective. In this sense, thinking for oneself involves a reflection upon one's own experience and upon one's own situation in the world. It requires appraisal of one's own values and in effect of one's own identity. It further involves a search for more and more reliable criteria so that the judgments one makes in the course of one's life can rest upon a firm and solid foundation.

Thinking and thinking for oneself are both necessary in any program of ethical inquiry. The encouragement of better thinking requires that children become aware of the logical patterns of reasoning, develop the capacity to read situations, learn to take all facts into account before making judgments, learn to classify and make distinctions, learn to generalize and develop hypotheses where appropriate—all these being characteristics of good thinking. On the other hand, that is not all there is to moral judgments. One must have a clear perception of oneself and the contents of one's consciousness. Since a sense of personal identity is an indispensable part of every moral judgment, one has to develop one's own sense of proportion—that is to say, develop an awareness of those matters that are of importance to oneself as distinguished from those that are not. Likewise, one has to have some feeling for one's own powers and capacities so as to be able to distinguish what may lie within one's powers to perform and what may be beyond those powers. Finally, thinking for oneself —or making moral judgments—involves developing a sense of personal direction towards the goals that one foresees, however dimly, for oneself. This is not to imply that the moral life is a journey by an individual with a fixed personal identity towards certain fixed and unalterable goals. It is rather that the ends that at any one time we hold to be desirable are held tentatively, and the self at any one time is always in a process of transition, contingent upon the means that are available to us to achieve the goals that are sought. Thus, the availability of means conditions and modifies our ideals and objectives, just as, conversely, the ends we have in view control the way we search for means to employ, and the selves that we are in process of becoming.

What thinking for oneself does is give guidance and regulation and direction to what would otherwise be a fluid and amorphous self with no continuity and no sense of unity. Each of us is subject to enormous stresses that fragmentize our world and disperse our energies in countless directions. To subject children to instructional processes that would result in helping them to think, without helping them to think for themselves, is neither good moral education nor good education in general. If the philosophy for children program alerts us to anything it is to the need to bring into education this component of thinking for oneself that is too often in danger of being lost sight of completely.

Appendixes

Appendix A

THE REFORM OF TEACHER EDUCATION

A philosophy for children program such as has been described in this volume will not be successful unless teachers competent to teach it begin to appear in the elementary classroom. But improvement of the quality of teachers will not take place unless the schools of education can attract young people with richer resources than are presently being attracted into the profession. This, in turn, will not occur unless teacher preparation programs can satisfy the intellectual and creative needs of these young people, who presently are repelled by the lack of intellectual challenge in many teacher education programs.

But a teacher education program cannot be designed without first considering the general aims of education. Once we know at least in very broad terms what sort of education we want to provide children with, we can have a clearer idea of the way we want to prepare teachers to provide such an education. It is true that education should prepare children to deal effectively with the lives they will lead once their educational preparation has been completed. But such education should also be intrinsically satisfying and meaningful in itself. Its values, therefore, should be both instrumental and consummatory. One could say that the main aim of education, in the broadest sense, is the upgrading of children's life experience, rather than preparing them to accept a level of experience that makes no use or inadequate use of their potentials and talents.

As long as education is viewed as a matter of learning what is already known—the acquiring of knowledge that has been passed on from generation to generation—it is unlikely that education can play a significant role in the upgrading or enhancement of life experience. At best, it can merely enable education to continue at its present level. Even where children are said to discover knowledge, that knowledge is often conceived of as something pre-existent, a possession of the adult world to which children have gained access, rather than something that they have had a part in shaping. It is only when the focus of the educational process is shifted from learning to thinking that education comes to be seen as a cooperative process in which children are active participants whose creativity is enlisted along with their memories.

207

If what we want ultimately are thoughtful, inquisitive, imaginative, reasonable children, then thinking skills must be integrated into virtually every aspect of the elementary educational process. This in turn would require that teachers be educated in such a way as to enable them to teach subject areas into which thinking skills have been integrated.

The traditional purpose of education has been to instruct children in certain specific subjects. Given such an objective, it was appropriate to construct a teacher-education process along two parallel tracks: courses in subject areas were separated from courses in the teaching methodology of those subjects. Thus there were "content courses" and "methods courses." The content was for the child and the method was for the teacher. If the objective of education is broadened so that what we are aiming to produce are children who not only know a certain content but can think readily and effectively in terms of that content, then the educational process must be revised. If the integration of thinking skills into the subject areas were to be the desired approach, then the only way teachers could be prepared would be by means of an educational process itself containing subject areas into which thinking skills have been integrated. This would mean an end to the dichotomization of content and methods courses, although in no way would it involve a watering-down of the subject areas.

Thinking is generic: it comprises the performance of a vast variety of mental acts of which knowing is, of course, one. An aim education should set itself accordingly is the enhancement of skills among a broad range of mental activities, together with the knowledge of specific subject areas. This entails, for example, children's not merely learning historical facts, but learning to think historically as well. It means helping children to think scientifically rather than just knowing scientific facts, to think artistically rather than merely knowing specific works of art. This broadened objective is already present in certain educational areas: in foreign languages, for example, one may learn words and phrases, declensions and conjugations, but such knowledge is considered insufficient by language teachers. One is educated in a language only when one begins to think in the language itself.

This shift in educational emphasis should not be thought of as simply a change in pedagogical style. It involves a broadening of the entire educational process so that the acquisition of thinking skills is included in every subject area. This revision would constitute a response to a serious and deeply felt need in society for educators to address themselves more directly to the crisis in contemporary education. The evidence of national test scores may be interpreted as suggesting that children are refusing to cooperate in their education because they find education irrelevant and meaningless. What can be done to counteract this trend? There is no way in which adults can give meanings to children. Meanings cannot be dispensed. All that educators can do is to develop the thinking skills among children that will enable them to ferret out and grasp the meanings of the subject matters to which they are exposed, with the end result that they begin thinking in terms of those subject areas, rather than merely becoming knowledgeable about subjects that remain basically alien to them.

Thinking skills by themselves, however, are atomistic and undirected. An adequate teacher preparation curriculum would have to enable the prospective teacher to master these thinking skills while at the same time offering the student the opportunity to experience what it is to participate in a community of inquiry that is purposive and relevant. Thus, it is a prerequisite of a teacher education program that it be reflective and that it establish each classroom as a locus of inquiry and each class as a community to which such inquiry is important. One way to measure the success of a teacher education program would be to the extent that, once teachers are in the classroom, they encourage their own students to engage in inquiry, rather than only to learn the results of past inquiry in specific subject areas.

Teachers who are convinced that knowledge in their chosen discipline is already complete feel little need for inquiry. And inquiry cannot proceed unless there is a felt need to do so. It is evident, therefore, that a teacher-education program must convey both initially and throughout its duration a sense of the partiality, incompleteness, and precariousness of human knowledge. Unless this is done, the prospective teacher is not likely to possess that sense of wonder and that persistent, restless doubt that urges an individual to inquire and to belong to a comunity that devotes itself to inquiry. And if teachers do not possess this wonder and doubt, there is little chance that they will communicate it to their students.

There are several ways in which the curriculum of a teacher preparation program can accomplish these ends. One is to include an adequate number of courses that encourage the student to be more open, inquisitive, and intellectually adventurous. Philosophy and the arts can serve such a purpose. In these areas there is a commitment to originality and individuality of formulation as well as a welcoming of a variety of perspectives, which can be most useful in correcting the passivity that many students bring to their studies by the first year of college. Philosophy is always wondering; it is continuous wonder and continuous re-examination. The arts do not represent formalized knowledge at all, but explorations, discoveries, prizing of similarities and dissimilarities without any attempt to coordinate them into a system of knowledge. It must be understood, of course, that in presenting philosophy and the arts to prospective teachers, the stress must be on the *practice* of these enterprises *prior to* the study of the tradition. This is exactly the opposite of what is done in the current preparation of teachers. Usually they are exposed to the history of philosophy, the history of literature, the history of art, the history of music, before they are encouraged to practice any of these disciplines in a way suitable for working with children. Often this inhibits students from perceiving themselves as active inquirers. They can easily be overwhelmed by the accomplishments of the tradition. Unfortunately, they often proceed to ensure that the very same thing happens to their own students.

In sequencing the courses for a teacher education program one general guideline can be followed: practice before theory. If one is interested in educating challenging teachers, one should enable these prospective teachers to encounter the tradition in a context of ongoing practice. The tradition can then be viewed with some sense of proportion. To attempt to engage in practice after exposure to the tradition often results in the abandonment of one's efforts as amateurish, futile, and hopeless.

But this brings us specifically to the question of how teachers are to be prepared, not only to integrate philosophy into the present school curriculum, but to encourage children to think philosophically. Certainly, in the case of philosophy, the method by which adults are taught is no different from that to be employed in the teaching of children. Not every applicant for certification as a teacher is necessarily a promising candidate to teach children philosophy. At the risk of considerable oversimplification, we could say that the prospective elementary philosophy teacher should be one who enjoys both children and ideas. That is, such a person should have a strong empathy with children's needs and interests and should have a love of ideas for their own sake. Teachers who have these characteristics can be recognized as being particularly delighted by the joy children reveal in their discovery of the possibilities of philosophical discussions and the pleasure they take in encountering philosophical ideas.

Assuming such prospective teachers can be found—and it is our impression that the number of those who would qualify would turn out to be quite large—who would teach them? They would have to be people who would share with the prospective teachers the love of children and of ideas. They would have to have an understanding of the relationship of philosophy to their particular discipline and have mastered the dialogical pedagogy that is philosophy. Further, they would have to be adept at modifying the curricula of their specific discipline so as to integrate thinking skills into that discipline.

Goals of the Program

The teacher-education program that follows has as its goals:

    1. To produce superior classroom teachers who have strong sympathies

with children, who manifest a commitment to the process of inquiry and who reveal a love of ideas such as they would be capable of encouraging among their students.

2. To teach prospective teachers as much as possible by the same methods and in the same fashion as they would teach their own students.
3. To equip teachers with the thinking skills that they will in turn encourage in their pupils.
4. To ground prospective teachers in the major areas of humanistic achievement, encouraging them to think in terms of various subject matters so that they in turn can encourage their pupils to do the same.
5. To provide prospective teachers with an adequate understanding of both the actualities and possibilities of children's behavior.
6. To provide ample opportunities for the prospective teachers to work with children in classroom situations.

Means and Procedures

The development of thinking skills is a complex and delicate operation. Thinking skills cannot be brought about in a vacuum, that is to say, independent of any subject matter. On the other hand, too close an identification with a specific subject matter can inhibit the development of the thinking skill appropriate to that subject matter. This means that there has to be a discipline that consists primarily of concepts, preferably concepts that have been of substantial importance in the history of civilization, upon which prospective teachers and children alike can hone their developing cognitive skills. Philosophy and, in general, the intellectual dimensions of civilization offer this kind of disciplinary subject matter. Encouraging teachers to be versatile in philosophical inquiry provides them with that kind of intellectual flexibility and resourcefulness that they can then apply to any concrete subject matter. Hence, a strong core of philosophical courses is indispensable, coupled with an additional core of courses in specific thinking skills for children. It is for this reason that the model calls for 24 credits in philosophy and 24 credits in thinking skills.

One of the underlying assumptions of this teacher education program is that thinking is the internalization of dialogical inquiry. This means that there is no better way of encouraging children to think than to engage them in classroom discussions concerning issues that are of primary importance to them. It is only the intellectual give and take of conversation that one has with one's peers that can stimulate reflection. When the conversation is itself disciplined and productive, children will internalize it in the form of critical and logical reflection. Therefore, the teacher education process should involve the prospective teachers in emerging communities of inquiry, just as those teachers

Model of a Pre-Service Curriculum Leading to an MAT in Philosophy for Children

		Subject Area Sequence (62 credits)		Pedagogy (31 credits)	Philosophical Sequences (24 credits)		Electives (24 credits)
YEAR 1	FALL	History of Civilization I (3 credits)	Writing of Prose and Poetry (3 credits)	Introduction to Reflective Education	Philosophical Thinking Skills for Children I	History of Philosophy I	
	SPRING	History of Civilization II (3 credits)	Mathematics for Teachers (3 credits)	Children and Literature (2 credits) Practicum (1 credit)	Philosphical Thinking Skills for Children II	History of Philosophy II	
	SUMMER	Earth Science for Teachers (3 credits)	Music for Elementary Teachers (3 credits)	(Month of June in Residential Setting)			
YEAR 2	FALL	Physical Education for Elementary Teachers (2 credits)	Communication Skills for Teachers (3 credits)	Child Psychology	Scientific Thinking Skills for Children	Metaphysics	
	SPRING	American History (4 credits)		Adolescent Psychology (2 credits) Practicum (2 credits)	Value Thinking Skills for Children I: Ethics	Introduction to Philosophy of Science and Mathematics	
	SUMMER	Art for Elementary Teachers (3 credits)	Environmental Studies for Teachers (3 credits)	(Month of June in Residential Setting)			

FALL	History of Literature I (3 credits)	Anthropology and Ethnic Studies (2 credits) Sociology (2 credits)	Educational Psychology (language acquisition and psychosocial development)	Value Thinking Skills for Children II: Aesthetics	Theory of Knowledge
YEAR 3 **SPRING**	History of Literature II (3 credits)	Economics (2 credits) Political Science (2 credits)	Psychology of Teaching the Special Ed. Child (learning disabilities and gifted children)	Language Thinking Skills for Children	History of Ethical Thought
SUMMER	Biology for Elementary Teachers (3 credits)	Reflective Acting (2 credits) Dance for Elementary Teachers (2 credits)	(Month of June in Residential Setting)		
FALL	History of Art (3 credits)	History of Music (3 credits)	Seminar in Philosophy of Education	Social Thinking for Children	Philosophy of Art
YEAR 4 **SPRING**			Practice Teaching (6 credits)	Mathematical Thinking Skills for Children	Social and Political Philosophy
SUMMER	Astronomy for Teachers (2 credits)	Seminar in the Relation of Philosophy to Psychology and Education	(Month of June in Residential Setting)		

Total Number of Credits Needed for Graduation—165
Degree Granted: MAT in Philosophy for Children

when themselves teaching in the classroom will encourage their pupils to develop communities of inquiry. The commitment to inquiry is thus central to the performance of thinking activity. The formation of communities is indispensable to the pedagogy that is to foster such thinking activity.

The prospective teachers in this program would take 62 credits of traditional academic disciplines. These would involve a broad spectrum of humanities, science, social science, and creative as well as performing arts. In general, opportunities to engage in the practice of these disciplines would be afforded prior to the theoretical explanation of such disciplines, since the explanation only makes sense in the context of the doing.

Each specific content area would be taught to the prospective teacher in a manner such that the thinking skills appropriate to that content area would accompany the materials to be mastered. Whatever the discipline, students would be encouraged to search out underlying assumptions, guiding reasons, possible implications, and alternative criteria for evaluation. Both prospective teachers and eventual pupils would be encouraged to see the field as one of ongoing inquiry in which they can participate. Prospective teachers and children alike must be able to envision themselves as agents in the process of inquiry rather than as learners of an inquiry process that has been completed.

The pedagogical sequence (31 credits) would enable teachers to recognize the advantages of intellectual cooperation in the classroom, such as is provided by a community of inquiry. Courses in philosophy of education, psychology, and the relation of philosophy to psychology and education would serve as the groundwork for the prospective teacher's understanding of what he or she will be seeking to achieve when he or she encourages dialogical education.

Each student will also have an opportunity to take 24 credits of electives to gain depth in those areas in which he or she is most interested.

Specific Student Outcomes

Prospective teachers who successfully complete this program would be able to:

1. Organize communities of inquiry in their elementary school classrooms.
2. Conduct dialogue in the classroom in such a way as to develop children's reasoning skills.
3. Hear the philosophical dimensions of children's dialogue and encourage them to explore these areas with their classmates.
4. Demonstrate adequate grounding in humanities, science, social science, and creative as well as performing arts, so as to bring these to bear upon the inquiries of elementary school children.

5. Model reflective inquiry in the classroom.
6. Demonstrate a mastery of such logic as is indispensable for promoting the reasoning skills of children.
7. Manifest an understanding of the history of philosophy and how it relates to children's inquiry.
8. Manifest an understanding of children, how they think, feel, and interrelate with each other, as well as with adults.
9. Manifest an understanding of the educational process, its history, its foundations, and its potential for developing thoughtful and reasonable children.

Admission Selection

Since this program puts a strong emphasis on prospective teachers' appreciation of the world of ideas, coupled with a strong empathy with children's needs and interests, the selection process would haave to be quite stringent. Guidance counselors throughout the country would need to be alerted to the opportunities for those of their high school seniors who manifest suitable motivation and abilities for success in this program. Screening would then take place among applicants so as to select the most promising candidates. This screening would involve a written essay as well as review of academic credentials and any other evidence of potential for success.

Academic Requirements for the Degree

Candidates for the MAT degree should have successfully completed 165 credits in various subject areas, pedagogy, thinking skills, and philosophy. Each student would be permitted to take 24 credits of electives so as to have the opportunity to explore alternative areas or concentrate on another subject of their choice. Each student would be expected to attend the normal school year plus one residential month each summer.

Appendix B

EXPERIMENTAL RESEARCH IN
PHILOSOPHY FOR CHILDREN

Can the philosophy for children program be demonstrated to be educationally significant? The first effort to answer these questions experimentally occurred in 1970. The hypothesis was that children needed help to improve their reasoning, and that such an improvement would in turn reflect itself in the enhancement of other academic skills. Further, it was hypothesized that to improve children's reasoning would be to improve their capacity to look for meaning in what they do. The 1970 experiment demonstrated that a nine-week program could produce impressive gains not only in reasoning but in reading as well. These reading gains remained highly significant two-and-a-half years later. This is a summary of the 1970 experiment:

> The first experiment with a Philosophy for Children program was carried out in 1970 by Lipman and Bierman, by means of a true field experiment in Montclair, New Jersey. The aim of the study was to determine the feasibility of teaching reasoning to fifth-grade children. It was carried out in an economically and racially heterogeneous school, two groups of 20 children each having been established by randomization. The control group was assigned to a social studies experiment. The experimental group held a total of 18 40-minute sessions over 9 weeks.
> Both groups were initially tested on the CTMM (1963 Revision Long Form). No significant differences appeared in the pretest. At the end of the 9 weeks, both groups were tested on the Short Form. The pilot group showed significant gains over the control group in the area of logic and logical reasoning ($p < .01$). The computed mental ages (as related to logical reasoning) were 13 years 11 months for the experimental group and 11 years 8 months for the control group (a gain of 27 months.)
> To determine if the experimental program might have had a lasting transfer effect, the reading scores on the Iowa tests taken by the students prior to the experiment and two years afterwards were examined. The differences between the two groups on reading was now significantly different ($p < .01$). (It was determined that the research design 2½ years later was still valid.) Bierman concludes that "the experiment conducted positively affected the reading scores of the students two and a half years later." *

While the 1970 experiment showed impressive gains in reasoning and reading, it had to be taken into account that the course was taught by a professor of

---

*Philosophy for Children," *Metaphilosophy* 7, no. 1 (Jan. 1976).

philosophy and not by a regular classroom teacher. The next step, therefore, was to arrange an experiment in which regular classroom teachers would be trained to encourage philosophical thinking in their own classrooms. This experiment was carried out in 1975, having been designed and evaluated by Ms. Hope Haas of the Institute for Cognitive Studies, Rutgers University. This is a summary of the results of that experiment:

> The Newark experiment employed Solomon's quasi-experimental four group design, which consists of two experimental and two control groups as the basic unit. Aside from the traditional control, this design controls for the effects of pretesting. The eight experimental classes in Newark comprised 200 students in two schools (Miller Street and Morton Street). The control group also comprised 200 students in two other schools.
>
> On the sixth-grade level, in Newark, there was a multi-faceted improvement. Sixth-graders made substantial improvements in reading, significant improvements in critical thinking involving listening, as well as highly significant gains with regard to interpersonal relationships. Fifth-graders showed significant improvement in their attitudes toward intellectual freedom. The combined fifth and sixth grades showed a significant improvement in reading (p was less than .02), the children in the experimental classes gaining an average of eight months in reading ability against five months for the control group. Some of the experimental classes had even more dramatic gains. One class jumped 2½ years, another, a year and four months.
>
> Unlike the other tests, which were administered by Ms. Haas of Rutgers, the reading scores were derived from the Metropolitan Achievement Tests, which are administered every year by the Newark school system. The scores used were those from the 1974 and 1975 administrations of the intermediate level MAT, a test which covers grades 5.0–6.9, and comes in alternate forms F and G. Students were tested with form G in 1974 and form F in 1975. The test taps several specific skills which have been identified as being critical components of the reading process:
>
> 1. ability to recognize the main idea of a reading passage;
> 2. ability to draw correct inferences from the material presented;
> 3. ability to perceive and understand details; and
> 4. ability to recognize the correct meaning of words in the context of the passage.
>
> Results in other categories tested were inconclusive. These included curiosity, logical thinking, and the use of analytical and creative questions. Since the 1970 pilot project, taught by a college logic instructor, showed significant improvement in logical reasoning, it would appear that the philosophy for children course is highly teacher-related. Teachers who stress reading can produce significant improvements in reading with it, while a teacher who stresses reasoning can produce significant improvement in reasoning using the materials.*

We would also like to summarize here the results of another experiment that has been brought to our attention by a researcher using our materials in an ex-

---

*Hope J. Haas, "Philosophical Thinking in the Elementary Schools: An Evaluation of the Education Program Philosophy for Children," unpub. mimeo., Institute for Cognitive Studies, Rutgers University, 1976.

perimental setting, Charlann Simon, speech-language clinician at the Devereux Day School, Scottsdale, Arizona, an educational facility for learning disabled and emotionally handicapped students.

In the fall of 1977, five boys were selected to participate in a philosophy for children seminar. The boys ranged in age from 11 to 16. Three controls were chosen. The mean IQ for the experimental group was 93, and for the control group, 102. Prior to entry into the experimental and control groups, the boys were given the following tests: CTMM Inference Subtest, Levels II and III, Auditory Association Subtest, ITPA, and Visual Association Subtest, ITPA. The five experimental subjects attended approximately 50 30-minute sessions from October 1977 and May 1978. The program used was the *Stottlemeier* program.

Pretests indicated the two populations were not significantly different on the initial test battery. On the pre and post test, the levels of significance were:

	Pre	Post
Level II (Inferences)	.55	.06
Level III (Inferences)	.63	.10
Auditory Association	.83	.20
Visual Association	.82	.10

Both groups improved, but the experimentals improved significantly more. Although the control group had advantages of age and IQ, the experimental group made greater gains in critical thinking skills. For example, while the control group made a 13% gain on the CTMMT-II Inferences test, the experimental group made a 35% gain.

By employing a t-test, it was possible to determine that participation in the group not only affected the absolute performance, but that the improvement pre-/post-testing was different to the following levels of significance:

Level II (Inferences)	.033
Level III (Inferences)	.068
Auditory Association	.042
Visual Association	.223

The research study was developed to test the validity of the Lipman and Sharp (1974) program and to assess whether clinician time should continue to be allotted to guiding the program. The data indicate the program is valid, and the degree of improvement in critical thinking skills merits the continuation of the philosophy for children program.*

Following the 1975 Newark experiment, the Educational Testing Service, Princeton, New Jersey, was engaged to design, monitor, and evaluate a two-year experiment at Pompton Lakes and Newark, New Jersey, to determine which aspects of reasoning were most substantially improved by the program.

The IAPC program in philosophy for children was subjected to an extensive experiment between September 1976 and June 1978. The study was conducted and

*Charlann Simon, "Philosophy for Students with Learning Disabilities," *Thinking: The Journal of Philosophy for Children* 1, no. 1 (Jan. 1979): 21–33.

evaluated by Educational Testing Service, and was supported by means of grants from the New Jersey Department of Education. The first year of the experiment was devoted to the construction of a new, criterion-referenced reasoning instrument, which is still in the process of development. The second year dealt with the impact of the philosophy for children program in urban and non-urban settings.

Two New Jersey communities were involved: Newark and Pompton Lakes, with approximately 200 experimental and 200 control subjects in each location. The children were in grades 5–8. Teachers were given one year of training in each site, meeting with a team of professors once a week for two hours per week. Classes of students were taught concurrently with the operation of the teacher-training workshops, and students were exposed to the program for approximately 2¼ hours per week.

The objective of the experiment was to determine whether such students would be able to attain:

1. Significant improvement in any or all of the three areas of reasoning treated in the philosophy for children program:
   a. drawing formal inferences and identifying fallacies
   b. discovering alternatives and possibilities
   c. providing reasons and explanations
2. Significant improvement in ideational fluency or productivity
3. Significant improvement in academic readiness as measured by teacher assessments
4. Significant improvement in basic skill (reading and mathematics) performance.

The instruments utilized in Newark for measurement of basic skills were the school-administered Metropolitan Achievement Tests; school-administered CTBS instruments were employed in Pompton Lakes.

The separate facets of the overall objective were distributed for measurement among a number of instruments within the test battery, as follows:

Subcategories of Objective	Instruments
1. Reasoning	
a. drawing formal inferences	Criterion-referenced formal reasoning test designed by ETS (also known as "Q-3") and CTMM
b. discovering alternatives, perceiving possibilities	Appropriateness aspects of "What Can It Be?" and "What Can It Be Used For?" tests
c. providing reasons	Appropriateness aspects of "How Many Reasons?" test
2. Ideational productivity	Total responses to "What Can It Be?" "What Can It Be Used For?" and "How Many Reasons?" tests
3. Academic readiness	Child Description Checklist
4. Basic Skills (reading and mathematics)	Newark: Metropolitan Pompton Lakes: CTBS

The following results are suggestive of the effectiveness of the program [and see Figures 2 and 3]:

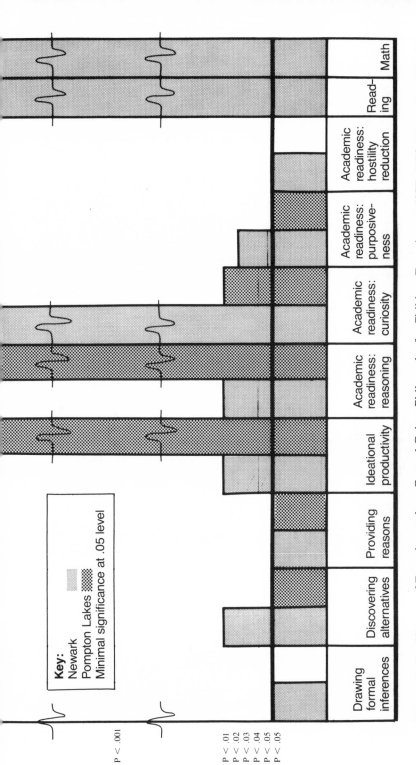

Figure 2. Significance of Experimental *vs.* Control Gains, Philosophy for Children Experiment, 1977–1978. Educational Testing Service, Princeton, N.J.

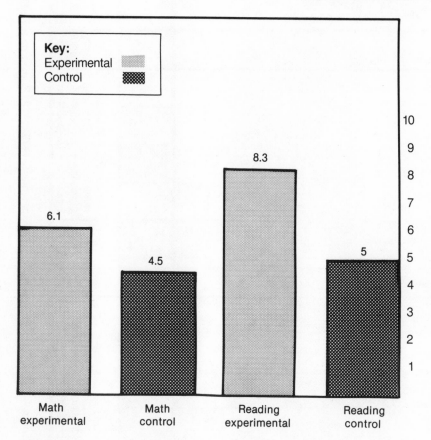

Figure 3. Comparison of Reading and Mathematics Gains in Terms of Average Standard Score, Newark Experiment in Philosophy for Children, 1977–1978. Educational Testing Service, Princeton, N.J.

Period of test: May 1977–May 1978
Instrument: Metropolitan (MAT)

Mathematics			Reading		
Experimental		Control	Experimental		Control
1978 mean	89.409	85.037	1978 mean	79.450	70.685
1977 mean	83.295	80.535	1977 mean	71.119	65.687
Gain	6.114	4.502	Gain	8.331	4.998

Conclusion: Experimental gain 36% larger than control

Conclusion: Experimental gain 66% larger than control

Instrument	Measure of Program Effects		Measure of Grade x Program Effects	
	Newark	Pompton Lakes	Newark	Pompton Lakes
CTMM		.02 for girls	.00	
Q-3			.04	
What Can It Be? (appr.)	.01			.00
Uses (appr.)	.00			
Reasons (approp.)	.06		.00	.11
Non-overlapping categories		.10		.05
(flexibility)	.10	.05	.01	.00
What Can It Be? (totals)	.01	.00		
Reasons (totals)	?	.00		
CDC-Reasoning	.01	.00		
Curiosity	.00	.01	.01	
Task Orientation	.02			
Hostility Reduction	.05			
Reading	.00			
Mathematics	.00			.03 for girls

Certain outcomes deserve to be pinpointed, as follows:

1. The overall program effect in Newark on *reading* and *mathematics*, using scaled scores so as to combine data across levels, was at the significance level of .0001.

2. With regard to the drawing of formal inferences, the program achieved significance (.02) for girls in Pompton Lakes for every grade except the 8th.

3. The teacher assessments of the program's impact upon the academic readiness of the students in the two communities suggest that, from the teachers' point of view, the program had a very favorable effect upon student motivation and interpersonal attitudes. It may be supposed that in the climate of more positive teacher expectations, children are more likely to fulfill such expectations. This is especially interesting in view of the fact that this improvement occurs in those middle grades where student performance often tends to go downhill.

4. Qualitative observation of the ideational fluency responses revealed very marked improvement in children's communication skills. The program was shown to be very effective for children identified as slow readers.

5. The length of exposure to the program was of critical importance. The more such exposure took place, the better such students performed. For example, in Newark, the longer children were in the program, the higher were their scores on the reasoning tests (.01 significance).

6. The results suggest that logical reasoning and intellectual creativity are not mutually inhibitive, and that both can be sharply stimulated by the same program. The conjunction of improvements is important, since the enhancement of critical skills alone can be superficial or empty without enhanced fertility of intellectual production.

7. The lesser frequency of significant ratings in Pompton Lakes as compared with Newark was due, in the opinion of ETS, to the overflow of program effects into the control group, causingthe latter's performance to improve along with that of the experimental group.

The results in brief:

1. *Reading and mathematics*. The overall impact of the philosophy for children program on the reading and mathematics performance of Newark Students was at the highest possible level of significance (.0001).

2. *Reasoning*. Highly significant improvement in creative reasoning (the capacity to generate new ideas, to discover feasible alternatives, and to provide reasons) was noted in many areas and on most grade levels in Newark, and on certain grade levels in Pompton Lakes. There was also a significant improvement in formal reasoning on three of the four grade levels in Newark.

3. *Academic Readiness*. Teachers' appraisals of the impact of the program upon their pupils was extremely favorable, both in Newark and in Pompton Lakes. Students appeared to teachers to be significantly more curious, better oriented toward their tasks, more considerate of one another, and better able to reason.*

*Educational Testing Service, Princeton, N.J., 1977–1978.

Bibliography

Aristotle, *Nichomachean Ethics*. New York: Random House, 1941.

Asch, Solomon E. *Social Psychology*. New York: Prentice-Hall, 1952.

Augustine, Saint. *Confessions*. New York: Modern Library, 1949.

————. *Divine Providence and the Problem of Evil*. Washington, D.C.: Catholic University of America Press, 1948.

————. *Soliloquies*. New York: Random House, 1948.

————. *Concerning the Teacher*. New York: Random House, 1948.

Baier, Kurt. "Good Reasons." *Philosophical Studies* 4 (1953): 1–15.

————. *The Moral Point of View*. Ithaca: Cornell University Press, 1958.

Bayles, Ernest E. *Pragmatism in Education*. New York: Harper and Row, 1966.

Beardsley, Monroe C. *Practical Thinking*. Englewood Cliffs, N.J.: Prentice-Hall, 1945.

Benjamin, Martin. "Can Moral Responsibility Be Collective and Non-Distributive?" *Social Theory and Practice*, Fall 1976.

Berlyne, D. E. "Children's Reasoning and Thinking." In *Carmichael's Manual of Child Psychology*, ed. Paul Mussen, 3rd ed. New York: Wiley, 1970.

Bettelheim, Bruno. *The Uses of Enchantment*. New York: Knopf, 1976.

Bruner, Jerome S. *On Knowing: Essays for the Left Hand*. New York: Atheneum, 1965.

————. *The Process of Education*. Cambridge: Harvard University Press, 1960.

————. *Toward a Theory of Instruction*. New York: Norton, 1968.

————, J. J. Goodnow, and G. A. Austin. *A Study of Thinking*. New York: Wiley, 1956.

Buber, Martin. *Between Man and Man*. New York: Macmillan, 1965.

————. *I and Thou*. New York: Scribner, 1958.

Buchler, Justus. "What Is a Discussion?" *Journal of General Education*, Oct. 1954.

Cohen, Morris, and Ernest Nagel. *An Introduction to Logic and Scientific Method*. New York: Harcourt, Brace and World, 1934.

225

Dearden, R. F., P. H. Hirst, and R. S. Peters. *Education and the Development of Reason*. London: Routledge and Kegan Paul, 1972.

Dewey, John. *Art as Experience*. New York: Minton, Balch, 1934.

―――. *The Child and the Curriculum*. New York: Macmillan, 1955.

―――. *Democracy and Education*. New York: Macmillan, 1944.

―――. *Experience and Education*. New York: Collier, 1971.

―――. *Experience and Nature*. New York: Norton, 1929.

―――. *Human Nature and Conduct*. New York: Modern Library, 1950.

―――. *Logic: The Theory of Inquiry*. New York: Holt, 1938.

―――. *The Theory of the Moral Life*. New York: Holt, Rinehart and Winston, 1908.

―――. *Theory of Valuation*. Chicago: University of Chicago Press, 1939.

Donaldson, Margaret. *Children's Minds*. London: Fontana/Croom Helm, 1978.

Doyle, J. *Educational Judgements*. London: Routledge and Kegan Paul, 1972.

Durkheim, Emile. *Moral Education*. New York: Teachers College Press, 1959.

Edel, Abraham. *Ethical Judgment*. Glencoe, Ill: Free Press, 1964.

―――. *Science and the Structure of Ethics*. Chicago: University of Chicago Press, 1961.

Edgeworth, Maria, and Richard Lovell Edgeworth. *Practical Education*. 1st Am. ed. New York: Hopkins, 1801.

Ennis, Robert H. *Logic in Teaching*. Englewood Cliffs, N.J.: Prentice-Hall, 1969.

Erikson, Erik H. *Childhood and Society*. New York: Norton, 1950.

―――. "The Golden Rule in the Light of New Insights." In Erickson, *Insight and Responsibility*. New York: Norton, 1964.

Evans, Clyde. *Critical Thinking and Reasoning*. Albany, N.Y.: University of the State of New York, 1976.

Firestone, Shulamith. *The Dialectic of Sex*. New York: Morrow, 1970.

Flavell, J. H. *Cognitive Development*. Englewood Cliffs, N.J.: Prentice-Hall, 1977.

―――. *The Developmental Psychology of Jean Piaget*. Princeton, N.J.: Van Nostrand, 1963.

Freire, Paulo. *Pedagogy of the Oppressed*. New York: Herder and Herder, 1972.

Hamlyn, D. W. *Experience and the Growth of Understanding*. London: Routledge and Kegan Paul, 1978.

Hare, R. M. "Adolescents into Adults." In *Aims in Education: The Philo-*

sophic Approach, ed. T. H. B. Hollins. Manchester: Manchester University Press, 1964.

————. *Freedom and Reason*. London: Oxford University Press, 1964.

Hirst, Paul H., ed. *Knowledge and the Curriculum*. London: Routledge and Kegan Paul, 1974.

Isaacs, Susan. *Intellectual Growth in Young Children*. New York: Harcourt, Brace and World, 1931.

James, William. *Talks to Teachers on Psychology*. New York: Holt, 1898.

Kagan, Jerome, and Nathan Kogan. "Individuality and Cognitive Performance." In *Carmichael's Manual of Child Psychology*, ed. Paul Mussen. 3rd ed. New York: Wiley, 1970.

Koffka, Kurt. *The Growth of the Mind*. New York: Harcourt, Brace, 1924.

Kohlberg, Lawrence. "Stages of Moral Development as a Basis for Moral Education." In *Moral Education: Interdisciplinary Approaches*, ed. C. M. Beck, B. S. Crittenden, and E. V. Sullivan. Toronto: University of Toronto Press, 1971.

Langford, Glen, and D. J. O'Connor. *New Essays in the Philosophy of Education*. London: Routledge and Kegan Paul, 1973.

Levit, Martin. *Curriculum*. Urbana, Ill.: University of Illinois Press, 1971.

Lewis, C. I. *An Analysis of Knowledge and Valuation*. LaSalle, Ill.: Open Court, 1946.

————. *The Ground and Nature of the Right*. New York: Columbia University Press, 1955.

Lipman, Matthew. *Contemporary Aesthetics*. Boston: Allyn and Bacon, 1973.

————. *Discovering Philosophy*. 2nd ed. Englewood Cliffs, N.J.: Prentice-Hall, 1977.

————. *Harry Stottlemeier's Discovery*. Upper Montclair, N.J.: Institute for the Advancement of Philosophy for Children, 1974.

————. *Lisa*. Upper Montclair, N.J.: Institute for the Advancement of Philosophy for Children, 1976.

————. *Mark*. Upper Montclair, N.J.: Institute for the Advancement of Philosophy for Children, 1979.

————. *Suki*. Upper Montclair, N.J.: Institute for the Advancement of Philosophy for Children, 1978.

————. *What Happens in Art*. New York: Appleton-Century-Crofts, 1967.

———— and Ann Margaret Sharp. *Growing Up with Philosophy*. Philadelphia: Temple University Press, 1978.

————, Ann Margaret Sharp, and F. S. Oscanyan. *Ethical Inquiry: Instructional Manual to Accompany Lisa*. Upper Montclair, N.J.: Institute for the Advancement of Philosophy for Children, 1977.

————, Ann Margaret Sharp, and F. S. Oscanyan. *Philosophical Inquiry: Instructional Manual to Accompany Harry Stottlemeier's Discovery*. 2nd ed. Upper Montclair, N.J.: Institute for the Advancement of Philosophy for Children, 1979.

Lynd, Helen M. *On Shame and the Search for Identity*. New York: Wiley, 1966.

Mandelbaum, Maurice. *The Phenomenology of Moral Experience*. Glencoe, Ill: Free Press, 1955.

Marcel, Gabriel. *The Mystery of Being*. Chicago: Regnery, 1951.

Matthews, Gareth B. "Philosophy and Children's Literature." *Metaphilosophy* 7, no. 1 (1976).

Mayeroff, Milton. *On Caring*. New York: Harper and Row, 1971.

Mead, George Herbert. "The Child and His Environment." *Transactions of the Society for Child Study* 3, no. 1 (April 1898): 1–11.

————. *Mind, Self and Society*, ed. Charles W. Morris. Chicago: University of Chicago Press, 1934.

————. *Movements of Thought in the Nineteenth Century*. Chicago: University of Chicago Press, 1936.

————. "The Relation of Play to Education." *University Record* 1, no. 8 (May 1896): 141–45.

————. *Selected Writings*, ed. Andrew J. Reck. Library of Liberal Arts, no. 177. New York: Bobbs-Merrill, 1964.

Merleau-Ponty, Maurice. *Consciousness and the Acquisition of Language*, trans. Hugh J. Silverman. Evanston, Ill.: Northwestern University Press, 1973.

Metcalf, Lawrence C. "Research on Teaching the Social Studies." In *Handbook of Research on Teaching*, ed. N. L. Gage. Chicago: Rand McNally, 1963.

Mill, John Stuart. *On Liberty*. London: Oxford University Press, 1969.

Montefiore, Alan. "Moral Philosophy and the Teaching of Morality." *Harvard Educational Review* 35 (Fall 1965).

Nelson, Leonard. *Socratic Method and Critical Philosophy: Selected Essays*, trans. Thomas K. Brown III. New Haven, Conn.: Yale University Press, 1949.

Nuthall, G. A., and P. J. Lawrence. *Thinking in the Classroom*. Wellington, N.Z.: New Zealand Council for Educational Research, 1965.

Oakeshott, Michael. "Learning and Teaching." In *The Concept of Education*, ed. R. S. Peters. London: Routledge and Kegan Paul, 1967.

————. "Political Education." In Oakeshott, *Rationalism in Politics*. New York: Basic Books, 1962.

Opie, Iona, and Peter Opie. *The Lore and Language of School Children*. New York: Oxford University Press, 1959.

Peirce, Charles. "Consequences of Four Incapacities." In *Collected Papers of Charles Sanders Peirce*, vol. 5, ed. Charles Hartshorne and Paul Weiss. Cambridge, Mass.: Harvard University Press, 1933.

―――. "Doctrine of Chances." In *Collected Papers of Charles Sanders Peirce*, vol. 2, ed. Charles Hartshorne and Paul Weiss. Cambridge, Mass.: Harvard University Press, 1932.

―――. "The Fixation on Belief." In *Philosophical Writings of Peirce*, ed. Justus Buchler. New York: Dover, 1955.

―――. "How to Make Our Ideas Clear." In *Philosophical Writings of Peirce*, ed. Justus Buchler. New York: Dover, 1955.

―――. "Pragmatism and Pragmaticism." In *Collected Papers of Charles Sanders Peirce*, vol. 5, ed. Charles Hartshorne and Paul Weiss. Cambridge: Harvard University Press, 1933.

Peters, R. S., ed. *The Concept of Education*. London: Routledge and Kegan Paul, 1967.

―――. *Authority, Responsibility and Education*. London: George Allen and Unwin, 1959.

Piaget, Jean. *The Birth of Logical Thinking from Childhood to Adolescence*. New York: Basic Books, 1958.

―――. *The Child's Conception of the World*. New York: Harcourt, Brace and World, 1932.

―――. *The Early Growth of Logic in the Child*. London: Routledge and Kegan Paul, 1964.

―――. *Judgment and Reasoning in the Child*. New York: Harcourt, Brace and World, 1928.

―――. *Language and Thought of the Child*. Cleveland, Ohio. World, 1959.

―――. *Logic and Psychology*. New York: Basic Books, 1957.

―――. *The Moral Judgment of the Child*. New York: Harcourt, Brace and World, 1932.

―――. *The Origins of Intelligence in Children*, trans. Margaret Cook. New York: International University Press, 1952.

―――. *To Understand Is to Invent: The Future of Education*. New York: Viking, 1975.

Postman, Neil, and Charles Weingartner. *Teaching as a Subversive Activity*. New York: Delacorte, 1969.

Raths, Louis E., et al. *Teaching for Thinking*. Columbus, Ohio: Merrill, 1967.

Raths, Louis E., Merill Harmin, and Sidney B. Simon. *Values and Teaching: Working with Values in the Classroom*. Columbus, Ohio: Merrill, 1966.

Ryle, Gilbert. *Collected Papers*. 2 vols. New York: Barnes and Noble, 1971.

―――. *The Concept of Mind*. New York: Barnes and Noble, 1949.

Sarason, Seymour. *The Culture of the School and the Problem of Change.* Boston: Allyn and Bacon, 1971.

Scheffler, Israel. *Conditions of Knowledge: An Introduction to Epistemology and Education.* Chicago: Scott Foresman, 1965.

————. *The Language of Education.* Springfield, Ill.: Thomas, 1960.

————. *Reason and Teaching.* Indianapolis: Bobbs Merrill, 1973.

Simmel, Georg. *Schulpädagogik.* Osterwieck/Harz: Verlag Von A. W. Zickfeldt, 1922.

Smith, B. O. "A Concept of Teaching." *Teachers College Record* 61 (1960): 229.

————. "Logic, Thinking and Teaching." *Educational Theory* 7 (1957): 225.

————. and Robert H. Ennis. *Language and Concepts in Education.* Chicago: Rand McNally, 1968.

Snook, I. A. "Teaching Pupils to Think." *Studies in Philosophy and Education* 8, no. 2 (Fall 1973).

Suchman, J. R. "The Child and the Inquiry Process." In *Intellectual Development: Another Look*, ed. A. H. Passow. Washington, D.C.: Association for Supervision and Curriculum Development, 1964.

Taba, Hilda. *Dynamics of Education.* New York: Harcourt, Brace and World, 1932.

————. "The Problems in Developing Critical Thinking," *Progressive Education* 28 (November 1950).

Thorndike, E. L. "Reading as Reasoning: A Study of Mistakes in Paragraph Reading." *Journal of Educational Psychology* 8 (1917): 323.

Toulmin, Stephen. *An Examination of the Place of Reason in Ethics.* Cambridge, Eng.: Cambridge University Press, 1950.

Urmson, J. O. "Saints and Heroes." In *Essays in Moral Philosophy*, ed. A. I. Melden. Seattle: University of Washington Press, 1958.

Vygotsky, L. S. *Mind in Society*, ed. Michael Cole, Vera John-Steiner, Sylvia Scribner, and Ellen Souberman. Cambridge, Mass.: Harvard University Press, 1978.

————. *Thought and Language*, ed. and trans. Eugenia Hanfmann and Gertrude Vakar. Cambridge: M.I.T. Press, 1962.

Wallach, Michael. "Creativity." In *Carmichael's Manual of Child Psychology*, ed. Paul Mussen. 3rd ed. New York: Wiley, 1970.

————. "Creativity and the Expression of Possibilities." In *Creativity and Learning*, ed. Jerome Kagan. Boston: Houghton, Mifflin, 1967.

Wees, W. R. *Nobody Can Teach Anyone Anything.* Toronto: Doubleday, 1971.

Werner, Heinz. *Comparative Psychology of Mental Development.* Chicago: Follett, 1948.

————. "The Conception of Development from a Comparative and Orga-
nismic Point of View." In *The Concept of Development*, ed. Dale B. Har-
ris. Minneapolis: University of Minnesota Press, 1957.

Wheelwright, Philip. *A Critical Introduction to Ethics*. 3rd ed. New York:
Odyssey, 1959.

————. *Valid Thinking*. New York: Odyssey, 1962.

Whitehead, Alfred North. *The Aims of Education*. New York: Macmillan,
1929.

Wilson, John. *Moral Thinking*. London: Heinemann, 1969.

————. *Thinking with Concepts*. Cambridge, Eng.: Cambridge University
Press, 1971.

Wittgenstein, Ludwig. *Lectures and Conversations on Aesthetics*. Berkeley,
Calif.: University of California Press, 1967.

————. *Philogosophical Investigations*, trans. G. E. M. Anscombe. Rev.
ed.Oxford, Eng.: Blackwell, 1958.

————. *On Certainty*. Oxford, Eng.: Blackwell, 1969.

————. *Tractatus Logico-Philosophicus*, trans. D. F. Pears and B. F. Mc-
Guinness. New York: Humanities Press, 1961.